Europe's Border Crisis

Europe's Border Crisis investigates dynamics in European border security and migration management and advances a new framework for thought, judgment, and action. It argues that a crisis point has emerged whereby irregular migrants are treated as both security threats to Europe and as lives that are threatened and in need of saving. This leads to paradoxical situations such that humanitarian policies and practices often expose irregular migrants to dehumanizing and lethal border security mechanisms. The dominant way of understanding these dynamics, one that blames a gap between policy and practice, fails to address the deeper political issues at stake and ends up perpetuating the terms of the crisis.

Drawing on conceptual resources in biopolitical theory, particularly the work of Roberto Espositio, the book offers an alternative diagnosis of the problem in order to move beyond the present impasse. It argues that both negative and positive dimensions of European border security are symptomatic of tensions within biopolitical techniques of government. While bordering practices are designed to play a defensive role they contain the potential for excessive security mechanisms that threaten the very values and lives they purport to protect.

Each chapter draws on a different biopolitical key to both interrogate diverse technologies of power at a range of border sites and explore the insights and limits of the biopolitical paradigm. Must border security always result in dehumanization and death? Is a more affirmative approach to border politics possible? *Europe's Border Crisis* advances research agendas for critical border and migration studies.

Nick Vaughan-Williams is Professor of International Security, University of Warwick.

Europe's Border Crisis

Biopolitical Security and Beyond

Nick Vaughan-Williams

OXFORD
UNIVERSITY PRESS

OXFORD
UNIVERSITY PRESS

Great Clarendon Street, Oxford, OX2 6DP,
United Kingdom

Oxford University Press is a department of the University of Oxford.
It furthers the University's objective of excellence in research, scholarship,
and education by publishing worldwide. Oxford is a registered trade mark of
Oxford University Press in the UK and in certain other countries

First published 2015
First published in paperback 2017

Published in the United States of America by Oxford University Press
198 Madison Avenue, New York, NY 10016, United States of America

British Library Cataloguing in Publication Data
Data available

Library of Congress Cataloging in Publication Data
Data available

ISBN 978–0–19–874702–4 (Hbk.)
ISBN 978–0–19–880679–0 (Pbk.)

For my mother

Acknowledgements

In the process of writing this book the chief debt I owe is to Madeleine for being such an extraordinarily brilliant wife, sparring partner, and mother to Helena. Among other things, she has developed a remarkable immunity towards my inabilities to be a better husband and father. Without her this book and all that I cherish most in life would be unimaginable.

The arrival of our daughter Helena during the latter stages of this project was the most joyous and violent event that I have ever experienced. Each day, her development has far outpaced that of this book, but I cannot take as much of the credit for that as I would like to. She is inspirational and has given me a new slant on things.

My mother and Ning have provided the everyday ballast and opportunity for retreat once in a while that ultimately made the final writing and preparation of this book possible: I am forever grateful to them both for all their unconditional love and lightness of touch in correcting me when I am wrong.

In Ann and Kieran I have been incredibly lucky to acquire an extended family notable for their wisdom, sense of fun, and penchant for gîtes and fine wine. Their greatest help, along with the following friends, has been in the form of distraction when I have needed it most: Rory Carson, Ollie Deakin, Owen Rawlings, and Tim Sismey.

In the research for this book I have been fortunate enough to be based at the Department of Politics and International Studies (PAIS), University of Warwick. Without a generous period of research leave in 2013–14 I would not have been able to complete the project and for that I am most grateful. In particular, I would like to thank the following colleagues and friends in PAIS and the Faculty of Social Sciences for supporting my work in their own inimitable ways: Richard Aldrich, Claire Blencowe, James Brassett, Chris Browning, Stuart Croft, Stuart Elden, Oz Hassan, Charlotte Heath-Kelly, Christopher Hughes, Chris Moran, Hidefumi Nishiyama, Shirin Rai, Vicki Squire, Maurice Stierl, Erzsebet Strausz, Illan Rua Wall, Matthew Watson, and all my PhD students past and present.

Beyond Warwick, I am especially grateful to the following colleagues and friends who, wittingly or otherwise, have at one point or another helped to inform, shape, and sharpen (but bear no responsibility for) many of the arguments presented in this book: Claudia Aradau, Victoria Basham, Luiza Bialasiewicz, Didier Bigo, Martin Coward, Dan Bulley, Sarah Bulmer, Tim Cooper, François Debrix, Michael Dillon, Roxanne Doty, Jenny Edkins, Elspeth Guild, Jef Huysmans, Jay Hwang, Debbie Lisle, Adrian Little, Joyce C. H. Liu, Tom Lundborg, Cetta Mainwaring, Anne McNevin, Claudio Minca, Andrew Neal, João Nunes, Cian O'Driscoll, Noel Parker, Columba Peoples, Kris Pollet, Sergei Prozorov, Simona Rentea, Chris Rossdale, Chris Rumford, Naoki Sakai, Andrew Schaap, Stephan Scheel, Michael J. Shapiro, James Sidaway, Philip E. Steinberg, Angharad Closs Stephens, Daniel Stevens, Hidemi Suganami, R. B. J. Walker, Marysia Zalewski, Maja Zehfuss, and Andreja Zevnik.

Many of the ideas for the conceptual backbone of this book were experimented with at the Gregynog Ideas Lab II in 2012 and I am indebted to those who came along to my seminars entitled 'Biopolitics, Thanatopolitics, Zoopolitics'. Arguments presented in Chapters 1–4 were also presented at Leiden University College, the University of Pittsburgh, the University of Helsinki, the University of Salford, the 2012 BISA Annual Conference, the 2013 International Studies Association Annual Convention, and the 2014 Monash–Warwick Workshop on 'Borders, Migration, and Sovereignty'. I am grateful to all those in attendance at these events who offered comments on my work.

Finally, I would like to thank the delegates of Oxford University Press and the editorial and production teams for supporting this book through to completion. Dominic Byatt has been an exceptional commissioning editor and I am truly grateful for his advice and encouragement at each stage. Earlier versions of different parts of the manuscript were also improved as a direct result of the input of François Debrix, Madeleine Fagan, Tom Lundborg, and eight anonymous reviewers whose constructive critiques I would also like to acknowledge as having an important bearing on the arguments presented here.

Part of the argument advanced in Chapter 4 is based on and further develops an article I published as ' "We are *not* animals!" Humanitarian Border Security and Zoopolitical Spaces in EUrope', *Political Geography* (March 2015) 45(1), pp. 1–10, and I am grateful to Elsevier for granting a copyright licence agreement in respect of this piece.

January 2015,
Kenilworth

Contents

Contents

List of Abbreviations

ABC	Automated Border Control
AoM	Autonomy of Migration
CBS	Critical Border Studies
CMS	Critical Migration Studies
CEAS	Common European Asylum System
ECDP	European Centre for Disease Protection
ECtHR	European Court of Human Rights
EEC	European Economic Community
EES	Entry/Exit System
EFTA	European Free Trade Association
EU	European Union
EURODAC	European Dactyloscopy
EUROSUR	European Border Surveillance System
Frontex	European Agency for the Management of Operational Cooperation at the External Borders of the Member States of the European Union
GAMM	Global Approach to Migration and Mobility
GPS	Global Positioning System
HCDPC	Hellenic Centre for Disease Prevention and Control
HIV	Human Immunodeficiency Virus
IBM	Integrated Border Management
ID	Identity Document
IOM	International Organization for Migration
ISPS	International Ship and Port Security
ISS	Internal Security Strategy
MEP	Member of European Parliament
MRCC	Maritime Rescue Coordination Centre
NATO	North Atlantic Treaty Organization
NGOs	Non-governmental Organizations
PACE	Parliamentary Assembly of the Council of Europe
PICUM	Platform for International Cooperation on Undocumented Migrants
RABIT	Rapid Border Intervention Team
RMA	Revolution in Military Affairs
RTP	Registered Traveller Programme

List of Abbreviations

SAR	Search and Rescue
SBI	Smart Borders Initiative
SIS	Schengen Information System
TB	Tuberculosis
TFM	Task Force Mediterranean
UAV	Unmanned Aerial Vehicle
UK	United Kingdom
UN	United Nations
US	United States of America
UNCLOS	United Nations Convention on the Law of the Sea
UNHCR	United Nations High Commissioner for Refugees
VIS	Visa Information System
WHO	World Health Organization

1

Borders, Crises, Critique

EUrope's Border Crisis

On 3 October 2013 at least 366 'irregular'[1] migrants from Eritrea and Somalia died within 800 m of the outcrop of Conigli on the Italian island of Lampedusa seeking entry to the European Union (EU). According to eyewitness accounts, the overcrowded vessel on which they were travelling—skippered by a Tunisian man, later accused of manslaughter by Italian authorities—had sailed from Misrata in Libya and began taking on water when its motor suddenly stopped working (BBC News 2013a, 2013b). Testimonies from the six known survivors suggest that a piece of material had been deliberately set alight in an attempt to attract attention to their situation. However, the fire rapidly got out of control and a spokesperson from the International Organization for Migration (IOM) reported that 'the migrants moved, all of them, to one side of the boat', which then capsized. Many were forced to throw themselves overboard in a bid for safety, but the majority—particularly the female passengers—could not swim to the shoreline (BBC 2013a).

The 'official' response of the EU Commission to the 3 October Lampedusa incident was characterized by a fusion of the language of security and humanitarian protection. In a 'Memorandum on the Tragic accident outside Lampedusa', the European Commissioner for Home Affairs, Cecilia Malmström, said that she was 'deeply saddened' by the 'terrible tragedy' and resolved that 'Europe has to . . . show solidarity *both* with migrants *and* countries that are experiencing migratory flows' (BBC News 2013b, emphasis added). This twinned 'solidarity' also framed the establishment of the Task Force Mediterranean (TFM) group designed to 'prevent such human tragedies from happening again' (EU Commission 2013b, 2). Thus, at the centre of the 'determined action' of the TFM, chaired by the EU Commission, is 'reinforced border surveillance' of the Mediterranean Sea in order to both 'protect the lives of migrants' and 'enhance the maritime situational picture' (EU Commission 2013b,16). Further reflecting this dual focus, the role of Frontex (the

European Agency for the Management of Operational Cooperation at the External Borders of the Member States of the EU) is presented as being 'key to ensuring effective border control in the region, whilst contributing to ensuring the protection of those in need and saving the lives of migrants' (EU Commission 2013b, 16).

Caught between the discourses of securitization and humanitarianism is the figure of the 'irregular' migrant seeking entry to the EU primarily via land and sea to the south and southeast (EU Commission 2014a). On the one hand, the 'irregular' migrant is cast in 'official' documentation as a political subject who potentially threatens the identity, economy, and security of the EU and its Member States (EU Commission 2010b; EU Commission 2011a). Far from a one-off tragedy the 2013 Lampedusa incident is connected to a longer history of violence in the field of EUropean[2] border security and migration management wrought in the name of protecting EU citizens in an 'area of freedom, security, and justice'.[3] Research undertaken by non-governmental organizations (NGOs)—often drawing upon 'irregular' migrants' testimonies—reveals habitual dehumanization in spaces of detention and exposure to death via abandonment in hostile environments both within the territory of EU Member States and beyond (Human Rights Watch 2011b; Migreurop 2012; Pro Asyl 2013; United Against Racism 2014).[4] On the other hand, alongside these dynamics there has also emerged a strong humanitarian discourse of 'migrant-centredness' associated with the EU Commission's 2011 renewed 'Global Approach to Migration and Mobility' (GAMM) (EU Commission 2011a). The GAMM claims not only to *observe* human rights in the management of the EU's external borders, but also pledges to use surveillance and screening methods in order to further *enhance* the humanitarian protection of endangered lives (EU Commission 2011e; EU Commission 2013a). In this way, as we also see in responses to the 2013 Lampedusa incident, the catch-all notion of the 'human' worthy of being saved has risen to prominence in the framing of EUropean border security: as well as being a potential threat, the 'irregular' migrant is simultaneously interpellated as a political subject whose life is threatened and must be empowered and saved at any point in their journey to the EU.

Both discourses—of securitization and humanitarianism—have histories of several decades in the EUropean context, but their interaction in the field of border security and migration management has intensified and gathered significant momentum in recent years, especially since the so-called Arab Spring. Indeed, the same border security authorities committed to saving the lives of 'irregular' migrants are also those complicit in creating the conditions that render them vulnerable to diverse forms of violence both directly and indirectly. Thus, while Frontex claims to have 'saved' 23,254 'irregular' migrants in 2011 alone (Fundamental Rights Agency 2013), research presented by NGOs alleges that the Agency has also been involved in illegal 'push-back' operations leading to an unknown number of injuries and deaths (PICUM 2010; Pro Asyl 2013; Watch The Med 2014). Taken together, these dynamics constitute what I refer to as EUrope's border crisis, which is characterized by a fundamental puzzle that this book seeks to outline and address as a whole, namely: *Why do EUropean humanitarian border security practices often* *expose the very 'irregular' migrants they are supposed to protect to dehumanization and death?*

EUropean Border Security and the Crisis of Humanitarian Critique

A dominant explanation for the dynamics associated with EUrope's border crisis—typically found across non-academic and academic critiques alike—is that of a perceived 'discrepancy' between the EU Commission's neo-liberal humanitarian policy 'rhetoric' and the violent 'reality' of many 'irregular' migrants' embodied experiences of their encounter with attempts to police their mobility. For example, in a high-profile United Nations (UN) Report on the Human Rights of Migrants in the EU, François Crepeau argues that there is a significant 'gap' between 'migration policy' and 'measures adopted on the ground' (UN 2013a, 9). The idea that the prospects for a less violent and more humanitarian form of EUropean border security would be enhanced *if only* existing policies such as the EU Commission's GAMM were better implemented is one that also pervades the extensive NGO and migrant activist literature (Amnesty 2013; Human Rights Watch 2011b; Migreurop 2012; Pro Asyl 2013). Similarly, to take one prominent example in the academic field of critical border and migration studies, Sandro Mezzadra and Brett Neilson (2013, 171) argue that the EU's humanitarian approach to border security can only ever remain 'a dream' because of 'the gap that separates policy from practice'.

The argument I advance here is that any explanation for the persistently violent nature of EUropean border security that relies on the 'rhetoric' versus 'reality' frame is both analytically limited and politically problematic. Such a framing is blind to the inherent ambiguity *within* EU border security and migration management policies and practices that (re)produces the 'irregular' migrant as potentially *both* a life to be protected *and* a security threat to protect against. This ambiguity is not merely discernible in the policy discourses of the EU and its agencies: more importantly still, it is prevalent in diverse sites of mutual encounter between EUropean border security apparatuses and 'irregular' migrants. It is often unclear, for example, whether enhanced surveillance methods and patrols at sea will lead to the humanitarian rescue or illegal

3

push-back of 'irregular' vessels in distress: those who call helplines can never fully know by which authorities they will be greeted and with what consequences for their personal safety (Pro Asyl 2013). Similarly, the rise of public health initiatives in detention centres across the EUropean borderscape may improve some detainees' access to life-saving medical services, but this provision often does not allow for long-term care of underlying illnesses (European Surveillance 2011). The medicalization of humanitarian border security may assist the immediate basic needs of some, but it also creates new opportunities to 'know' and thereby potentially better manage otherwise unknown and ungovernable 'irregular' populations. Furthermore, the conventional rhetoric/reality framing ultimately fails to appreciate and tackle head-on the coalescence of interests among seemingly diverse actors—including NGOs and the EU Commission and its Agencies—around the human rights of the 'irregular' migrant.

The convergence between authorities associated with EUropean border security and some of their fiercest critics in this way poses a significant challenge for the possibility of engaging critically with the question of the persistence of border violence. While humanitarian ideals have long provided the foundation from which a critique of the effects of bordering practices on the lives of 'irregular' migrants can be mounted, this move is severely compromised—assuming that it ever was 'effective'—because it has now become openly co-opted by the very authorities associated with that violence. This means that the call for a humanitarian response to the lived 'reality' of the situations in which many 'irregular' migrants find themselves is ultimately a position that appeals back to and reinforces the ground already occupied by the EU and yet in whose name some of the most egregious abuses of human rights continue to persist. For this reason it is not only that EUrope's borders are in crisis in the ways illustrated above: so too is the hitherto dominant basis upon which border security authorities might be challenged and held to account, which amounts to what I call a *crisis of humanitarian critique*. This book argues that alongside sociologically driven analyses of specific sites of border struggles there is also a pressing need for alternative critical-conceptual diagnoses of the nature of EUrope's border crisis in order to generate new insights and questions beyond the 'rhetoric' versus 'reality' framing and the reliance on abstract notions of the human subject, human rights, and humanitarianism: to ignore this formidable challenge is otherwise to remain stuck within and further perpetuate—rather than critique—the terms of the crisis as a whole. But while many resources for responding to such a challenge already exist in the interdisciplinary field of critical border and migration studies, this burgeoning body of scholarship is beset by its own conceptual crises to which a response is also urgently required.

Conceptual Crises in Critical Border and Migration Studies

Over the past few decades, the concept of the border has attracted renewed scholarly interest across a range of disciplinary areas including Politics and International Studies, Political Geography, Anthropology, and Sociology. In the context of what John Agnew (2003) has referred to as the idealized 'modern geopolitical imagination', this concept has traditionally been tied to that of the state: borders are typically understood to be the territorial markers of the limits of sovereign juridical-political authority (see also Agnew 1994; Albert et al. 2001; Elden 2006). A simplifying device for under-standing the location of political authority, the concept of the border of the state organizes the otherwise messy, overlapping, and interconnecting nature of global politics into two supposedly distinct realms: the 'inside' of the state characterized by normality, friendship, security, and progress; and the 'out-side' of the international associated with enmity, insecurity, and anarchy (Walker 1993). As well as problematizing the work that the concept of the border of the state does in shaping and maintaining interests bound up with the modern geopolitical imagination, more recent critical scholarship has sought to diagnose the various ways in which the nature and location of borders are not what or where they are supposed to be according to that idealization (Walker 2010).

While there is no doubt that many stubborn territorially identifiable borders persist in contemporary political life, bordering practices are not only to be found at 'regular' entry and exit points and neither are they always linked with 'territory' in the conventional sense (Albert et al. 2001). Indeed, one of the central arguments presented in this book is that EUrope's border crisis is characterized by increasing uncertainty about what the very concepts of 'the border' and 'border security' refer to. Bordering practices are increasingly spectral and undergoing a series of spatial and temporal displacements: these practices are largely invisible to citizens of the EU in whose name they are legitimized and yet they are no less violent in their effects for those who are produced by them as 'irregular' migrants. As is already well documented, the *offshoring* of EU bordering practices beyond the territorial limits of EU Member States has become a hallmark of migration management and broader initia-tives to performatively secure the external dimension of EUropean space (Bialasiewicz, 2011; see also Migreurop 2012). These practices are illustrated by the work of Frontex, whose missions have extended far beyond the Medi-terranean Sea into West Africa and increasingly come to resemble military operations (Balibar 2009; Borderline Europe 2013; PICUM 2010). Extra-territorial projections of the border have also given rise to the *outsourcing* of bordering practices involving a transfer of governance from the EU to states in North Africa and to the east (Bialasiewicz 2012). In turn, third states often pursue a strategy of further sub-contracting border control to private security companies and local militias who profit from amplifying the perceived threat of 'irregular' migration as part of a cyclical industry (Andersson 2014, 121).

For these reasons, traditional understandings of the border—and accompanying metaphors of 'lines', 'walls', and 'limits'—have been plunged into *conceptual crisis*, and various authors—working within and beyond the EUropean context—have called for the development of alternative border vocabularies and imaginaries (Balibar 1998; Salter 2012; Sidaway 2006; Vaughan-Williams 2009; Walker 2010). R. B. J. Walker (2010, 6) sums up the scale and significance of the task when he argues that the future of social and political analysis will need to 'think much more carefully about how complex practices of drawing lines have come to be treated as such a simple matter'. In response to this conceptual crisis by now a considerable body of scholarship has sought to develop a more theoretically and methodologically reflective and self-consciously 'critical' approach to the study of borders globally (see *inter alia*: Johnson et al. 2011; Kumar Rajaram and Grundy-Warr 2007; Mezzadra and Neilson 2013; Parker and Vaughan-Williams et al. 2009, Parker and Vaughan-Williams 2012; Rumford 2009; Squire 2011). Seeking to move beyond the limits reached in zero-sum debates about the continued 'presence' or increasing 'absence' of borders under globalizing conditions, the interdisciplinary field of Critical Border Studies (CBS)—broadly conceived—has shown that borders are increasingly fractured throughout society in ways that do not respect traditional understandings of the inside/outside distinction but are often no less violent in their effects. Much of this work has sought to 'decentre' the border so that it is not taken as a straightforward foundation for political analysis, but treated precisely as a site of interrogation in its own right. Central to this decentring has been a move towards a more sociological treatment of borders as a set of contingent *practices* throughout societies with performative effects. The move from 'border' to 'bordering practice' gives added weight to routine and everyday attempts to control mobility alongside more spectacular and exceptional sites and events (Côté-Boucher et al. 2014). In turn, this enables greater attention to the role that state and non-state actors play in performing what Chris Rumford (2009) has referred to as 'borderwork'. Once the analytical focus is reorientated in this way from 'the border' as a given to the more active notion of 'bordering practices'—understood broadly as *attempts* by diverse actors to identify and control the mobility of certain people, services, and goods—then the concept of the border becomes fuzzier, but arguably more apposite to the complexity of contemporary conditions.

In the continued quest to 'extrapolate new border concepts, logics, and imaginaries that capture the changing perspective on what borders are supposed to be and where they may be supposed to lie' (Parker and Vaughan-Williams 2009, 2), some CBS scholars have argued for a paradigm shift from a geopolitical to a biopolitical horizon of analysis (Amoore 2006; Bigo 2007; Kitagawa 2011; Vaughan-Williams 2010; Walters 2002). Whereas the traditional geopolitical paradigm of border studies focused primarily on the defence of territory at its physical outer-edge, the latter, influenced by Michel Foucault's paradigmatic account of biopolitics (1998, 2003, 2007), encourages greater attention to the relationship between populations and government.[5] Foucault (1998) used the concept of biopolitics in order to trace the emergence from the eighteenth century of new forms of knowledge that brought biological life into the heart of political calculations and mechanisms. On Foucault's view, changes associated with industrialization and demographic growth meant that modern politics were increasingly driven by the optimization of the life of man-as-species. Biopolitical modes of governance from this perspective operate not by enclosing and disciplining individual bodies, but via the management of and intervention in the population as a whole. As such, the biopolitical paradigm has potentially very significant implications for rethinking the concept of the border in a way that is not beholden to the limits of the modern geopolitical imagination. In this context, 'border security' refers not to the fixing and demarcation of territory as per the geopolitical paradigm, but rather to the *enhancement* of mobility and circulation of populations in order to create new opportunities to sift and cancel out perceived risks within the population.[6] As François Debrix and Alexander Barder (2012, 10) have argued, however, this does not mean that the inside/outside distinction is erased under biopolitical conditions, but rather that 'differentiations, classifications, and categorizations' are no longer 'primarily territorially defined' (see also Vaughan-Williams 2009). Despite the insights of the Foucaultian biopolitical frame, however, its adoption in the study of contemporary bordering practices has nevertheless proved controversial—particularly when approaching the politics of border security from the perspective of migration—and has precipitated yet another crisis in terms of what it means to be 'critical' in this field of research.

On one side of the debate, a number of CBS and 'Critical Migration Studies' (CMS) scholars have turned to the work of Giorgio Agamben as a supplement to the Foucaultian frame in order to better understand the 'negative' dimensions of biopolitical bordering practices: the so-called 'thanatopolitical' dynamics (*thanatos* is the Greek personification of death), which often expose 'irregular' migrants to dehumanizing and lethal conditions (Bigo 2007; Diken 2004; De Genova and Peutz 2010; Doty 2009; Edkins and Walker 2000; Gregory 2006; Khosravi 2010; Minca 2007; Kinnvall and Nesbitt-Larking 2013; Rajaram and Grundy-Warr 2004; Shewly 2013; Vaughan-Williams 2011a). Modifying Foucault's account, the work of Agamben (1998, 1999, 2000) has sought to reintroduce the role of sovereign power in order to recover the violent potentiality for thanatopolitical drift within biopolitical forms of

7

governance. Via the concept of the sovereign ban—a spatial-ontological device used to refer to the 'potentiality of the law . . . to apply in no longer applying'—Agamben (1998, 28) draws on Carl Schmitt's (2005) theory of sovereignty as the decision on the exception in order to understand the constitutive violence underpinning the juridical-political order. For Agamben, sovereignty is originally biopolitical because it rests on the division of natural life (*zoē*) from the politically qualified life of the polis (*bios*): the former is the negative foundation against which the latter is defined. Throughout his oeuvre, Agamben uses the figure of *homo sacer* from Roman law—a subject position that can be exposed unconditionally to death—in order to illustrate the way in which the sovereign ban operates. This paradigm has become popular in some quarters of CBS and CMS for diagnosing the logic according to which contemporary biopolitical border security practices attempt to produce forms of subjectivities that are amenable to being governed.

On the other side of the debate, however, a number of other scholars across critical border and migration studies have more recently urged caution regarding what they consider to be a prevalent control bias, particularly within Agambenian approaches to biopolitical border security, which they largely reject (Garelli and Tazzioli 2013; Johnson 2013; McNevin 2013; Mezzadra and Neilson 2013; Nyers 2013; Papadopoulos et al. 2008; Puggioni 2014; Scheel 2014; Squire 2011; Stierl 2014). What is common to this otherwise diverse body of scholarship is the argument that an exclusive focus on thanatopolitical drift is empirically and politically problematic because it privileges sovereign power and control over political struggle and contestation, fails to account for the role of migrant agency in shaping and resisting contemporary border regimes, and tends to flatten and generalize across diverse border sites and migrants' experience. By contrast, the work of scholars associated with the 'Autonomy of Migration' (AoM) approach in particular derive inspiration from an alternative genealogy of biopolitics—one most commonly linked to the work of Antonio Negri (1993, 2004, 2008)—which gives greater emphasis to the more 'positive' or vitalist dimension of the Foucaultian account: the power *of* life rather than power *over* life (Mezzadra and Neilson 2013; Papadopoulos et al. 2008). Thus, according to the AoM perspective, the mobility of people is reinterpreted as ontologically prior to any attempts by border security authorities to control them—'Escape comes first!'—and sovereign regimes prompted by the constitutive creativity of migrants will always ultimately be outwitted and rendered porous (Papadopoulos et al. 2008, xv).

While there remain nuances within and between both 'sides' of the debate, critical border and migration studies are nonetheless in a state of crisis because the field as a whole remains caught in an impasse between these two poles: the analyst must seemingly 'choose' either to privilege border control ('negative' biopolitics) or migrant agency ('positive' biopolitics), respectively (McNevin

2013). The very terms of this debate, however, are problematized by the central puzzle with which this book engages, as outlined above: the EU's humanitarian approach to border security at once encompasses *both* the (discourse of control *and* that of migrant agency.) An alternative approach is therefore required beyond the limits of the extant debate stemming from 'negative' and 'positive' views of biopolitics. The ambition of this book is, therefore, to contribute to recent attempts to move critical border and migration studies beyond this tired and totalizing dichotomy. In this regard, the work of Vicki Squire (2011) and Anne McNevin (2013) is of particular importance in focusing on the politics of 'irregularity' and 'ambivalence' at diverse sites of border struggles, respectively.[7] But whereas Squire and McNevin advocate a sociological turn to practice, the conceptually driven approach offered here draws on complementary resources for deconstructing 'negative' versus 'positive' poles in contemporary (post)biopolitical theory. In particular, I argue that the otherwise overlooked works of Roberto Esposito (2008, 2010, 2011, 2012a, 2012b, 2013)—especially his treatment of the relationship between biopolitics and the paradigm of immunity—bridge the gap between thanatopolitical and vitalist perspectives. Via his concept of the immunitary *dispositif*, Esposito shows the way in which both impulses—the negation and affirmation of life—are not separate from each other, but part of the same biopolitical logic. Inspired by Esposito's deconstructive approach to biopolitics, this book proposes a reconceptualization of border security as a form of immune system with the potentiality not only for the protection of life, but also its destruction: when bordering practices develop excessively defensive immunitary mechanisms they acquire the characteristics of an autoimmune disorder, which ultimately comes to threaten the very lives, communities, and values such practices are designed to optimize. While the potential for thanatopolitics is ever-present, however, there is nothing inevitable about this drift and, ultimately, I will argue that Esposito's thought—in conversation with Jacques Derrida's (2009, 2005, 2003, 2002) more recent engagements with the biopolitical paradigm and the concept of autoimmunity—paves the way for rethinking the border along more affirmative lines and a critical response to EUrope's border crisis beyond the dominant 'rhetoric' versus 'reality' frame.

Key Themes and an Outline of the Book

In addressing the central puzzle expressed above, this book seeks to investigate the insights and limitations of (post)biopolitical theory for diagnosing diverse aspects of EUrope's border crisis. The notion of (post) biopolitical theory refers to a heterogeneous range of thought that engages with and in different ways seeks to move beyond the paradigmatic Foucaultian frame.[8] But while certain key departures are made from this frame—often controversially so—it is important to emphasize that the various positions within (post)biopolitical debates do not necessarily abandon that which they seek to develop. Rather, in recent years, the work of Agamben, Negri, Esposito, and Derrida—and a range of interdisciplinary literatures inspired by them—has used Foucault's account as a platform for opening up new understandings of the relationship between politics and life. In this context, as Nikolas Rose (2007, 54) has argued, biopolitics must be seen more in terms of a 'perspective than a concept': one that focuses in various ways on 'attempts by authorities to intervene upon the vital characteristics of human existence'. Similarly, Thomas Lemke (2011, xi) refers to biopolitics as an 'interpretive key', which despite inspiring rival and sometimes conflicting perspectives, takes as its focus 'how the production and protection of life is articulated with the proliferation of death'. While biopolitics has been interpreted in both 'major' and 'minor' keys, the overall approach taken here is that this diversity makes it a rich and agile—though not always unproblematic—register for understanding seemingly contradictory practices in the field of contemporary EUropean border security and migration management beyond the limits of extant approaches.

One of the central features of this book is that its engagement with debates in (post)biopolitical thought is connected with and illustrated by different aspects of EUrope's border crisis. Each chapter explores a different understanding of and engagement with the biopolitical key in order to identify and interrogate different technologies of power[9] at diverse border sites: Chapter 2 explores the paradigmatic Foucaultian account via a discussion of EUropean border security and migration management from the Schengen Agreement to the Arab Spring; Chapter 3 presents a reassessment of Agamben's treatment of thanatopolitical drift in the context of illegal push-backs and acts of abandonment at land and sea across the EUropean borderscape; Chapter 4 investigates Derrida's concept of zoopower drawing upon some 'irregular' migrants' own narratives of their animalization, particularly in spaces of detention; Chapter 5 examines the implications of Esposito's paradigm of immunity against the backdrop of the increasing medicalization of EUropean border security; and Chapter 6 synthesizes the insights of Esposito and Derrida for addressing the question of what it might mean to rethink EUrope's borders along more affirmative lines from within the horizon of biopolitics. In this way, a key theme of the book is that it seeks to offer a disaggregated approach to the study of contemporary EUropean border politics: 'the border' does not exist as such beyond diverse biopolitical *attempts* to striate space and produce subjects. In this way, the analysis seeks to apply and further develop R. B. J. Walker's (2010) insight that greater attention is necessary to the complex ways in which certain borders, divisions, and distinctions must be read as enabling other borders, divisions, and distinctions in contemporary political life. Most notably, the Foucaultian account of biopolitics demands a greater appreciation of how the anterior border between life and death operates at diverse sites of encounter between EUropean border security authorities and 'irregular' migrants. Further still, the Derridean concept of the zoopolitical threshold emphasizes how biopolitical security not only relies on and reproduces borders between life and death, but also between human and animal subjectivities.

Taken as a whole, the book seeks to foreground the notion of encounter as a way of avoiding an essentialized understanding of what and where 'the borders' of EUrope must be while retaining an analytical focus on bordering practices as attempts to produce and police 'irregular' mobility. Focusing on the encounter in this way also allows for closer analysis of the mutually constitutive field of interaction between policymakers, border security authorities, and 'irregular' migrants, rather than seeking to privilege one set of actors over another. Ultimately, drawing on Esposito and Derrida, I will argue for a recovery of that encounter, which has otherwise been offshored, outsourced, and folded within biometric technologies, as an ethical-political response to EUrope's border crisis that does not advocate either tougher border security or the opening up of borders—both are attempts at a politics of escape (Walker 2010). While the investigation is unapologetic in making the case for a conceptually driven approach in order to better diagnose the stakes of EUrope's border crisis and step outside the 'rhetoric/reality' frame, it also draws extensively on official policy documentation published by the EU Commission and key agencies such as Frontex, research materials produced by a range of NGOs—including 'irregular' migrants' testimonials—and insights from fieldwork visits in order to highlight the insights and limitations of various aspects of (post)biopolitical theory and to propose new interpretations of seemingly familiar positions within relevant conceptual debates.

The following chapter offers a brief historical account of the policy background to the integration of EU border security and migration management from the 1985 Schengen Agreement to the Arab Spring. It focuses on the neoliberalization of EU border security, the move to enhance flows of 'regular' people, services, and goods, and a series of accompanying spatial-temporal displacements of the border. While these elements have been covered extensively in the literature with regards to the securitization of migration, the emergence of a strong discourse of humanitarianism—associated with the EU Commission's GAMM—and the relationship between the two has received less attention. With the shift from securing territory to populations, the effort to increase circulation of people, services, and goods over an ever-expanding space, and an emphasis on optimizing the health and well-being of both 'regular' and 'irregular' populations, I argue that developments in EUropean border security and migration management closely resemble Foucault's paradigmatic account of biopolitical forms of governance. The discussion offers an overview of this account and considers the extent to which it is apposite to diagnosing tensions at the heart of contemporary EU border security and migration management concerning the unstable and ambiguous figure of the 'irregular' migrant. While Foucault's work goes a considerable way in helping to discern the 'positive' characteristics of biopolitical bordering practices, however, it is argued that more attention needs to be given to the 'negative' dimensions that expose 'irregular' populations to dehumanization and death.

Chapter 3 examines contemporary contexts in the field of EU border security and migration management where—alongside the humanitarian discourse of migrant-centredness—some 'irregular' migrants are often exposed to life-threatening conditions on land and at sea. Reports by NGOs and the testimonies of 'irregular' migrants highlight brazen human rights abuses and offer a counter-archive to official narratives considered in the previous chapter. Dominant explanations focus on a 'gap' between 'policy' and 'practice', but this framing fails to capture the ambiguous subject position of the 'irregular' migrant within 'policy' discourses or the problem that humanitarian appeals ultimately reinforce the aims and outcomes of the GAMM. What is required, therefore, are alternative conceptual resources for diagnosing and problematizing the relationship between the humanitarianism of the GAMM and the persistence of border violence. Foucault's understanding of biopolitical governance as to '*make* live and *let* die' is inadequate as a diagnosis of situations in which some 'irregular' migrants are endangered precisely by the authorities associated with humanitarian border security: the 'letting die' part of his equation entails a passivity that belies concerted efforts to police 'irregularity' via lethal modes of biopolitical abandonment. This is investigated in the context of 'push-back' operations and failures to respond to 'irregular' migrants' distress calls, typically in the Mediterranean and Aegean seas. While Agamben's thanatopolitical theses have been strongly criticized, in these contexts I argue that it is important to recognize the operation of the sovereign ban in order to understand the systemic conditions that lead to the loss of life: otherwise, deaths continue to be read as one-off tragic accidents used to justify more security and surveillance measures under the rubric of humanitarianism. However, the analysis also seeks to modify Agamben's arguments in the light of testimonies by rethinking the concept of the sovereign decision and the everyday material potency of the ban. In this way, a more nuanced exegesis and application of Agamben is advanced for critical border and migration studies.

While Agamben's conceptualization of the thanatopolitical potential of the sovereign ban provides a compelling diagnosis of acts of abandonment and the loss of life at sea, Chapter 4 agrees with extant criticisms of the inapplicability of his work in the context of contemporary spaces of detention across the EU and beyond. Drawing extensively on 'irregular' migrants' protests against their dehumanization and, in some contexts, animalization in such spaces—some of which are, indeed, former public zoos—the discussion argues that a different technology of power is at play, which demands a conceptual understanding beyond the sovereign exposure to death. After a detailed exploration of conditions of detention particularly in the Evros region of Greece—with a special focus on what is at stake in the systematic denial of access to vital critical infrastructure networks—the move to police populations via their dehumanization is examined in relation to Agamben's (2004a) lesser-known work on the 'anthropological machine' and Derrida's (2009) concept of zoopower. While to some extent complementary, Derrida's recent reflections on the relationship between the human/animal distinction, biopolitics, and sovereignty are shown to offer greatest insight into what is at stake in the move to animalize the human. Beyond simply a gap between the neo-liberal rhetoric of the GAMM and the realities on the ground, Derrida offers critical resources for conceptualizing how the animalization of 'irregular' migrants reveals the bestial potential of EU border security practices and, in turn, how these depend on and reproduce prior zoopolitical distinctions and spaces. Derrida's zoopolitical critique demands a keener awareness and interrogation of the operation of the human/animal distinction under biopolitical conditions, not only in the context of border security practices, but also in the context of responses to them in which we find calls for 'rehumanization'.

Having charted thanatopolitical and zoopolitical drift within biopolitical border security practices across a range of sites in EUrope, Chapter 5 tackles head-on the research puzzle at the heart of this book. It is argued that Esposito is instructive in the crucial task of understanding how the dichotomous terms of existing debates in critical border and migration studies set up a false 'choice' in interpreting contemporary biopolitical conditions as *either* essentially 'negative' or 'positive'. Via the concept of immunity, Esposito deconstructs this binary and shows that, rather than reflecting merely divergent schools of thought within (post)biopolitical theory, these poles represent deeper contradictory dynamics within biopolitics. The substantive analysis focuses on the spatial-ontological devices found in Esposito's work and their implications for theorizing political space in general and the concept of the border in particular. As well as developing new understandings of security in terms of immunitary protection, Esposito paves the way for reconceptualizing the border as an immune system that seeks to defend the life of the body politic. But the immunitary features of the border mean that there is always potential for excessive defence, which runs a risk of negating the very lives it seeks to protect. On this view, EU border security practices are neither intrinsically 'good' nor 'bad', but precisely a biopolitical immune system with Janus-faced potentialities. The insights of Esposito's immunitary paradigm are set against the contemporary problematization of 'irregular' populations as 'contagion' and the creeping medicalization of EU border security as a form of therapeutic intervention. In this way, a further technology of power is explored: one associated with immunitary bordering practices.

Must biopolitical border security practices always result in death and/or animalization? Are humanitarian discourses sufficient for critiquing contemporary biopolitical forms of border violence? Is a more affirmative approach to borders possible within the biopolitical frame? The final chapter acknowledges that bordering practices are only ever *attempts* at controlling mobility and that some 'irregular' migrants—as well as biopolitical apparatuses of security—have agentic capacities. However, instead of rushing to prioritize an ontology of escape, agency, appropriation, and/or resistance, I urge for an approach that steps back and considers very carefully what is at stake in the attempt to articulate a more affirmative border imaginary from within the biopolitical horizon. Initially, the discussion mobilizes resources found within Esposito's thought for thinking biopolitics affirmatively beyond the 'negative'/thanatopolitical versus 'positive'/vitalist frame. His search for alternative biopolitical grammars is mounted from within the terms of the immunitary *dispositif*, which refuses to gloss over the potential for thanatopolitical and zoopolitical drift. With a subversive reading of *communitas* as an opening on to the common and the notion of 'impersonal politics' as an alternative register to that of the modern sovereign subject, Esposito is suggestive of an approach that reconceptualizes the border as a site of encounter between self and other: too much protection or too little protection will lead to an autoimmune crisis. But while Esposito's work gets us so far, I argue that Derrida's reworking of autoimmunity as a productive force—and, in particular, his autoimmune figure of 'hostipitality'—goes even further in paving the way for a critical and politically engaged response to the dynamics of EUrope's border crisis.

Notes

1. 'Irregularity' is used in inverted commas in order to denaturalize the category as one that is performatively produced by apparatuses of border security (Squire 2011; see Chapter 3 for a fuller discussion).
2. The term 'EUrope' is used throughout this book in order to acknowledge that the spatial and legal limits of the 'European Union' are related to but not coterminous with that of 'Europe' (Bialasiewicz 2011; Walker 2000; see Chapter 2 for a fuller discussion).

3. According to the IOM (2014), in 2014 more than 3,500 'irregular' migrants are estimated to have died while attempting to cross the Mediterranean Sea, making it the most deadly stretch of water in the world despite also being one of the most monitored.

4. Since 1993 the NGO United Against Racism has compiled a list of documented 'migrant deaths' linked with EU immigration and asylum policy, border control and management, and detention and deportation systems. As of 1 January 2015 the total figure stands at 18,759 deaths, but clearly this tells only a part of the story and an unknown number of people have also perished without trace; others have experienced the embodied violence of EUropean border security in various ways and have nonetheless survived (United Against Racism 2014). The detail of each entry on the list reveals that some deaths arise from direct encounters with EUropean border security authorities; others are accounted for by suicide and personal accidents and injuries (see Chapters 3 and 4 for a fuller discussion).

5. Debrix and Barder (2012, 10) offer a helpful distinction between geopolitics and biopolitics as follows: 'Whereas geopolitics of security are driven by the need to protect and defend the territory of the sovereign nation-state, biopolitics of security are geared towards constantly promoting and improving the conditions of life of a population or species.'

6. Gros (2014, 25) usefully characterizes the shift to biopolitical apparatuses of security when he argues: 'It is striking the way in which the question of security is no longer posed in terms of closure as in the modern age, where the two symbols of security were the prison, for internal security, and the border, for external security, but, instead, in terms of the control of circulations and exchanges.'

7. For an extended engagement with Squire (2011) and McNevin (2013) and the literature in critical border and migration studies more generally see Chapter 3.

8. By now there is a considerable body of interdisciplinary scholarship associated with (post)biopolitical theory (see *inter alia* Clough and Willse 2011; Debrix and Barder 2012; Lemke 2011; Lemm and Vatter 2014; Prozorov 2013; Rose 2007; Sakai and Solomon 2006; Wolfe 2012). While heterogeneous, a common goal of this work is to engage the paradigmatic Foucaultian account of biopolitics and explore its insights and limitations in relation to dynamics in contemporary political life. In this context, (post)biopolitics does not signal the rejection of biopolitics, but rather an attempt to work through what is at stake in thinking beyond the Foucaultian account. For a fuller discussion see Chapter 2.

9. In this context, the concept of technology refers in a broad sense to technological aspects of government characterized by Bröckling et al. (2010, 12), as follows: 'The concept of technology . . . includes technical artifacts, strategies of social engineering, and technologies of the self; it refers to both arrangement of machines, medical networks . . . and so forth, and to a range of procedural devices through which individuals and collectives shape the behavior of each other or themselves.'

2

Biopolitical Borders

Introduction

The global migration of people has increased dramatically in recent years. According to data produced by the UN (2013b) in 1960 there were 75 million international migrants; by 2005 this figure had doubled to 191 million; and in 2013 it is estimated that 232 million—or 3.2 per cent of the globe's population—are international migrants living abroad with the largest concentration in the EU (72 million). In the policy rhetoric of the EU Council the issue of the mobility of people is framed passively as an inevitable 'reality that will persist as long as there are differentials of wealth and development between the various regions of the world' (EU Council 2008, 2). Distancing itself from the roles that EUrope has historically played in perpetuating these inequalities, the Council claims that migration and the external dimension of asylum in particular is a fact of life that will become increasingly important.

Migration and its effects on the EU are typically presented throughout official discourse in ambivalent terms. For example, in the 2008 'Pact on Asylum' the Council emphasizes that 'legal' international migration must be seen as an 'opportunity' that can 'contribute decisively to the economic growth of the EU and of those Member States which need migrants because of the state of their labour markets or of their demography' (EU Council 2008, 2). Similarly, in the Stockholm Programme Action Plan it is stated that 'Immigration has a valuable role to play in addressing the Union's demographic challenge and in securing the EU's strong economic performance over the longer term. It has great potential to contribute to the Europe 2020 strategy, by providing an additional source of dynamic growth' (EU Commission 2010a, 7). However, the same policy documents also assert that the economic benefits of 'legal' migration need to be weighed up against other social factors: 'poorly managed immigration may disrupt the...cohesion of the countries of destination. The organisation of immigration must consequently take account of Europe's reception capacity in terms of its labour market, housing, and health, education and social services, and protect migrants against possible exploitation by criminal networks' (EU Council 2008, 2).

More recently, particularly in the light of austerity measures and the vision for sustainable growth put forward in 'Europe 2020', EU elites have stressed the importance of neo-liberal 'flexible migration policies' that are able to respond quickly to likely future demands of labour markets (EU Council 2010, 27). Yet, despite the stated need for flexible labour in response to domestic shortages, opportunities for unskilled migrants to seek work in person—particularly those from Morocco, Algeria, Tunisia, and other African states—have been severely curtailed since the introduction of strict visa requirements in the early 1990s (UN 2013a; Guild and Carrera 2013). Without the existence of 'regular' channels open to those seeking employment an unknown number of migrants have sought to enter the EU via methods and points of entry deemed to be 'irregular'. Indeed, a moral panic surrounding 'irregularity' has emerged as part of EUrope's border crisis—particularly in the aftermath of population upheavals across North Africa associated with the 2011 Arab Spring and the NATO-led bombing of Libya (Garelli and Tazzioli 2013)—which, as subsequent chapters will go on to explore in greater detail, has also severely compromised access to asylum and international protection and led to dehumanizing conditions and deaths (UN 2013a). These dynamics—associated with the 'turbulent excess' of migrant mobilities (Mezzadra and Neilson 2013, 102–3)—animate contemporary EU border security policies and practices as much as they are produced by them.

This chapter examines the problematization of enhanced border security as the 'solution' to the 'problem' of 'irregular' migration in the EUropean context and argues that this perpetuates and further entrenches the crisis it purports to respond to. It begins by offering a brief account of the historical, political, and policy contexts in which this problematization has taken place from the 1985 Schengen Agreement to the 2011 Arab Spring and its immediate aftermath. The discussion then traces the evolution of the crisis of EU border security as a series of spatial displacements and temporal deferrals, which I argue has produced the 'irregular' migrant as a highly ambivalent and unstable subject. On the one hand, this figure is presented in elite policy discourse as a security threat to idealized notions of the economy, identity, and solidarity of the EU as a sovereign political community: there has been significant investment in pan-EUropean military-style coordination via Frontex, 'homeland security' surveillance systems, and new legislation such as the controversial Return Directive. On the other hand, in the EU Commission's renewed 2011 GAMM the 'irregular' migrant is also increasingly presented as a political subject whose life is threatened and must be protected, saved, and *empowered* by EU border security apparatuses: the imperatives to mount search and rescue missions at sea, enhance surveillance to prevent 'unnecessary' deaths, and

ensure human rights throughout 'irregular' migrants' journeys were all underscored by the Commission in response to the October 2013 Lampedusa incident, for example.

While the securitization of migration and the strengthening and pluraliza-
tion of EUrope's borders has already attracted significant critical attention, the
rise of bordering practices under the rubric of humanitarianism—and the
relationship between these dynamics—has not been subjected to the same
degree of scrutiny (Walters 2011, 138; see also Garelli and Tazzioli 2013;
Mezzadra and Neilson 2013; Stierl 2014; Ticktin 2011). However, instead
of viewing securitization and humanitarianism as essentially contradictory
elements within the field of EUropean border security and migration
management—or the difference between 'rhetoric' and 'reality' (UN 2013a;
Mezzadra and Neilson 2013)—the argument I advance here is that they can be
more instructively interpreted as twinned elements of what Michel Foucault
outlined as biopolitical forms of governmentality.[1] In the following discussion I summarize this account and consider the extent to which it is apposite
to diagnosing tensions at the heart of contemporary EU border security and
migration management concerning the unstable and ambiguous figure of the
'irregular' migrant. While I suggest that Foucault's work goes a considerable
way in helping to discern the 'positive' characteristics of biopolitical bordering
practices (associated with the humanitarian urge to 'protect', 'save', and
'empower' 'irregular' migrants), ultimately I will argue that the 'negative'
dimensions (practices that habitually expose 'irregular' populations to dehumanization and death) exceed the diagnostic capacity of the Foucaultian
frame. The latter dimensions form the basis for further investigation and
alternative diagnoses via engagements with the modified (post)biopolitical
accounts of Giorgio Agamben, Jacques Derrida, and Roberto Esposito in
Chapters 3, 4, and 5, respectively.

EUropean Border Security and Migration Management: From Schengen to the Arab Spring

The lifting of internal border controls between France, Germany, Belgium,
Luxembourg, and the Netherlands—originally provided for in the 1985
Schengen Agreement—is often posited as an important milestone in prominent narratives of the trajectory of EUropean integration (Walters 2002). Yet, it
was not until the meeting of the Tampere Council in 1999 that Member States
agreed in principle to the establishment of a 'Common European Asylum
System' (CEAS). Under the Hague Programme, border security and migration
management—historically two of the most sensitive topics and the preserve
of Member States (UN 2013a)—were brought closer together in policy and

practice. Between 1999 and 2005 the policy emphasis was on harmonizing legal frameworks in respect of both external border controls and asylum standards. In a second phase, from 2005 to 2010, attempts were made to align the conditions for legal migration and establish areas for cooperation in the attempt to control 'irregular' migration. One of the most significant developments in the practice of integrated border security and migration management was the establishment in May 2005 of Frontex to coordinate and promote a pan-EUropean model. Since 2010 this fusion of the two fields has continued under the auspices of the Stockholm Programme of the European Council, which has sought to both mainstream human rights and strengthen external border controls (UN 2013a).

As of 2013 the expanded Schengen area of internal free movement comprises a total of twenty-six states (twenty-two of which are EU Member States together with European Free Trade Association (EFTA) states Iceland, Liechtenstein, Norway, and Switzerland), encompassing 42,673 km of external sea borders and 7,721 km of land borders (UN 2013a, 5). While data presented by the UN indicate that the majority of migrants deemed to be in the EU 'irregularly' are those who enter legally and then overstay their visa, considerable policy, media, and academic attention has been given to formal land and sea borders as sites of encounter between enforcers and challengers of the Schengen regime—again particularly since 2011 (UN 2013a; see also Mainwaring 2012). Alongside what many authors have referred to as the 'securitization of migration' (Bigo and Guild 2005; Guild 2009; Huysmans 2000, 2006; van Munster 2009)—the process whereby migration is read through the lens of security as an existential threat to the identity, economy, and welfare of the EU—the strengthening of border security has gradually become posited as the primary 'solution' to the 'problem' of 'irregular' migration. Moves towards the securitization of migration and the enhancement of EU border security predate the attacks on the World Trade Center and Pentagon of September 2001. In 1989 the so-called Trevi group—originally set up in 1976 to coordinate policing and counter-terrorism in what was then the European Economic Community (EEC)—expanded its remit to include immigration and asylum matters. In 1990 the Convention implementing the Schengen Agreement—which entered into force in 1995—further consolidated the connection between immigration, asylum, transnational crime, and terrorism in the formal constitutional structure of the EEC: what was formerly an issue considered resolvable in the sphere of politics had been shifted, albeit subtly, into the 'domain of security' (Huysmans 2006, 4). Together with the lifting of internal controls among Schengen states a series of 'compensatory measures' were introduced over a number of years in order to develop what Walters (2002, 573) has called a 'more diffuse, networked, control apparatus', which interlaced 'internal' and 'external' attempts to monitor 'irregularity' into and throughout the

Schengen area. Since the formal incorporation of the Schengen *acquis* into the legal framework of the EU and the establishment of the 'Area of Freedom, Security, and Justice' under the 1999 Treaty of Amsterdam, the attacks of 9/11, the bombings in Madrid and London, and the Arab Spring have all been responded to by EUropean elites in ways that further intensify and entrench these long-standing trends: far from being a fixed control on movement at the outer-edge of Member States' territories, the EU border has evolved into a complex, multiform, and highly dynamic apparatus (Bigo and Guild 2005; Bigo et al. 2007; Huysmans 2006; Walters 2002).

Border security and migration management cannot be separated and at base are inextricably interlinked via multiple efforts to differentiate and categorize people (Guild 2009). Ever more 'sophisticated' border security measures are continually justified on the grounds of the perceived requirement to 'better' categorize, risk assess, and sift out 'irregular' migrants from 'citizens', 'refugees', 'legal economic migrants', and those eligible for 'subsidiary protection'. However, the attempt to distinguish between individuals and populations in this context is performative of the social reality it purports merely to reflect: through their encounter with border security apparatuses political subjectivities are (re)produced via the deployment of specific juridical-political terminologies— 'regular'/'irregular', 'voluntary'/'involuntary', 'asylum seeker'/'refugee', and so on—each with very significant consequences for individuals' immediate circumstances and longer-term livelihoods. The figure of the 'irregular' migrant is at the heart of EU border security and migration management because this subject position is *both* the alleged 'cause' of the need for tougher measures *and* the performative 'effect' of those very measures. What this amounts to is a powerful—albeit paradoxical—teleology, whereby the more 'successful' EU border security practices become the greater the number of 'irregular' migrants are performatively identified as such. It is paradoxical because ultimately the 'effect' (greater numbers of 'irregular' migrants) becomes referred to as the cause of the 'cause' (the perceived need for greater border security) (see Culler 1982; Derrida 1982).

The following discussion considers in greater detail the above trajectory of border security and migration management in EUrope by positing three inter-related analytical axes: first, the neo-liberalization, technologization, and outsourcing of border controls; second, the external, pre-emptive, and increasingly militarized projection of bordering practices beyond the physical territory of Member States; and third, the emergence of a strong discourse of 'humanitarian' border security accompanying this militarization of the EUropean borderscape. Taken together, I argue that these developments constitute a series of spatial and temporal displacements of 'the border' such that not only has its nature and location been fundamentally transformed, but also that access to asylum and international protection is increasingly curtailed.

The Neo-liberalization, Technologization, and Outsourcing of the Border

Nikolas Rose (2007, 3–4) argues that contemporary advanced liberal demo-cratic societies are characterized by three primary features: the reorganization of the state so that it is increasingly directed towards the imperatives of global market capitalism; the devolution of responsibility for the management of populations from what were formerly state authorities; and the notion that individuals are increasingly responsible for their own welfare and security and that of their families. These elements of Rose's pithy characterization are reflected in what a number of critical analysts have already referred to as the 'neo-liberalization' of EUropean border control in recent years, marked by: the rise of a €multimillion EUrope-wide homeland security industry (Hayes 2009; Prokkola 2013); the shift from state monopolies on the provision of border security to an increasing reliance on for-profit public–private partnerships (Amoore 2006; Bialasiewicz 2011); and a new twinned emphasis on the role of the EU citizen in the risk-management cycle and levels of 'customer experience' among 'trusted travellers' at 'regular' border crossings in the con-text of land, sea, and air travel (Rumford 2009; van Houtum 2010; Vaughan-Williams 2010).

Since the 1985 Schengen Agreement there has been a technological trans-formation in EU border security designed to performatively establish and police the distinction between 'regular' and 'irregular' mobilities. Early initiatives such as the development of the 'Schengen Information System' (SIS) allowed for better communication and closer cooperation between national police forces, customs officials, and judiciaries. In 1999 the Treaty of Amsterdam gave the EU Commission a greater role in managing Member States' external borders for the purpose of managing immigration and asylum. A year later the legal framework was established for EURODAC—the EU-wide biometric database of the finger-prints of 'irregular' migrants aged fourteen years and above—which as of January 2014 holds the personal data of more than 2.3 million individuals (Jones 2014c). This system, implemented in January 2003 and designed for the purposes of applying the Dublin Convention on the reception and processing of asylum seekers, informs operating staff whether an applicant has previously claimed asylum or been apprehended for illegal entry in another Member State. EURODAC was followed in 2004 by the creation of the EU Visa Information System (VIS) comprising of 'National Interfaces' in each Member State and an overarching communication infrastructure network. A further milestone came in 2008 with the announcement by the Commission of the 'Smart Borders Initiative' (SBI), which committed the EU to a further technologization of its borders (see Dijstelbloem and Meijer 2011).

According to the EU Commission's 2011 communication 'Smart Borders—options and the way ahead', the SBI has the 'dual objectives of enhancing security and facilitating travel' (EU Commission 2011d, 2). The SBI comprises two key components: an Entry/Exit System (EES) and a Registered Traveller Programme (RTP). The former is an automated system designed to calculate the length of an authorized stay and verify the individual travel history of 'regular' travellers in order to replace passport stamping with 'an electronic registry of the dates and places of third country nationals admitted short stays' (EU Commission 2011d, 4). It is designed to speed up the border crossings of 4–5 million 'regular' passengers *per annum* and reduce time spent at the traditional border flashpoint from between one and two minutes to less than thirty seconds. The RTP programme facilitates this use of automated border controls by pre-vetting and pre-screening third-country travellers at the Schengen external border, which, according to the Commission, provides 'a tangible confirmation of the EU's openness to the world and commitment to facilitating travel and cross-border contacts including for business' (EU Commission 2011d, 12).

The growing consensus around technological solutions to the policy and practical 'challenges' of 'irregular' migration has given rise to the increased involvement of the private sector in the field of EUropean border security. In one direction, this has entailed an ever more significant role for multinational companies such as Safran Morpho, Thales International, and Raytheon Systems in the research and development of new border security technologies, which underpin EUropean industry. Each year there are a burgeoning number of high-profile international conferences that bring together representatives of industry, EU Member States and agencies, and policymaking communities.[2] At these events it is possible to identify a cyclical culture whereby the presentation of new technologies not only responds to, but also enables and drives the formulation of new policies and practices in the field of border security and migration management. Thus, for example, at the 2011 Round Table Symposium on European Border Security organized by the International Centre for Parliamentary Studies, a sales director from the French defence firm Safran Morpho pitched her company's 'perfect border solution' to an audience of no more than thirty including EU Commissioner for Home Affairs Celia Malmström and former Frontex Director Ilkka Laittenan.[3] Gillian Ormiston presented the new system, which she claimed was the next market-leader in improving both EUropean security and 'customer experience' before, during, and after travel. New technologies developed by Safran Morpho include quadrupole resonance technology to scan footwear while it is still being worn, tomographic 3D detection systems to identify the nature and quantity of explosives hidden in items such as laptops, and x-ray defraction methods to measure the density of suspicious liquids—all designed to achieve an 'optimal encounter' of less than thirty seconds. In this way the company's vision for the 'perfect border' is said to be fast, unobtrusive, and 'smart' for those deemed to be 'trusted travellers'.

Aside from research and development capacity, for several decades the private sector has also acquired an augmented role in the implementation of EUropean border security and migration management. The outsourcing of border security—formerly the preserve of the authority of Member States— to commercial interests has given rise to new dynamics whereby responsibility not only for bordering practices but also for access to asylum and international protection is deferred and in some cases displaced altogether. A prominent example of the outsourcing of the border in this context is the transferal of the governance of 'irregular' mobility at sea to the maritime industry (Migreurop 2012; Maquet and Zartea 2013). With 75 per cent of all global trade trans- ported on the high seas, 'irregular' migrants often use commercial routes as a mode of obtaining access into EUrope. Since the 1990s the use of shipping agents to police 'irregularity' on maritime trade routes has been common- place. The heightened securitization of maritime space following the attacks of 11 September 2011 has meant an enhanced role for these private agents. The introduction of the 'International Ship and Port Security' (ISPS) code in 2004 established an international framework for detecting and managing a range of security risks associated with 'irregular' migration including piracy and terrorism. Many private shipping companies—such as UK-based Robmar- ine Insurance—are indirectly involved in preparing risk analyses of sea-based 'irregularity'. More directly still is the involvement of the maritime industry in dealing with the issue of 'irregular' stowaways at sea (Maquet and Zartea 2013).

According to the NGO Migreurop (2012), the phenomenon of the 'irregular' migrant stowaway—defined by the International Maritime Organization as someone who hides on a vessel at sea without the captain's consent and is discovered after the ship has left port—is especially common in southern Mediterranean ports, although the overall scale of the issue in EUrope is largely unknown. In the context of attempting to police 'irregular migration' from the south, the port at Tangiers is the most heavily securitized in the Mediterranean: 'At the port's entrance, the lorries are checked by customs officers, particularly the seals on containers. Then the lorries enter what we call the lock where, at first, the cargo's radioactivity is verified. Afterwards, we auscultate each lorry with the help of heartbeat detectors. Finally, we examine the lorries using two scanners. We conduct between two hundred and one thousand controls every day and, in this way, we catch between six and eight stowaways every month' (Tangiers Port official quoted in Migreurop 2012, 55). Sometimes on inspection there are only material traces of individuals' passage such as empty water bottles, the remains of food, and so on (Migreurop 2012, 35). However, the maritime industry has negotiated a series of procedures in the event that stowaways are found at sea. Under these circumstances the captain of the vessel will conduct an interview and complete a questionnaire in order to collect a range of personal data including height, weight, eye colour, hair colour, skin colour, and facial shape, and in some cases a photograph is also attached to the document (Migreurop 2012, 59). The interview also seeks to ascertain the reason for the journey, and details of the date, place, and method of embarkation. This information is then typically passed on to legal representatives of ship-owners' Protection and Indemnity (P&I) Insurance Clubs who, in turn, make further arrangements with external private security companies for stowaways to be repatriated (Maquet and Zartea 2013). In such cases, as the Migreurop report has pointed out, a process purporting to be merely an administrative exercise turns effectively into policing, policymaking, and decision-making on the spot. The commercial objectives of shipping companies—together with the fact that some Member States including France and Spain have powers to fine firms that allow the disembarkation of stowaways at their ports—means that any other outcome is highly unlikely irrespective of the specificities of the case: 'The main goal for a crew that discovers one or several of them on board is to get rid of them as quickly as possible in order for them not to delay the boat's schedule and not to cause excessively high costs for ship-owners' (Migreurop 2012, 83). With border security practices outsourced from Member States and the EU to the maritime industry, from the maritime industry to insurance companies, and from insurance companies to private security personnel, the case of the 'management' of stowaways, therefore, provides a powerful example of the contemporary spatial and temporal deferral and displacement not only of 'the border'—understood in terms of an attempted control on 'irregular' movement—but also that of access to asylum and international protection. Another form of externalization—in some cases thousands of miles away from the territories of EU Member States and often characterized by a pseudo-military nature—can also be found in the context of the outward projection of offshore bordering practices.

The Outward Projection and Militarization of the Border

In an effort to export the border and pre-empt the arrival of 'irregular migrants' on the shores of EUrope, the Commission and Member States have established a complex web of networks with a range of neighbouring third countries. While the outward projection of Europe's borders is, of course, an historic practice—and one that could certainly be traced further back to colonial logics of striating space to control subjects overseas—in recent years it has been diversified and further entrenched as part of official EU border security and migration management. Since the early 2000s immigration and asylum controls have effectively been outsourced not only to private security companies, but also to historically undemocratically elected regimes—

particularly, though not exclusively, across North Africa. The EU Commission's response to the Arab Spring further enhanced these dynamics via the launch in December 2011 of the renewed GAMM. The GAMM has become the overarching policy framework for the field of EU border security and migration management, and it has played an important role in bringing these two dimensions even closer together. François Crepeau, the UN Special Rapporteur on the human rights of migrants, refers to the GAMM as 'shaping and influencing all other management decisions by all entities of the EU' in this field (UN 2013a). One of the chief aims of the renewed GAMM was to 'include "mobility"', thereby stressing the importance of fostering well-managed mobility of third country nationals across the external EU borders' (EU Commission 2014a, 2). The primary mechanisms for achieving this 'mobility' are a series of bilateral frameworks known as 'Mobility Partnerships' (MPs): mechanisms that project EUrope's ability to control movement far beyond what are traditionally considered to be the territorial limits of EUrope.

As of September 2014, MPs have been signed with Moldova (2008), Cape Verde (2008), Georgia (2009), Armenia (2011), Morocco (2013), and Azerbaijan (2013), and shortly after the Jasmine Revolution proposals for a 'Dialogue for Migration, Mobility, and Security' were discussed with Tunisia, Egypt, and Libya. Since 2011 the 'Regional Protection Programme for North Africa' has received funding of €5.5 million with separate agreements for Morocco and Libya worth €11 million and €30 million, respectively (EU Commission 2014a, 6). MPs are designed to promote 'regular' migration, particularly economic migration, in order to meet the supply and demand needs of the EUropean labour market (Martin 2014). In exchange for enhancing the mobility of 'regular' economic migrants via visa assistance under the terms of these agreements the EU expects third countries to play a more active role in the policing of 'irregular' migration. Separate agreements also exist between Frontex and third countries, which allow for enhanced cooperation, the deployment of liaison officers, and the use of local authorities to effectively police the EU's borders, albeit thousands of miles away from Member States. For example, in 2012 agreements were signed with Nigeria and Armenia: the former to curb cross-border crime, human trafficking, and 'irregular' entry of Nigerian nationals; the latter to manage 'irregular' migration from the south Caucasus. In these ways—reflecting the emergence of a strong humanitarian discourse as the analysis will go on to examine—the EU Commission claims that agreements have been put in place 'in order to avoid that migrants embark on hazardous journeys towards the EU' (EU Commission 2014a, 5).

However, despite the EU Commission's presentation of MPs and cooperation with third countries on border security and migration management as being (i) in the economic interests of both third countries and EU Member States, and (ii) orientated around the technical pooling of expertise and resources, the outsourcing of bordering practices raises a number of ethical-political issues. A number of NGOs have pointed out that agreements reached under the terms of MPs have not been subjected to democratic debate in the EU Parliament, are not legally binding, and there are no monitoring mechanisms in place in order to ensure that third-country authorities respect the human rights of 'irregular' migrants whose movement they are tasked with controlling (Migreurop 2012; Martin 2014). As Luiza Bialasiewicz (2011) has highlighted, the *de facto* transference of access to asylum and international protection from EUrope to third countries has placed responsibility for 'irregular' migrants in the hands of former dictatorships with dismal human rights records. The effect of the outward projection of the common refugee protection framework away from EUrope is the advent of what Thomas Gammeltoft-Hansen (2011, 146) refers to as 'protection lite', which has given rise to the 'eclipse of a range of legal constraints'. Moreover, Ruben Andersson (2014) demonstrates that, in a further extension of the neo-liberal market logic identified earlier, authorities of third states often sub-contract border control to private security companies and local militias who then profit from amplifying the perceived risk of 'irregular' migration as a part of a cyclical industry. For example, he argues that the externalization of EUrope's bordering practices to the Sahel and Sahara has reduced West African migration to the Canary Islands and that private African forces have attracted increased EUropean funding by exaggerating the criminality of travellers who have often 'only committed an administrative infraction' (Andersson 2014, 123). Finally, as Chapters 3 and 4 will explore in greater depth, the work of NGOs has traced the egregious effects of the outsourcing of EUrope's border controls, which have exposed thousands of 'irregular' migrants to death at sea and on land routes and also to degrading, inhuman, and animalized conditions in detention centres: 'This war against migrants that has led thousands of people trying to escape patrols and other military devices to die in the Mediterranean and tens of thousands more locked up in the camps of Algeria, Egypt, Libya, Tunisia' (Migreurop 2012, 103–4).

Alongside the neo-liberalization, technologization, and outsourcing of EUropean bordering practices, another trend has emerged in recent years: the increasing use of military and military-style measures in managing the risk of 'irregular' migration (Balibar 2009; Borderline Europe 2013; PICUM 2010). While Frontex has sought to characterize itself as a technocratic risk manager and mere coordinator of EUrope's borders, its profile and the nature of many of its operations are now more akin to those of military-style forces. As of 2014, Frontex has access to a pool of 2,484 border officers, 196 coastal patrol vessels with a range of 600 nautical miles, 26 offshore patrol vessels with a range of 1,500 miles, 53 helicopters, 224 'mobile laboratories' including heartbeat and carbon dioxide detectors, and 43 fixed-wing aircraft (Jones

2014a). Since the mid-2000s, Frontex missions—including Operation HERA II in the Canary Islands and the West African coastlines—have deployed military equipment supplied by Member States in order to mount surveillance and controversial 'push-back' operations at sea and on land (Carrera 2007; Vaughan-Williams 2011a; see Chapter 3). In 2010 the first 'Rapid Border Intervention Team' (RABIT)—a SWAT-style unit designed to respond to urgent and exceptional migratory pressure—was deployed in the Evros region of Greece (see Chapter 3). Moreover, while their potential use remains controversial, the legal framework for the deployment of 'Unmanned Aerial Vehicles' (UAVs or 'drones') within forty nautical miles of EU Member States' shores is in place and often referred to in official policy documentation (EU Commission 2011c; Hayes and Vermeulen 2012, 38).

One of the central characteristics of the so-called 'Revolution in Military Affairs' (RMA) is, of course, the harnessing of new information technologies to avoid what Clausewitz famously referred to as the 'Fog of War' (Peoples and Vaughan-Williams 2015). In this context, alongside the potential use of drone technology, EUropean border security practices are increasingly reliant upon various forms of military-style aerial surveillance techniques. The use of satellites, GPS, and other forms of virtual communications to gain real-time information about the battlefield between border security authorities and 'irregular' migrants is most notably reflected in the emergence of the 'European Border Surveillance System' (EUROSUR). Alongside the EES and RTP programmes, EUROSUR is a €250 million multiplatform surveillance system—operational from December 2013—that aims to 'reinforce the control of the Schengen external borders' by assisting EU Member States and Frontex to 'share information and improve cooperation' (EU Commission 2011c, 1). The legal framework establishing EUROSUR draws on the militarized language of 'situational awareness and reaction capability', which the Commission claims will reinforce border control on land and at sea (EU Commission 2011c, 2). Here 'situational awareness' refers to 'the ability to monitor, detect, identify, track and understand cross-border activities in order to find reasoned grounds for control measures on the basis of combining new information with existing knowledge' (Article 3a) (EU Commission 2011c, 9). Data produced by EUROSUR are designed to assist national and supranational border security authorities by providing 'analysis of irregular migration, cross-border crime, crisis situations and other events, categorized on the basis of either a low, medium, or high impact level' (EU Commission 2011c, 9). Consistent with other attempts to elongate the reach of EUrope's borders above, Article 12 refers to the projection of EUROSUR's capability beyond the territorial limits of EU Member States to include the 'selective monitoring of 3rd country ports and coasts identified through risk analysis' and surveillance of the 'prefrontier area' (EU Commission 2011c, 9). The concept of the 'pre-frontier area'—outlined in Article 3(f) as 'the geographical area beyond the external border of the member state, which is not covered by a national border surveillance system' (EU Commission 2011c, 9)—thus reflects a further offshored spatial technology of control with pre-emptive capacities.

EUROSUR has received considerable criticism from NGOs and migrant activist groups for its military-style surveillance of 'irregular' migrants (Heller and Jones 2014; Borderline Europe 2013). As well as the potential for significant infringements of the right to privacy and data protection laws, NGOs claim that the monitoring of the 'pre-frontier area' will enhance the possibility for pre-emptive 'push-back' operations in contravention of the legal principle of *non-refoulement* (Borderline Europe 2013). However, the Commission insists that the purpose of EUROSUR is not to gather data about particular individuals or to prevent 'irregular' movement using force, but rather to detect and monitor 'incidents and depersonalized objects, such as the detection and tracking of vessels' (EU Commission 2011c, 2). Further still, particularly in the aftermath of the October 2013 Lampedusa incident discussed in Chapter 1, EUropean elites have increasingly sought to frame EUROSUR not only as a mechanism for enhancing 'the control of the Schengen borders', but also for search and rescue missions: a 'life-saving instrument' (EU Commission 2013a) that is 'crucial to . . . protecting lives at the EU's external borders' and 'enabling more effective prevention of loss of life' (EU Commission 2013b, 16–17). Thus, following his visit to the Italian island, the President of the EU Commission Jose Manuel Barroso said: 'We . . . need to strengthen our capacity for search and rescue, and our surveillance system to track boats, so that we can launch a rescue operation and bring people to safe grounds before they perish. I think the kind of tragedy we have witnessed here so close to the coast should never happen again. Our initiative "EUROSUR" is meant to do that' (quoted in Heller and Jones 2014, 9). Far from a unique framing, however, the discourse of 'saving lives' associated with EUROSUR is symptomatic of a further development: the increasing entanglement of securitizing and humanitarian logics.

Humanitarian Border Security, the Ambiguous Figure of the 'Irregular' Migrant, and the Possibility of Critique

Alongside the securitization of migration—a move that took place in the late 1980s/early 1990s (Huysmans 2000, 2006)—a strong humanitarian concern for the lives and well-being of 'irregular' migrants has also developed in the field of EUropean border security and migration management. While the focus of existing critical literature has typically been directed towards the former, less attention has been paid to what William Walters (2011, 138) has referred to as the 'birth of the humanitarian border' in EUrope and the relationship between the two discourses. Building on Walters, it is instructive to consider what is at stake in the recent emergence of the humanitarian discourse of 'migrant-centredness' found in the 2011 GAMM and its implementation. Eschewing traditional 'statist' paradigms, the renewed GAMM calls explicitly for a 'migrant-centred' approach to border security and migration management and commits EU Member States to being 'among the frontrunners' in promoting international protection (EU Commission 2011a, 6). A particular feature of the GAMM is its catch-all focus on the human rights, safety, and well-being of each *individual* migrant rather than on formal juridical-political categories of migrants: 'In essence, migration governance is not about "flows", "stocks", and "routes", it is about *people*' (EU Commission 2011a, 6, emphasis added). Elsewhere, it is argued that this approach reflects and reinforces the EU Commission's respect for the Charter of Fundamental Rights and the importance of protecting migrants not only within the territorial limits of EU Member States, but also 'along the migratory routes, in countries of origin, transit and destination' (EU Commission 2011e, 14). While the GAMM emphasizes the particular need to protect 'vulnerable' migrants—classified as unaccompanied minors, asylum seekers, victims of trafficking, stranded migrants, and women—it also refers more generally to mainstreaming democratic principles and human rights for *all* migrants as human beings irrespective of their origin, destination, or 'legal status': 'A migrant-centred approach is also about *empowering migrants*, and ensuring that they have access to all relevant information about the opportunities provided by legal migration channels and the risks of irregular migration' (EU Commission 2011e, 14, emphasis added). This discourse of empowerment is again featured in the Commission's 'Report on the Implementation of the GAMM 2012–13', which underlines the need for 'constant attention' to be given to all migrants in the EU's strategic priorities for the future (EU Commission 2014a, 18).

It is against this broader backdrop that the framing and justification of EUROSUR as a mechanism for humanitarian intelligence can be located. A number of EUropean elites joined Barroso in using the occasion of the Lampedusa incident not only to reiterate but also to strengthen this nascent humanitarian approach to border security and the aims of the GAMM more generally. As discussed in Chapter 1, Cecilia Malmström also drew attention to the need for 'quicker tracking, identifying, and the rescuing of more vessels and boats' in order to 'prevent the loss of lives at sea' (EU Commission 2013a). The emphasis on 'saving lives' while 'enhancing border security' was further reflected in Operation 'Mare Nostrum'—a military-humanitarian initiative launched in October 2013 by the Italian Navy—which Italian Interior Minister Angelino Alfano referred to as a 'proud' mission designed to prevent both human smuggling and the Mediterranean from becoming the 'lake of death' (*Times of Malta* 2014).[4]

In the case of EUROSUR and each of the examples above, the securitization of migration has become increasingly entangled with discourses of humanitarianism such that a fundamental ambiguity now surrounds the figure of the 'irregular' migrant. On the one hand, this subject is cast as one of the primary security risks to EUrope viewed as a whole. Thus, for example, in the 2010 'Internal Security Strategy' (ISS) launched by the EU Council, the 'Other' against which the 'internal' security of the EU is defined is not framed in terms of *particular* states or geopolitical regions: it is the imagined and generalized 'non-EU citizen'. While EU citizens are *not* perceived to be potential security risks, the 'non-EU citizen'—more specifically the unknown 'irregular' migrant—is interpellated as the figure associated with the primary 'crime-related risks and threats facing Europe today' listed in the ISS as: terrorism; serious and organized crime (including cyber and cross-border); drug trafficking; sexual exploitation and child pornography; economic crime and corruption; and trafficking in arms and cross-border crime (EU Commission 2010b, 3). Similarly, in its 'Communication on Migration' published on 4 May 2011, the EU Commission unambiguously framed the 'problem' of 'irregular' migration in terms of a 'threat' to: good governance (EU Commission 2011a, 2); employment rates among EU citizens (EU Commission 2011a, 3); economic competitiveness, health systems, and the social cohesion of Member States (EU Commission 2011a, 4–5); and the effectiveness and credibility of the external Schengen border (EU Commission 2011a, 7).

On the other hand, as we have also seen, the 'irregular' migrant is *simultaneously* cast in official EUropean discourse as a life that is perpetually placed in jeopardy and in need of 'saving' by border security authorities, especially Frontex. Thus, for example, within one month of the launch of the EUROSUR programme, the EU Commission sought to claim its first humanitarian victory:

> For the very first time the satellite images obtained in the framework of EUROSUR cooperation enabled [sic] to save the lives of migrants. On 16–17 September, the satellite imagery obtained ... enabled [sic] to locate and rescue a migrant rubber boat in the Mediterranean with 38 people on board, including 8 women and 3 children that has [sic] spent three days in an open sea and was drifting outside the area where search and rescue activity for the boat was ongoing originally. (EU Commission 2014a, 8)

Furthermore, in a twist to a familiar strategy used by NGOs, the Fundamental Rights Agency's 2013 report into Europe's southern sea borders includes testimonials from border security personnel who have put their own lives at risk in mounting search and rescue missions: 'Once I dived in the sea to save them but I shouldn't have done it. But when you see people drowning, sometimes you don't think straight. They can drag you down, they don't know how to hold you' (Hellenic Coast Guard interviewed in Greece, quoted in Fundamental Rights Agency 2013, 33). The same report also features testimonials from 'irregular' migrants who have had positive experiences of search and rescue missions: 'Italians picked us up at sea. A helicopter came near us. We have seen it. He turned around us about 10 times and then told us to move in this direction (indicating direction). But the boat did not go, and they realized that the boat could not go, because they gave us directions, but we stood still. Then they came back with a bigger boat after about 30–45 minutes' (unnamed male from Ivory Coast, crossed to Lampedusa, quoted in Fundamental Rights Agency 2013, 33).

The use of testimonial material to resonate with audiences is one conventionally associated with what Walters (2011, 152) calls the 'epistemic strategies' of migrants' rights activists seeking to hold a mirror up to the violence and suffering of those targeted by border security practices: 'the move is significant both in that it accords "voice" to subjects who are presumed to have no place as political subjects in official debates ... and that it acts as a tactic of empathy' (see also Fassin 2009, 2012). However, the deployment of similar strategies by EUropean agencies in order to portray a more 'positive' counter view to the field of contemporary border security and migration management is a recent phenomenon, which challenges conventional notions about the nature of migrant testimony as if it were automatically a site of resistance and contestation (Puggioni 2014; see Chapter 3). Moreover, the appropriation of migrant testimonies for radically different political purposes can be interpreted as part of an increasing propensity—exemplified in the GAMM—of the co-option of the language and posture of humanitarianism by the very authorities associated with the violence of EUropean border security and migration management. These dynamics are reflective of what I sketched in Chapter 1 as a 'crisis of humanitarian critique' for both migrant activist groups and critical border and migration studies, which have formerly relied upon methods of criticism that have now themselves become folded into official discourses and thus increasingly co-opted and neutralized.

Indeed, the increasing ambiguity and instability of the figure of the 'irregular' migrant *within* discourses and practices of EUropean border security and migration management means that humanitarianism is no longer—if it ever was—an effective check on logics of securitization: the former is not external to the latter, but inseparable from it as part of a more complex topological relation between the two (see also Walters 2011, 147; Mezzadra and Neilson 2013, 187). In this context, it is important to note that the Stockholm Programme, in particular, has consistently sought to 'balance' the imperatives of maintaining access to asylum while introducing tougher controls on mobility: 'The Union must continue to facilitate legal access to the territory of its Member States *while in parallel* taking measures to counteract illegal immigration and cross-border crime and maintaining a high level of security' (EU

Council 2010, 26, emphasis added). For these reasons it is too simplistic to portray EUropean elites as straightforwardly privileging the enhancement of border controls at the expense of human rights concerns: the latter have been mainstreamed throughout border security and migration management for some time. On the contrary, the crisis of humanitarian critique has come about because the terrain of 'official' EUropean border security and migration management has embraced the values that many of its fiercest critics have been calling for.

The dominant stance employed by those critical of the persistent violence of contemporary EUropean border politics is one that points to the seeming 'discrepancy' between the humanitarian 'rhetoric' of the GAMM and the lived 'reality' of 'irregular' populations targeted by EU border security practices. Thus, for example, in his high-profile 'Report on the Human Rights of Migrants in the EU', UN Special Rapporteur François Crepeau argues explicitly that there is a significant 'gap' between 'policy and practice': 'The EU has certainly progressively developed a more rights-friendly approach with regard to migration policy [but] the Special Rapporteur did not necessarily see this reflected in measures adopted on the ground' (UN 2013a, 9). This logic of critique is also found in the work of many NGOs, which, despite the 'saving lives' discourse of the EU Commission and Frontex, highlights 'irregular' migrants' habitual abandonment on land and at sea, dehumanization in detention centres, and even death both within and beyond the territory of Member States (Amnesty 2013; Borderline Europe 2013; Human Rights Watch 2011b; Migreurop 2012; Pro Asyl 2012a, 2012b, 2013; see also Chapters 3 and 4). Common throughout this literature is the notion—echoing long-standing Realist critiques of moral discourses in international politics (Morgenthau 1948)—that the aspiration of 'humanitarian borders' is laudable and to be welcomed in theory, but is nevertheless a smokescreen for everyday *realpolitik*. Chris Jones, writing for Statewatch, highlights this position when he argues that EU border security and migration management practices are characterized by 'a superficial adherence to European values concerning respect for rights, access to asylum, and humane treatment', which work to conceal 'a brutal reality driven by base politics' (Jones 2014a, 1).

A similar line of argument is also detectable in Sandro Mezzadra and Brett Neilson's claim that the EU's 'program of humanitarian and rational migration governance could only ever be a dream, leaving the violent face of sovereign power to intervene whenever this frame was broken or fractured in the gap that separates policy from practice' (Mezzadra and Neilson 2013, 171). Equally, for Dimitris Papadopoulos, Niamh Stephenson, and Vassilis Tsianos (2008, 182), humanitarianism is merely a 'pretext' and 'the moral panic it creates is also an excellent opportunity to generate billions for new border control projects'. According to this position the conditions for 'irregular' migrants would improve and a solution to the problem of systematic human rights abuses would be found if only the humanitarian aims of the GAMM were implemented *more successfully*. However, a major limitation of this 'rhetoric/reality' framing as the basis for mounting a critique of violent practices carried out in the name of EUropean humanitarian border security is that it ultimately makes an appeal back to rather than challenges the terms on which those practices have already been established—and continue to be justified—in the context of the GAMM. Arguing for 'better' adherence to already existing policies—as Crepeau, Jones, Mezzadra and Neilson, and Papadopoulos et al. all imply—serves to further entrench 'humanitarian border security' and its attendant ethical-political ambiguities and violence.

The content of the GAMM and its emergent 'migrant-centred' approach also poses a direct challenge to 'critical' approaches to border and migration studies in a more general sense. Many of the strategies for critique advanced by the latter have effectively been stymied by their projection into the very heart of official EUropean border security and migration management policy and practice. For example, Elspeth Guild (2009) argues that what combines mainstream approaches to migration in Political Science and the 'overarching framework promoted by political actors' is one that relies upon the massifying and statist language of 'flows', 'stocks', and 'routes'. From Guild's perspective this obscures the diverse experiences and perceptions of individual migrants and allows for their 'manipulation' in ways that lead to human rights abuses (Guild 2009, 6). In response, Guild's vision for CMS is one that refuses 'to accept the disappearance of the individual into an undifferentiated flow of or people', which she claims leads to an alternative outlook: 'When the flow is disaggregated into the individuals with their individual struggles and objectives...a very different analysis is possible' (Guild 2009, 5). Similarly, in seeking to reorientate the study of borderzones and 'irregular' migration away from what some perceive to be a prevailing exclusive and totalizing focus on the control of movement, a growing number of critical scholars have also sought to emphasize the political agency of migrants in empirical studies (Guild 2009; Johnson 2013; Mainwaring 2012; McNevin 2013; Nyers 2013; Scheel 2014; Squire 2011; Stierl 2014). I offer an extended engagement with some of these works in Chapter 3, but for now I wish to point out that such strategies of critical engagement rely on a particular problematization of actuality that is increasingly challenged by EUropean border security and migration management policy and practice. That is to say, in its stated commitment to a 'migrant-centred approach', the emphasis on the rights of each and every individual migrant irrespective of their formal juridical-political status, and a new priority given to their personal empowerment, the GAMM already pre-empts the lines of critique associated with some of this work. What we are left with, then, is a pressing policy and conceptual need to step back and search for critical resources for diagnosing and problematizing the relationship between the humanitarianism of the GAMM and the chronic continuum of border violence that continues to beset EUrope in the twenty-first century: a different interpretive key is required.

In the rest of this chapter—and, indeed, over the course of the book as a whole—I aim to respond to this task and the crisis of critique outlined above by arguing that Foucault's paradigmatic account of biopolitics offers a productive starting point for challenging dominant frameworks of understanding and developing alternative diagnoses of the Janus-faced nature of EUrope's border crisis. I will argue that the adoption of biopolitics as a grid of intelligibility offers an important and yet hitherto underexploited intellectual basis for rethinking the fundamental ambiguities surrounding the 'irregular' migrant as both a security 'risk' and life in need of 'saving': not simply in terms of the difference between 'rhetoric/reality', but as conjoined elements within the same governmental technique. Moreover, the adoption of a biopolitical framework of analysis opens up new problematizations of contemporary crisis conditions, which in turn allow for new lines of critique and different avenues for political practice in view of the transformations in EUropean border security and migration management laid out above.

Foucault and the Biopolitical Paradigm

Towards the end of *The Will to Knowledge: The History of Sexuality: Volume 1* [1976], Foucault famously argues that: 'For millennia, man remained what he was for Aristotle: a living animal with the additional capacity for a political existence; modern man is an animal whose politics places his existence as a living being into question' (Foucault 1998, 143). Whereas for Aristotle 'life' and 'politics' were treated as separate domains, Foucault traces an historical shift whereby life became the primary referent object of politics. For Foucault, the eighteenth century witnessed the emergence of new forms of scientific knowledge in Europe—made possible by disciplines such as statistics, demography, epidemiology, and biology—that brought about the entrance of biological life (*zoē*) into the modalities of state power (*bios*). He argues that these dynamics led to a fundamental transformation in the order of politics since Aristotle and constituted a specifically modern way of exercising power characterized by a politics of caring for and maximizing life: a politics that Foucault eventually refers to as 'biopolitics'.

Before delving further into the biopolitical paradigm and its implications for (re)conceptualizing contemporary EUropean border security and migration management, it is instructive to recall briefly Foucault's distinctive approach to the concept of power. In Part 4, Chapter 2 of *The History of Sexuality* on 'Method' it is well known that Foucault seeks to move away from a model of power that emphasizes subservience, domination, and, indeed, the notion of sovereignty. On his view, power does not emanate from a single source or point: it cannot be 'acquired, seized, shared', held onto, or relinquished (Foucault 1998, 94). Rather, Foucault's alternative propositions for how to study power emphasize that 'power must be understood in the first instance as the multiplicity of force relations immanent in the sphere in which they operate and which constitute their own organisation' (Foucault 1998, 92). Central, here, is the idea that power is first and foremost a relational phenom- enon: it is not concentrated in the hands of the prince, but to be found dispersed throughout society 'through ceaseless struggles and confrontations' (Foucault 1998, 92). Importantly, Foucault argues that power relations are always 'imbued with calculation', but these 'aims and objectives' do not emanate from 'the choice or decision of an individual subject' (Foucault 1998, 95). Although power relations are characterized by tactics 'it is often the case that no one is there to have invented them, and few who can be said to have formulated them' (Foucault 1998, 94). Finally, because power is 'strictly relational' for Foucault 'where there is power there is resistance': the latter is part of the former as its 'irreducible opposite' (Foucault 1998, 96).

In Part 5 of *The History of Sexuality* and Lecture 11 given at the *Collège de France* in 1975–6 published as *Society Must Be Defended*, Foucault (2003) offers an historical delineation of various mechanisms of power and seeks to differ- entiate between sovereign power and biopower: an important distinction for understanding both Foucault's notion of biopolitics and later attempts by Agamben, Derrida, and Esposito at critiquing and modifying his paradigmatic account. Historically, Foucault argues that the privilege of the sovereign was the unconditional right to decide over life and death. The origin of this right lay in the notion of *patria potestas* or the power of the father in the Roman family to dispose of children and slaves (Foucault 2003, 240). According to this model, the sovereign can either '*take* life or *let* live' (Foucault 1998, 136; 2003, 241), but there is always a skew towards the former. This is because the sovereign cannot *give* life in the same way that he can *take* it: 'Sovereign power's effect on life is exercised only when the sovereign can kill' (Foucault 2003, 240). For Foucault, the defining characteristic of modernity is the tran- sition from an unconditional understanding of this power to one that only permits the sovereign to kill whenever his own life is in jeopardy. The move- ment from an absolute right to 'a sort of right of rejoinder' meant that the ancient unconditional power over life and death became conditional on 'the defense of the sovereign, and his own survival' (Foucault 1998, 135). However, Foucault goes on to argue that the social and economic changes wrought by industrialization and demographic growth in seventeenth-century

goes against right to life (take life)
HR framework but can be justified

35

Europe—followed by a surge in medical knowledge about the human body in the eighteenth century—meant that the concept of sovereign power was increasingly anachronistic (Foucault 1998, 136; 2003, 241).

Over the course of these two centuries Foucault claims that sovereign power was not abandoned, but rather co-opted by the emergence of two new non-antithetical forms of power: disciplinary power and biopower. The former is a type of power based on the training and surveillance of the individual human body at a local level. This 'anatomo-politics' sought to localize, discipline, and normalize individual bodies, which was reflected spatially by the emergence of terraced housing and enclosed institutions such as barracks, schools, and universities, for example. While allowing for political subjugation, this form of power also enabled the enhancement of economic productivity and increased the machinic qualities and usefulness of the body. By contrast, biopower is associated with the development of a new technology of power that dovetails with disciplinary power, but one that is addressed to 'man-as-species'—in other words the population as a whole—rather than to individual bodies. This was made possible via new forms of knowledge—birth rates, death rates, rate of reproduction, fertility rates, and so on—that gave rise to the very category of the population: 'biopolitics deals with the population, with the population as a political problem that is at once scientific and political, as a biological problem and as power's problem' (Foucault 2003, 245).

Whereas disciplinary power involved supervising and controlling, Foucault associates biopolitics more specifically with regulation and intervention in order to maximize and enhance the population. Thus, to return to the example above, alongside the disciplining power of terraced housing came the regularizing biopolitical mechanisms of workers' pensions, health insurance, and so on. Furthermore, these biopolitical dynamics—alongside disciplinary power—were essential to the rise of modern capitalism, which 'would not have been possible without the controlled insertion of bodies into the machinery of production and the adjustment of the phenomena of population to economic processes' (Foucault 1998, 141). For these reasons, Foucault suggests that the old sovereign right to '*take* life or *let* live' was gradually replaced by the power to '*foster* life or *disallow* it to the point of death' (Foucault 1998, 138). But while the new formula that Foucault proposes is 'to make live and let die', he also argues that sovereignty and the power over life never disappeared entirely. On the contrary, the lethal dimension of sovereign power is inextricably woven into biopolitics: the formidable power of death 'now presents itself as the counterpart of a power that exerts a positive influence on life, that endeavors to administer, optimize, and multiply it, subjecting it to precise controls and comprehensive regulations' (Foucault 1998, 137).

In his 1978–9 lectures at the *Collège de France* (published as *The Birth of Biopolitics*), Foucault locates biopolitics in the context of the wider emergence of liberal forms of government: 'only when we know what this governmental regime called liberalism was, will we be able to grasp what biopolitics is' (Foucault 2008, 22). On Foucault's view, liberalism is not a political ideology or an economic theory, but rather a specific art of governing human subjects. In particular, he argues that from the mid-eighteenth century, government became a question about 'how not to govern too much' (Foucault 2008, 13). Liberalism, however, is understood in this context not simply to be about freedom of the market and individual, property rights, and political expression, and so on, but revolves more specifically around 'the management and organization of the conditions in which one can be free' (Foucault 2008, 63–4). At the centre of liberal government, therefore, is a core tension between the attempt to produce freedom and the risk of destroying it in providing those very conditions of possibility: 'Liberalism … as the art of government found in the eighteenth century, entails at its heart a productive/destructive relationship with freedom. Liberalism must produce freedom, but this very act entails the establishment of limitations, controls, forms of coercion, and obligations relying on threats, etcetera' (Foucault 2008, 64). These limitations, controls, and the biopolitical attempt to regulate and intervene in the government of populations is precisely what Foucault refers to as *security*: technologies that involve 'forecasts, statistical estimates, and overall measures' in order to establish and maintain an equilibrium 'around the random element inherent in a population of living beings so as to optimize a state of life' (Foucault 2003, 246).[5]

Seeking to update the Foucaultian paradigm for the twenty-first century, Rose (2007, 54) has remarked that biopolitics 'is more a perspective than a concept'. He argues that biopolitics today must not be seen as an homogenous mode of government, but can and does take many diverse forms in contemporary political life, which consists of: 'a fragmented field of contested truths, heterogeneous and often conflicting authorities, diverse practices of individual and collective subjectification, competing ways of thinking and acting, and divergent opinions about what [are] the most important, and most appropriate, objectives for authoritative action' (Rose 2007, 54). Moreover, for Rose, the core distinction that Foucault introduced between the anatomo-politics of discipline and the regulation of the population as a whole ultimately 'blurs, as different authorities seek to act upon the one through action upon the other' (Rose 2007, 53). At base, biopolitics in advanced liberal societies on his view refers to 'a variety of strategies that try to identify, treat, manage, or administer those individuals, groups, or localities where risk is seen to be high' (Rose 2007, 70). In this context, biopolitical security practices refer primarily to the identification and management of risk: 'ways of thinking and acting that involve calculations about probable future in the present followed by interventions into the present in order to control that potential future' (Rose 2007, 70).

However, this influential account retains an analytical focus on biopolitics from within the context of society as if it were a pre-existing political community: Rose does not probe how membership is itself performatively (re)produced via biopolitical bordering practices. Thus, for example, in his discussion of 'biological citizenship', a term used to describe 'the ways that citizenship has been shaped by conceptions of the specific vital characteristics of human beings', at no point does Rose consider the role of the 'non-citizen' as the other against which the 'proper' citizen-subject of advanced liberal societies is (re)produced. By contrast, one of the ambitions of this study is to consider the various spatial and temporal technologies of (bio)power that attempt to identify, manage, and (re)produce the 'irregular' migrant as a constitutive outside of 'normal' EUropean political community. Indeed, the reading that I seek to advance here is that it is precisely the pursuit of the (re)production of the figure of the 'irregular' migrant—understood as an individual subject and the category of an entire population—that animates the contemporary biopolitics of EUropean border security and migration management. Furthermore, the fundamental tension found in Foucault's paradigmatic account of biopolitical governance—between the vitalist urge to optimize life on the one hand and yet the simultaneous need for security interventions on the other—is reflected in the liminal subject position of the 'irregular' migrant as *both* a potential risk to contemporary EUropean society *and* a life that must be saved. Indeed, as we have already seen in the foregoing analysis, it is arguably this fundamental tension that characterizes the field of biopolitical border security and migration management today.

Biopolitical Border Security in EUrope

The various spatial and temporal displacements of 'the border' charted above resemble diverse aspects of biopolitical governance as paradigmatically set out by Foucault. Extant work on biopolitical border security—particularly in the EUropean and North American contexts—has already traced the way in which the increasing emphasis on the enhancement of mobilities resonates with the Foucaultian notion of the incitement of circulation in the liberal art of government (Amoore 2006, 2007; Bialasiewicz 2011; Bigo and Guild 2005; Bigo 2007; Walters 2002; Vaughan-Williams 2010). Whereas border controls prior to the 1985 Schengen Agreement were more commensurate with traditional geopolitical conceptualizations of the prevention of movement, the recent prioritization of mobility and impetus to govern subjects across an ever-expanding space reflects Foucault's argument that under biopolitical conditions: 'We see the emergence of a completely different problem that is no longer that of fixing and demarcating the territory but that of allowing circulations to take place, of controlling them, sifting the good from the bad, ensuring that things are always in movement, constantly moving around, continually going from one point to another, but in such a way that the inherent dangers of this circulation are cancelled out' (Foucault 2003, 65). Indeed, as Shinya Kitagawa, among others, has argued, biopolitical border security implies a different spatial technology of power to that associated with the border in the context of the modern geopolitical imagination: 'biopolitical borders . . . do not aim to territorialize geographical spaces, but instead function to deterritorialize borders in order to govern the deterritorialized, namely, the un-localizable' (Kitagawa 2011, 212; see also Vaughan-Williams 2010, 2011a). But while biopolitical border security fundamentally relies upon movement this is not to say that the 'freedom' to be mobile is without constraint; it is, of course, the product of a series of orchestrated moves—or security mechanisms in the Foucaultian sense—that condition its very possibility. For this reason, the ability of the 'regular' citizen-subject—the 'trusted traveller'—to glide across the surface of the globe with minimal delays and inconvenience (at least in principle) is permitted only by prior risk-based interventions throughout the course of their travel that, to use Foucault's terminology, 'sift' out subjects considered to be 'bad'. In this way, the advent of 'Smart Border' technologies, for example—with their targeting of the movement and behaviour of entire populations—typify the biopolitical aim of 'achieving an overall equilibrium that protects the whole from internal dangers' (Foucault 2003, 249).

Once the Foucaultian paradigm of biopolitics is adopted as an alternative starting point for analysing border security and migration management in EUrope then the seemingly 'paradoxical' subject position of the 'irregular' migrant as both a 'security risk' and 'life to be saved' can be placed within the same grid of intelligibility: the bodies of 'irregular' populations—their basic needs, vulnerabilities, and potentialities—are targeted and managed with ambivalent ethical and political effects. It is precisely this targeting and management of the body—albeit in often divergent directions—that performatively (re)produces *both* the 'irregular' migrant *and* the various apparatuses of power that attempt to produce this form of political subjectivity. In one direction, the biopolitical border security mechanisms already discussed in this chapter—SBI, EES, RTP, EUROSUR, and so on—can then be understood as responses to what Michael Dillon (2003, 537) has called the 'virtual potential' of living things, in this case the figure of the 'irregular' migrant, to 'become dangerous'. For Dillon, the imperative of biopolitical security apparatuses is to first acquire knowledge of 'life' if those mechanisms are to succeed in securing it: 'Life that remains not knowable, unknown or intractable to knowing for whatever reason—it might be a form of life that simply does not show up on the radars of knowing in acceptable ways, or, as an excess of being over apprehension, it may simply not be knowable in principle—is the ultimate danger' (Dillon 2003, 533). Central to this biopolitical notion of security is the production of knowledge about the becoming-dangerous of some risky subjects through algorithmic models of risk management based on the profiling of populations and behaviour: 'Security becomes a boundless science of the very engendering of mutating form and of the tracking of the virtual potential for what are now essentially conceived as bodies-in-formation in the process of becoming dangerous' (Dillon 2003, 538). While recognizing that the elimination of risk is impossible, the desire to simulate the effect of maximum security means that biopolitical EUropean border security and migration management has been shaped by diverse attempts to better identify and govern 'irregular' populations as quickly and efficiently as possible. But whereas this dimension has already been explored extensively in the literature on biometric borders, risk, and technology, the more vitalist dimension of Foucaultian biopolitics—that which emphasizes the optimization of life as core to contemporary biopolitical governance—and the relationship between the two has not been explored to the same extent.

In another—albeit related—direction, the biopolitical paradigm as set out by Foucault also applies to the contemporary field of EUropean border security and migration management in the context of the nascent humanitarianism typified by the 'migrant-centredness' of the GAMM and efforts not only to 'protect' the rights of 'irregular' migrants, but also to 'save' their lives and 'empower' them.[6] William Walters (2011, 145) argues that the 'birth of the humanitarian border' in EUrope complicates what he considers to be a prevailing focus on 'surveillance and control' in critical border and security studies, which on his view 'risks a rather linear and developmental narrative about borders'. Walters sees humanitarian border security in EUrope as 'a singularity, something new', but locates this phenomenon in the broader historical context of what Didier Fassin (2009, 2012) has referred to as 'humanitarian reason'. Fassin's work, focusing on immigration in the French case, emphasizes that humanitarianism—'the vocabulary of suffering, compassion, assistance, and responsibility to protect'—is itself a highly political mode of governance (Fassin 2012, 2; see also Feldman and Ticktin 2010; Fassin and Pandolfi 2013; Ticktin 2011). He locates the emergence of 'humanitarian reason'—understood as a particular moral economy that enjoins 'us' to 'help' and/or 'save' 'them'—against the backdrop of the Christian tradition of empathy and the abolitionist movement in the eighteenth century in France, the UK, and the US (Fassin 2012, 4). As a mode of governing otherwise 'threatened and forgotten lives', humanitarianism encompasses a set of procedures and actions designed to 'manage, regulate, and support the existence of human beings' (Fassin 2012, 1). Fassin stresses that his Foucaultian-inspired approach is one that rejects the Realist idea that morality in international politics is merely a veil for power—if this were the case, he argues, then 'Why does it work so well'—and neither does he seek to judge the effectiveness of NGOs or other humanitarian actors (Fassin 2012, 2). Rather, Fassin considers the effects of humanitarian reason, the political dimension of its affective capability, and the blind spots and dilemmas that it gives rise to. For example, in the case of immigration in France he argues that the shift in the 1990s from struggles over political asylum to the humanitarian language of compassion constituted an important political moment whereby the body of the undesirable 'irregular' subject—'the primary site on which the imprint of power is stamped'—was removed from public life and given shelter in camps such as Sangatte (Fassin 2012, 112). In this way, humanitarianism and securitization, compassion and repression, and hospitality and hostility were not straightforwardly in contra-diction with each other or indeed, we might add, reflective of a disjuncture between 'rhetoric' and 'reality' (a key theme to which Chapter 6 will return). Rather, he argues, these seemingly contradictory elements must be seen as being inextricably intertwined as part of the same terrain and logic of biopolitical governance, which in turn gave rise to ambivalent spaces like Sangatte characterized by the dual presence of aid agencies and French riot police (Fassin 2012, 135–52).[7] While Fassin's overall approach is self-characterized as Foucaultian he nevertheless seeks to introduce a distinction between his notion of humanitarian reason and Foucault's paradigmatic account of biopolitics. On the one hand, Fassin argues that humanitarian action 'is indeed a biopolitics in the sense that it uses techniques of the management of populations in setting up refugee camps, establishing aid corridors, making use of communication around public testimony to abuses perpetrated, and conducting epidemiological studies of infectious diseases, malnutrition, trauma, and even violations of the laws of war' (Fassin 2012, 226). Moreover, humanitarian reason is also said to be biopolitical on Fassin's account inasmuch as its referent object is unambiguously the 'biological life of the destitute and unfortunate' as opposed to the 'biographical life' of migrants—'the life through which they could, independently, give a meaning to their own existence' (Fassin 2012, 254). On the other hand, however, Fassin also claims that humanitarianism is in another sense distinct from biopolitics because the former is primarily about saving individual lives, 'which presupposes not only risking others but also selecting those that have priority for being saved' (Fassin 2012, 226). It is because humanitarian-ism 'qualifies and measures the value and worth of lives' that Fassin sees it as being in tension with Foucault's biopolitical emphasis on the optimization and regulation of the population as a whole (Fassin 2009, 242). Nevertheless, the difference between Fassin's notion of humanitarian reason and Foucaultian biopolitics is perhaps somewhat overdrawn by Fassin and begins to fade away once Foucault's concept of racism—an essential component of biopolitical logics of governance—is taken into account. Furthermore, as I will go on to argue and explore, Foucault's treatment of racism is an important—if ultimately somewhat limited—starting point for diagnosing the violence with which biopolitical EUropean border security and migration management policies and practices draw borders within and between 'regular' and 'irregular' populations and thereby create 'hierarchies of humanity' (Fassin 2009, 239; see also Debrix and Barder, 10).

In *Society Must Be Defended*, Foucault identifies a fundamental paradox in his own account of biopolitics; namely: 'How . . . is it possible for a political power to kill, to call for deaths, to demand deaths, to give the order to kill, and to expose not only its enemies but its own citizens to the risk of death? Given that this power's objective is essentially to make live, how can it let die? How can the power of death, the function of death, be exercised in a political system centred upon biopower?' (Foucault 2003, 254). He goes on to argue that the 'letting die' element of the equation 'to make live and let die' is accounted for by the emergence of racism within populations, which introduces a break between 'what must live and what must die' (Foucault 2003, 254). Accompanying the shift from sovereignty to biopolitics, Foucault identifies the eclipse of a 'political-military discourse' and the emergence of a 'racist-biological' one (Lemke 2011, 40). Racism was not new, on his view, but from the nineteenth century it became a novel function of the state, which was provoked by the biopolitical idea that the social body required continual cleansing (Lemke 2011, 40). With the rise of 'state racism' a fissure emerges in society between life that is deemed to count on the one hand and life considered to be abnormal, degenerate, and thus a risk to the health of the population as a whole on the other hand (Foucault 2003, 254–61). In this way, Foucault argues that the category of race is an essential element of biopolitics and allows for killing to become acceptable under biopolitical conditions: 'The fact that the other dies does not mean simply that I live in the sense that his death guarantees my safety; the death of the other, the death of the bad race, of the inferior race (or the degenerate, the abnormal) is something that will make life in general healthier: healthier and purer' (Foucault 2003, 255).

While Foucault claims that Nazism took this racist logic of biopolitics to the furthest possible point, he also warns that 'the play between the sovereign right to kill and the mechanisms of biopower . . . is in fact inscribed in the workings of all states' (Foucault 2003, 261). Indeed, for Foucault, death as a result of state racism does not only refer narrowly to killing in the sense of the Nazi *lager*, but also what he refers to as 'indirect murder: the fact of exposing someone to death, increasing the risk of death for some people, or, quite simply, political death, expulsion, rejection, and so on' (Foucault 2003, 256). For these reasons, Fassin's diagnosis of the work that humanitarian reason does in creating hierarchies within populations is not at odds with Foucaultian biopolitics once the concept of racism—broadly understood as that which differentiates between worthy and unworthy forms of life—is brought back into the analytical frame.

In conclusion, the logic of racism is crucial for understanding the coexistence of both 'positive' and 'negative' impulses towards life that are internal to biopolitics as understood by Foucault. Instead of viewing these impulses dichotomously they can be co-located within the field of biopolitical governmentality, which moves an understanding of the seemingly contradictory nature of EUropean border security and migration management beyond that of a 'gap' between humanitarian 'rhetoric' and the 'reality' of security imperatives. In turn, it is precisely this fundamentally Janus-faced characteristic that is further reflected in the experiences of the embodied subject of biopolitical border security practices in EUrope today: the figure of the 'irregular' migrant who can never be sure whether they will be cast as a potential security risk or a life in need of saving. But while the paradigmatic account of biopolitics advanced by Foucault is apposite in developing an understanding of the conjoined nature of the optimization and abandonment of lives, I want to argue that its core emphasis on 'making live and letting die' is insufficient to address the specific spatial and temporal technologies of biopower that, as we shall go on to see, not only actively expose some 'irregular' migrants to death, but also operate in some cases via dehumanization and animalization. Taking Foucault's account as an important point of departure, subsequent chapters will, nevertheless, make the case—against the backdrop of diverse 'irregular' migrants' experiences—that alternative (post)biopolitical frames are required in the light of the complexity and differential effects of the contemporary crisis in border security and migration management in EUrope.

Notes

1. Bröckling et al. (2010, 23) outline the intersection between biopolitics and governmentality in Foucault's work as 'the question of how the government of individuals and populations interact with the biological categories and concepts of life and death, health and disease, normality and pathology'. For a detailed exploration of the relationship between biopolitics and governmentality in Foucault see Lemm and Vatter (2014).
2. Some of these events are organized by Frontex; for example, the annual Automated Border Control (ABC) conference, which I attended in Warsaw in 2012 and 2013. Others are organized by for-profit policy-facing event-management companies, such

as the International Centre for Parliamentary Studies' annual European Border Security Symposium, which I attended in 2011.

3. For a policy-orientated report on the content of discussions at this event and the context in which it was held more generally see Vaughan-Williams (2011b).

4. According to the EU Commission (2014a), Operation Mare Nostrum led to a 250 per cent increase in the number of 'irregular' border crossings detected between May and July 2014 as compared with the same period in 2013.

5. Lemke (2014, 60) understands Foucault's notion of 'technology of security' as the regulatory control of populations: 'It aims at the mass phenomena characteristic of a population and its conditions of variation, seeking to prevent or compensate for dangers that result from its existence as a biological entity.'

6. As Adorno (2014, 104) argues, 'biopower guarantees itself . . . by taking the subject's well-being into account'.

7. Similarly, Ticktin (2011, 5) has also argued in the context of France's response to 'irregular' migration that humanitarian and security imperatives conjoin as part of what she refers to as 'armed love': 'the moral imperative to act is accompanied . . . by practices of violence and containment'.

3

Thanatopolitical Borders

Introduction

On 26 March 2011 a small rubber boat carrying seventy-two passengers departed from Tripoli only to be washed up back on the Libyan coast near Misrata fifteen days later with just nine survivors. According to the Strik Report produced by the Parliamentary Assembly of the Council of Europe (PACE 2012), the dinghy bound for Lampedusa was carrying seventy men and women aged between twenty- and twenty-five-years-old together with two babies. The passengers were all from Ethiopia, Nigeria, Eritrea, Ghana, and Sudan, and fleeing Tripoli at the height of the internal Libyan conflict and aerial bombardment coordinated by NATO. Based on testimonial evidence obtained from the survivors of the so-called 'boat-left-to-die' incident, the Strik Report details how, after having travelled for eighteen hours and with no sign of land in sight, the passengers began to worry about their where-abouts. Seeking assistance, the captain—a man understood to be from Ghana and travelling with his wife—used his mobile phone to contact someone he knew in Italy called Father Zerai, an Eritrean priest living in Rome, who on 27 March alerted the Italian coastguard. The Rome Maritime Rescue Coordin-ation Centre (MRCC) gave the captain instructions on how to provide the boat's coordinates, but during the call his mobile phone ran out of battery power and this was the last contact that he or the rest of the passengers had with the MRCC. A short time afterwards, an unmarked military helicopter appeared overhead and passengers believed that they were about to be res-cued, only for it to then leave the area. Another helicopter (possibly the same one) came and raised hopes of assistance once more, but while the crew of the helicopter dropped bottled water and packets of biscuits—believed to have been of Italian origin—no additional assistance was forthcoming. Conditions aboard the dinghy deteriorated as it ran out of fuel, began to drift, and encountered adverse weather conditions. Some passengers were thrown overboard—others are reported to have jumped—and the remaining few began to suffer the hallucinatory effects of starvation and drinking untreated seawater. On the tenth day the boat drifted close to a military vessel thought to be a NATO aircraft carrier stationed in the area as part of Operation Unified Protector. Personnel on board were seen using binoculars to observe the stranded vessel, but failed to respond to their distress signals. After that point, despite being in an area of the Mediterranean Sea patrolled by Frontex and used frequently by commercial fishing vessels, the stranded passengers began to drink their own urine and some members of the group started to die. On 10 April the boat was finally washed up on rocks close to Zilten, 160 km east of Tripoli and at that point only eleven of the original seventy-two passengers had survived the journey. However, two additional passengers died subsequently—one woman collapsed on disembarkation and another is reported to have been denied crucial medical attention during her immediate incarceration in a Libyan detention centre on arrival, pending an investigation into the circumstances of the incident (PACE 2012, 6–10).

As discussed in Chapter 2, the neo-liberalization of EU border security, the humanitarian focus of the GAMM, and the increasing emphasis on the health, well-being, and protection of 'irregular' as well as 'regular' populations are all characteristics associated with what Foucault paradigmatically outlined as biopolitical techniques of government (Foucault 1998, 2003). Yet, while the Foucaultian frame offers important insights into the orientation of EU border security towards the management and enhancement of populations under the rubric of humanitarianism, this chapter explores the extent to which the concept of 'letting die' adequately addresses contexts such as the 'boat-left-to-die' case where the lives of 'irregular' migrants are routinely exposed to death by the very authorities associated with humanitarian border security. A greater emphasis on the lethal—or 'thanatopolitical'—dimension of biopolitical governance is found in the somewhat controversial work of Giorgio Agamben (1994, 1998, 1999, 2000, 2013). As is well known, Agamben argues that Foucault was too hasty in diminishing the role of sovereign power in contemporary political life and argues for its recovery—albeit according to his own modified account—*within* the biopolitical frame (Campbell 2011; Debrix and Barder 2012; Lemke 2011; Prozorov 2013; Wolfe 2012).[1] By now, Agamben's concepts of sovereign power, bare life, and the camp are widely known and many significant critiques of his *homo sacer* series have been advanced not least by a number of scholars working in critical border and migration studies and related fields. Indeed, as I will go on to discuss, it has become almost customary in the critical literature to acknowledge the impact that Agamben's work has had only to then challenge if not dismiss on empirical grounds its implications for analysing the concrete lived realities of 'irregular' migrants in the EUropean context and beyond. On the one hand, I am attuned and sympathetic to concerns about certain secondary readings of the Agambenian framework and its apparent potential for totalizing caricatures of sovereign power, unhelpful generalizations about the nature of subjectivity and space across diverse geopolitical contexts, and inability to recognize scope for resistance and political claim-making among 'irregular' migrants. On the other hand, when read in less deterministic terms and with greater attention to the nuances of his arguments, I seek to make the case that several otherwise overlooked aspects of Agamben's work—particularly the concept of the sovereign ban and its *material* effects—provide important insights into the thanatopolitical dimensions of contemporary humanitarian bordering practices and *some* 'irregular' migrants' experiences of them.

Running somewhat against the grain of both extant applications of Agamben and critiques of the implications of his work, I will argue that on its own terms the *homo sacer* thesis is actually *least* instructive in diagnosing the study of contemporary spaces of detention across the EUropean borderlands. Despite the persistence of well-known human rights abuses, such spaces should not be equated with the Nazi *lager* and nor is it appropriate or helpful to draw parallels between the experience of contemporary detainees and that of the *Muselmänner* as outlined in Agamben's *Remnants of Auschwitz* (1999). Rather, I will suggest that another (post)biopolitical key is required in order to understand the specific technology of power that seeks to control some 'irregular' migrants via dehumanization and animalization—rather than their death—in particular at contemporary sites of detention, which is the focus of Chapter 4. However, in the immediate discussion that follows I seek to make the case that Agamben's unique treatment of biopolitical abandonment offers deeper insight than Foucault's concept of 'letting die' in the task of diagnosing thanatopolitical drift *within* the humanitarianism of the EU Commission's GAMM. I consider this to be an important task because without developing such diagnostic accounts some of the worst examples of thanatopolitics may otherwise appear merely as tragic accidents, where the 'reality' of EU border security has simply failed to live up to the neo-liberal humanitarian rhetoric, rather than as a more intrinsic feature of biopolitics.

In order to advance this alternative diagnosis of EUrope's border crisis beyond the 'rhetoric/reality' frame I focus on two related sites in the field of contemporary EU border security practices where I argue that the thanatopolitical impulses of the sovereign ban are especially visible: in the context of 'push-back' operations and the linked practice of failing to respond to the distress signals of 'irregular' migrants. At both of these border sites I argue that it is important to recognize the activity of sovereign power, which is expressed in terms of the protection or abandonment of 'irregular' migrants by a range of petty and temporary sovereigns. Without an appreciation of the work that this expression of sovereign power does I argue that it is not possible to understand the systemic nature of the conditions that lead to the routine loss of life, which are otherwise reduced to the mere status of regrettable accidents used to justify *more* security measures in the name of humanitarian protection. As well as performing and reproducing the borders between 'regular' and 'irregular' populations, such practices also serve as an *attempt* to authorize and legitimize the authority of EU border security.

Drawing upon some 'irregular' migrants' testimonies of their embodied encounter with and experiences of EU border security practices, however, I argue for an expanded understanding and modification of Agamben's thesis in order to: first, rethink the sovereign decision as a more complex and diverse set of acts of omission undertaken by various border authorities that lead to the everyday exposure of many 'irregular' migrants to life-threatening conditions; and second, to develop a greater appreciation of the active role that materiality—in particular, the hostility of the physical environment in which 'irregular' migrants are often abandoned—plays in imbuing the sovereign ban its everyday potency. In this way I hope to outline ways in which it might be possible not only to draw on Agamben's thought to diagnose the changing nature and location of the border in contemporary political life in abstract terms, but also to conceptualize what is at stake when 'biopolitical' borders turn 'thanatopolitical' from the perspective of populations produced by them as 'irregular'.

The Sovereign Ban and Thanatopolitical Spaces

Seeking to 'correct' the Foucaultian account of biopolitics, Agamben has (in)famously sought to reintroduce sovereignty and 'thanatopolitics', or the politics of the embodied exposure to death) back into what the latter theorist considers to be the more vitalist account of biopolitics of the former. Whereas Foucault read the movement from politics to biopolitics as an historical transformation involving the inclusion of what the Greeks referred to as 'natural life' (*zoē*) into the politically qualified life of the polis (*bios*), for Agamben the political realm is originally biopolitical. What has changed, on the Agambenian view, is that the nature of the relationship between politics and life has become more visible in the context of the modern sovereign state and its practices (Agamben 1998, 6). While the visibility of the relationship between politics and life is thus historically contingent the political realm is 'originally' biopolitical because it is founded precisely upon the sovereign exclusion of *zoē*: the putting to one side of natural life acts as the negative foundation against which *bios* is defined. It is precisely this division of natural life from *bios* that marks out the function and activity of sovereignty in the Agambenian account and hence sovereign power is considered to be always already biopolitical. However, Agamben also argues that *zoē* is not straightforwardly separated from *bios* in the sovereign operation: the relationship between the two is marked by a more complex topology than one of a simple inside/outside relation. Rather, the connection between *zoē* and *bios* is characterized by the structure of the exception: that which is excepted (*zoē*) nevertheless maintains a relationship to the norm (*bios*) despite or rather precisely because of its exclusion. According to this formula, the link between *zoē* and *bios* is therefore one of an 'inclusive exclusion'. As a result, *zoē* neither falls strictly outside the realm of *bios* and yet nor is it fully synonymous with *bios*. What is produced instead by all political structures born of the sovereign exception is a third term: a hybrid form of life that occupies a 'threshold of articulation' between *bios* and *zoē*. It is this very specific form of life that Agamben refers to throughout his work as 'bare life'.

Bare life has been the source of much confusion and controversy and, as I have argued elsewhere, it is important *not* to mistake bare life for *zoē* in Agamben's account (Vaughan-Williams 2009). Bare life cannot be *zoē* because any form of politically qualified life—'bare' or otherwise—is a move away from what the Greeks referred to as natural life (Murray 2010). Whereas *zoē* refers to the pure fact of living, bare life has already been captured and contaminated by the sovereign operation and does not pre-exist it. Moreover, while the former is a universal category, the latter takes on historically and culturally contingent forms. In order to both establish and illustrate his thesis on the relationship between sovereignty and bare life, Agamben draws on the figure of *homo sacer*: a figure initially found in archaic Roman law. To fully appreciate the nature of the *homo sacer* thesis, however, it is necessary to pause momentarily and note Agamben's methodology, which draws heavily on the idea of the paradigm.

As outlined in *The Signature of All Things* (2009), Agamben claims inspiration from Foucault and his particular use of paradigmatic analysis. For example, in *Discipline and Punish*, Agamben notes Foucault's treatment of Jeremy Bentham's figure of the panopticon as both a specific architectural form and a model for understanding the relationship between surveillance and the body. In this way, Agamben argues that Foucault uses the figure of the panopticon—and that of the confession and the care of the self in other contexts—as a paradigm in the strictest sense of the concept: 'a singular object that, standing equally for all others of the same class, defines the intelligibility of the group of which it is a part and which, at the same time, it constitutes' (Agamben 2009, 17). On this view, the work of paradigmatic analysis is then to identify figures such as the panopticon in order to illuminate the features of a broader context 'that they both constitute and make intelligible' (Agamben 2009, 17). Elsewhere, Agamben argues that his political-philosophical attempt to diagnose dominant matrices of intelligibility 'should not be confused with a sociological investigation' (Agamben 2004b, 610).

On this basis, it is possible to better grasp the figure of *homo sacer* through which Agamben attempts to diagnose the relationship between sovereign power and bare life. *Homo sacer* or 'sacred man' was the subject in Roman law who had committed a crime and was banned from both human and divine law. The nature of this ban meant that *homo sacer* could in effect be killed by anyone without that act constituting homicide and at the same time his death would not be celebrated as a sacrifice. As such, what Agamben sees in the specificity of the figure of *homo sacer* is a glimpse of the broader logic of sovereignty that operates by banning subjects from 'normal' juridical-political order and thus exposing them to violence and death: '*Homo sacer* presents the originary figure of life taken into the sovereign ban and preserves the memory of the originary exclusion through which the political dimension was first constituted' (Agamben 1998, 83). Here, it needs to be underscored that Agamben does not argue that the Roman figure of *homo sacer* is somehow the historical origin of sovereign power, but that this liminal figure acts as a paradigm—understood in the terms above—for conceptualizing the sovereign operation more generally. The role of the 'ban', referred to above, is also central in this conceptualization, but unlike the figure of *homo sacer*, which is in effect an historically located symptom of the operation of sovereign power, the ban is considered by Agamben to be a central mechanism internal to that operation. For this reason, the ban deserves special attention and arguably more than has been devoted to it in the secondary literature.

Borrowed from Jean-Luc Nancy's essay 'Abandoned Being' (1993), Agamben uses the spatial-ontological device of the ban in order to understand the 'potentiality...of the law [...] to apply in no longer applying' (Agamben 1998, 28). In this context, the ban refers to the peculiar topological relationship discussed above that the sovereign operation relies upon in both excepting and capturing bare life: 'He who has been banned is not, in fact, simply set outside the law and made indifferent to it but rather abandoned by it, that is, exposed and threatened on the threshold in which life and law, outside and inside, become indistinguishable' (Agamben 1998, 29). As such, the ban is the element that fulfils the potential of the law not to apply by suspending it in respect of certain subjects deemed to be unworthy of protection and thus exposed to 'an unconditional capacity to be killed' (Agamben 1998, 85). Thus, while the ban occupies a privileged place in Agamben's schema he stresses that it is much more than a 'formal structure': it has a 'substantial character, since what the ban holds together is precisely bare life and sovereign power' (Agamben 1998, 109). The ban, then, is the relation that enables the biopolitical abandonment of the subject and renders that subject 'consigned to the mercy of the one who abandons it' (Agamben 1998, 110).

Agamben notably fuses Nancy's concept of the ban with Carl Schmitt's (2005) theory of sovereignty as the decision on the exception. In this way,

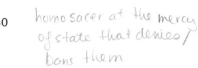

the ban features in Agamben's work as a quasi-decision on whether certain subjects are to be protected by the law or excepted from it and abandoned 'to an unconditional power of death' (Agamben 1998, 90). What is less commonly appreciated, however, is that in a modification of Schmitt the ban is only a 'quasi-' decision for Agamben: 'not the expression of the will of a subject hierarchically superior to all others' as per Schmitt's sovereign, but rather 'the inscription within the body of the *nomos* of the exteriority that animates it and gives it meaning' (Agamben 1998, 26). In this way Agamben is working with a more Derridean understanding of the decision not as originating from a singularly identifiable source or origin: 'The juridical order does not originally present itself simply as sanctioning a transgressive fact, but instead constitutes itself through the repetition of the same act without any sanction, that is, an exceptional case' (Agamben 1998, 26). The ban's suspension of the law enables sovereign power to inclusively exclude the bare life it needs to operate by producing a desubjectified form of subjectivity (Agamben 2013).

Nevertheless, on the reading advanced here, the sovereign operation is neither inevitable nor successful in Agamben's account and across a number of texts—notably *The Coming Community* (1993), *The Time That Remains* (2005), *Profanations* (2009), and several interviews and shorter interventions (Agamben 2004b, 2013)—he has explored the concept of profanation as a means of illuminating how the sovereign ban may be deactivated and put to a different use.[2] While this dimension of Agamben's thought is the focus of a number of revisionist readings of his *homo sacer* thesis (see Basham and Vaughan-Williams 2013; Prozorov 2013; Vaughan-Williams 2009), the argument presented in this chapter is an injunction to pay closer attention to the operation of the sovereign ban in spaces that suspend the law and create the conditions of possibility for the desubjectification of certain subjects and their potential exposure to death in contemporary political life: 'We must learn to recognize the structure of the ban in the political relations and public spaces in which we still live . . . The banishment of sacred life is the sovereign *nomos* that conditions every rule, the originary spatialization that governs and makes possible every localization and every territorialization' (Agamben 1998, 111).

Agamben's own attempts at identifying and interrogating the substantive historical operation of the sovereign ban have notoriously focused upon the concentration camps of early twentieth-century European dictatorships. He notes the absence of a discussion of the camps in Foucault's account of biopolitics and argues that it is in this context that 'the decision on life becomes a decision on death, and biopolitics can turn into thanatopolitics' (Agamben 1998, 122). Elsewhere, in *Remnants of Auschwitz* (1999), Agamben uses the Nazi *lager*—specifically Auschwitz—to illustrate the limits of Foucault's aphorism 'making live and letting die' in order to capture the nature of biopolitics: 'In Hitler's Germany, an unprecedented absolutization of the biopower to *make* life intersects with an equally absolute generalization of the sovereign power to *make die*, such that biopolitics coincides immediately with thanatopolitics' (Agamben 1999, 83). But while Agamben refers to Auschwitz as the place in which the state of exception coincides with the norm and the production of bare life is most visible, the concept of the camp in his work again operates according to the status of a paradigm.

Confusingly, the camp in Agamben's work extends beyond the Nazi *lager* to refer to the paradigmatic space in which the sovereign ban is realized: 'If sovereign power is founded in the ability to decide on the state of exception, the camp is the structure in which the state of exception is permanently realized' (Agamben 2000, 40; see also Debrix 2013). Hence, the status of the camp is similar to that of *homo sacer*: it operates as a figure in which the spatiality of the operation of the sovereign ban may be caught sight of. The space of the camp emerges as a materialization of the state of exception in which bare life and juridical rule enter into a threshold of indistinction (Agamben 2000, 171–2). Understood in these terms, the camp in Agamben may exceed the limits of concentration camps such as Auschwitz: 'We must find ourselves virtually in the presence of a camp every time such a structure is created' (Agamben 1998, 174). For this reason Agamben's thesis does not rule out the potentiality for the space of the camp to emerge anywhere in which the sovereign ban operates—the latter defines the former, which is not delimited by pre-existing borders.[3] Equally, however, the figure of the camp does not apply to spaces where the sovereign ban does not operate such as in prisons: 'The camp is merely an expression of [the] deeper logic of the exception: the camp is outside the juridical order whereas the prison is not' (Agamben 1998, 20). Indeed, Agamben goes even further in order to stress that the figure of the camp in his work is inapplicable to more general spaces of detention: 'As the absolute space of exception, the camp is topologically different from a simple space of confinement' (Agamben 1998, 28). In the following discussion I want to suggest that these points are of special importance when assessing contemporary critiques of Agamben's work and applications of it in order to diagnose certain aspects of EUrope's border crisis, which the analysis will move on to consider.

Reassessing Agamben in Critical Border and Migration Studies

By now there has been a spirited—if controversial—uptake of Agamben's theses in order to diagnose both the logic of contemporary bordering practices on the one hand and the experiences of 'irregular' migrants in the EUropean context and beyond on the other, although these two strands have not been brought together in the literature as closely as might be expected. Regarding the former, the spatiality of Agamben's thought—understood in terms of his treatment of political spaces via the lens of the exception and the range of spatial-ontological devices he develops to analyse sovereign power—has inspired a range of scholarship associated with CBS (Johnson et al. 2011; Parker and Vaughan-Williams et al. 2009, Parker and Vaughan-Williams 2012). This work has explored various ways of reconceptualizing 'the border' apposite to contemporary conditions and has often sought to connect bordering practices with what Claudio Minca has referred to as 'the normalization of a series of geographies of exceptionalism in Western societies' (Minca 2006, 388; see *inter alia* Bigo 2007; Doty 2009; Edkins and Walker 2000; Gregory 2006; Minca 2005, 2007; Kinnvall and Nesbitt-Larking 2013; Minca and Vaughan-Williams 2012; Salter 2012; Vaughan-Williams 2009). Didier Bigo (2007), for example, draws on Agamben in order to develop the concept of the 'ban-opticon': a play on Bentham's figure of the panopticon, which refers to logics of surveillance that form a transnational field of unease and (in)security management) in the EUropean context. Such a field combines practices of exceptionalism, acts of profiling, the containment and detention of foreigners, together with enhanced mobility for trusted liberal subjects. Moreover, this field destabilizes conventional understandings of the relationship between sovereignty, territory, and security, and associated divisions between inside/outside, internal/external, and domestic/international. For my own part, elsewhere I have developed the concept of the 'generalized biopolitical border' in order to characterize the reformulation of bordering practices that can be identified in Agamben's work. Instead of conceptualizing borders as thin lines located in a fixed position at the outer-edge of the modern sovereign territorial state—as per the Weberian paradigm underpinning the dominant ontology of the discipline of 'International Relations'—these are recast from an Agambenian perspective as mobile, pre-emptive, and performative dividing practices) zigzagging throughout social space (Vaughan-Williams 2009). Such practices *attempt* to (re)produce the limits of sovereign political community and are 'biopolitical' in that they involve a decision (in the Agambenian sense) on the worthiness of different lives: the politically qualified life of the citizen (whose identity, rights, and security are assured) is produced in contradistinction to that of contemporary *homines sacri* (whose subject position is often indistinct, unable to access 'normal' structures of protection, and placed in insecure zones of habitual jeopardy).

From a different angle, Agamben's work has also informed a range of scholarship associated with CMS. Much of this research draws particularly on the Agambenian figures of the camp and *homo sacer* in order to identify and investigate the subject-positions of 'irregular' migrants in diverse geopolitical contexts across the EUropean borderscape and beyond (Diken 2004; De Genova and Peutz 2010; Khosravi 2007, 2010; Rajaram and Grundy-Warr

2004; Shewly 2013). However, in recent years a heated debate has emerged within critical border and migration scholarship concerning the applicability of these figures and (a certain reading of) Agamben's theses. In particular, this debate centres on the figure of the 'irregular migrant', his/her lived experience of borders, and the issue of 'political agency'. To some extent, the stakes of the debate relate to an ontological question frequently framed in terms of whether priority should be given to border control or migrant mobility. While the thanatopolitical dimensions of Agamben's arguments and certain secondary applications of them are often cast by critics as being associated with the former, the latter is typically linked with AoM approaches and the notion that migrant mobility always exceeds the attempted grasp of sovereign power (Hardt and Negri 2004; Mezzadra and Neilson 2013; Papadopoulos et al. 2008; see Chapter 6 for an extended discussion).

The primary charge commonly made against Agamben is that the 'bare life' thesis does not adequately grasp the 'reality' of contemporary borderzones from the perspective of the lived experiences of irregular migrants (Johnson 2013; McNevin 2013; Puggioni 2014; Squire 2011; Scheel 2014). This line of critique is one that often mobilizes a range of empirical evidence from diverse border contexts as a ground for identifying three main perceived weaknesses: the misplaced focus on the politics of exceptionalism and the camp as a paradigm for analysing the global politics of mobility, which in turn denies migrant agency; the tendency to generalize about the nature of borders and the experiences of migrants across time, space, and subject positions, rather than offering a more nuanced, grounded approach; and the normative implications of a reductionist and politically impoverished account of the lived experiences of migrants, respectively.

While some scholarship above has drawn a parallel between 'the border' as a site of attempted control over movement and Agamben's characterization of the camp as a space of exception, Vicki Squire claims that, on the contrary, contemporary borderzones are not exceptional spaces and should more accurately be conceptualized as sites of political struggle, rather than of biopolitical control (Squire 2011, 15). This is because, on Squire's view, 'borderzones may be marked by struggles around abjectification, but do not necessarily produce abject subjects' (Squire 2011, 14). To focus on such abjection, which Squire claims that the Agambenian account does, is to ignore what she considers to be the political agency of irregular migrants—'the different ways in which irregularity is contested, resisted, appropriated and/or re-appropriated—often by those who are constituted or categorized as such' (Squire 2011, 8). In a similar vein, Anne McNevin rejects Agambenian approaches in the light of her fieldwork with irregular migrant communities in Berlin, which revealed them not to be akin to the figure of *homo sacer*, but rather as 'politically active people' (McNevin 2013, 184). Dissatisfied with approaches that accept the biopolitics of sovereign power and the futility of human rights discourses as a given, McNevin argues that the main problem with what she takes to be Agambenian perspectives is that they 'fail to acknowledge any generative potential in precisely the sort of ambivalence and indeterminacy that constitutes political struggles in the everyday' (McNevin 2013, 195).

For Heather Johnson, an Agambenian perspective may account 'for the spatial structure of the Camp', but the problem with equating borderzones and camps is that such an approach ultimately 'fails to account for the agency of the migrant, except to render it impossible' (Johnson 2013, 84). Moreover, whereas, on Johnson's reading, the camp refers to a localized space—one that is defined by 'closure and limits, captured by borders'—the phenomenon of irregular migration is characterized more by 'mobility through space, across borders, and along routes' (Johnson 2013, 84). Based on fieldwork conducted in the Melilla border region of Spain and Morocco in 2008, Johnson argues that the migrants she spoke with challenged 'conventional understandings of Camp space' in which typically 'the political agency of the irregular migrant is not simply controlled, but excised' (Johnson 2013, 78). While on her view an Agambenian account 'situates migrants in a state of exception, unable to participate in any further mobility . . . and seemingly unable to participate in the politics of migration', Johnson points to the way in which this depiction is at odds with the 'moments of insurrection and challenge' she found in Melilla: 'as migrants fail to cross the border, but still return to try again, there is . . . a demand to enter the space cordoned off by the fence' (Johnson 2013, 76, 87). For Johnson, these 'fleeting interruptions and flashes of resistance' demonstrate migrants' ability to 'create politics itself within this space of exception' and allow them to 'find a voice and demand an equality of place' (Johnson 2013, 88).

What is common to all the critiques above is the argument that the failure of Agambenian approaches 'to begin from the position of the migrant' means that there is a tendency within this literature to treat every borderzone and all 'irregular' migrants as the same, rather than appreciating how the contested politics of mobility and struggles around border control play out differently across multiple sites with varying effects and implications (Johnson 2013, 84). This line of criticism also shares similar ground with those, particularly though not exclusively in Political Geography, who have argued that Agamben has a tendency to flatten space and to foist a totalizing frame onto diverse sites in global politics as if they all constituted an undifferentiated exceptional space (Coleman and Grove 2009; see also Connolly 2004). Similar arguments about the universalizing pretensions of (a certain reading of) the concept of 'bare life' have also been raised in respect of the assumed racial and gendered homogeneity of subjects banned from juridical-political community and the lack of any nuanced sensitivity to the way in which certain populations are more likely to be excluded from political communities than others (Butler 2004; Lemke 2011; Masters 2009). Cristina Masters, for example, has argued that the figure of *homo sacer* is inadequate to the task of theorizing women's experiences in the context of the global war against terrorism and to the ways in which gender has acted as a 'significant category of political exclusion' historically (Masters 2009, 32).[4]

A final line of argumentation targets what a number of critics consider to be the normative implications of adopting an Agambenian frame in critical border and migration studies. Central, here, once again, is the distinction drawn between approaches that are said to focus on border control on the one hand versus those that give greater weight to migrant mobility and agency on the other hand. An Agambenian approach is usually associated with the former and for Squire the act of omitting the latter is itself an ethically and politically loaded move: 'To suggest that irregularity is merely produced through a politics of control... is to erase the struggles inherent to... the contested politics of mobility' (Squire 2011, 8). The normatively undesirable consequences of locating theoretical and methodological starting points for the study of irregular migration within the Agambenian paradigm are also stressed by McNevin: 'Adopting the terms of reference ("bare life" in particular) that rely on an overdrawn account of sovereign power to describe, analyse and strategically orient the predicament of irregular migrants may well have the perverse effect of reinforcing the discursive tools through which the incarceration and degradation of irregular migrants are justified' (McNevin 2013, 189).

A number of alternative frames for the study of contemporary border control and migration have been proposed, which are animated by the above critiques of—and in some cases set up in contradistinction to—Agambenian approaches. Thus, for Squire, analysts should look at migration and border security via a lens of *irregularity* rather than exceptionality: 'while Agambenian analyses of border practices generally focus on the exceptional moments of a politics of control, an analytics of irregularity examines a range of processes of (ir)regularization that are manifest across various sites through various rhythms and in various forms—the standard and the everyday, as well as the extraordinary and the spectacular' (Squire 2011, 14). Thinking in terms of irregularity refuses to accept the framing of migrants in terms of 'illegality'—a frame said to be common to both dominant statist and Agambenian approaches—in favour of an approach that foregrounds the political agency of migrants and considers how they move in and out of 'irregular' conditions via 'processes of securitization and criminalization' (Squire 2011, 6).

Yet, while Squire argues that such a viewpoint demands a 'careful' consideration of migrant agency, she also warns that 'to reduce irregularity to a politics of migration or movement would be to overlook the struggles inherent to the formation of irregularity as a condition' (Squire 2011, 8). In other words, the focus on migrant agency in Squire's account is not one that simply seeks to re-privilege it over border control as if there were no conditions circumscribing the movement of migrants in the first place. This argument, one associated particularly with AoM accounts, is considered equally problematic from McNevin's perspective because it mistakenly represents migration as a 'social movement that resists incorporation into administrative systems aligned with the modern state system' (McNevin 2013, 192). Where Agambenian *and* AoM approaches go wrong, in the opinion of both Squire and McNevin, is the tendency to think in binary terms about whether sovereign power or human mobility should be considered as 'primary'. Such a move, on both perspectives, works within a reductive framework for understanding power and consequently there is a need to think beyond a zero-sum 'subjection-agency register' (McNevin 2013, 197). One way of addressing this impasse is to adopt *ambivalence* as an alternative framing to both, which McNevin characterizes as a way of coming 'to terms with the transformative potential of claims that *both* resist *and* reinscribe the power relations associated with contemporary hierarchies of mobility' (McNevin 2013, 183). By focusing on ambivalence rather than abjection or agency *tout court*, she argues that it might be possible to adopt an approach that has greater sensitivity to the complex, multifaceted, and contradictory imperatives that can be seen at work in specific, grounded sites of encounter between contemporary regimes of border control and migration. This perspective shifts the starting point from assuming an ontological primacy given to either border control or migration to one that considers political claim-making and acts that may potentially have generative potential: 'The transformative dimension of political claims is better discerned via a dialogical relationship between theory production and concrete migrant struggles—an approach that goes hand in hand with an emphasis on the *act of making claims* and the broader social environment that contextualizes that act' (McNevin 2013, 197).

Taken together, these critiques amount to a strong urge within the contemporary critical border and migration studies to abandon Agamben's work altogether and to begin analyses from an array of alternative starting points. But while some critics raise a number of perceptive insights and important challenges that require serious engagement, all too often the signifiers 'Agamben' and/or 'Agambenian-inspired approaches' are assumed to do the work of critique in and of themselves. Indeed, it is as if the limitations and failures of this scholarship are axiomatic such that the details of Agamben's argument—and those of other authors' who work with (and often modify and develop) it—do not deserve careful engagement. A further troublesome leap is to treat 'Agamben', 'Agambenian-inspired' scholarship, and 'biopolitical perspectives' as essentially synonymous with each other: this is problematic because, as the unfolding chapters of this book seek to explore, it overlooks important divergences within and between such perspectives, which cannot be reduced to one homogenous, coherent position. Indeed, I will make the case that the more nuanced perspective advocated by Squire (2011) and McNevin (2013) can be conceptualized from within (a modified account of) the biopolitical paradigm. This is important in order to counteract the prevailing view that such paradigm leads to a binary choice in critical border and migration studies between prioritizing 'border control' or 'migrant agency'.

Nevertheless, there are several reasons why an unproblematized turn to the lived 'reality' of individual 'irregular' migrants is not as secure a ground for dismissing the *homo sacer* thesis as some critics suggest. First, as I have already established, the precise content and nature of this 'thesis' is itself open to interpretation. Critics such as Raffaela Puggioni (2014, 1) refer to the 'sovereign-power/camps/*homo sacer* triad' as if the meaning of this 'triad' and its apparent limitations were self-evident and not already the subject of extensive debate within more theoretically orientated literature. Rather, as with any body of philosophical thought, Agamben's work is riddled with inconsistencies, areas of incoherence, and *aporia*, and so there is considerable scope for divergent understandings of what the *homo sacer* thesis actually 'is' and, therefore, what its implications for the critical study of borders and migration might be, as attested to by the earlier discussion of the concept of 'bare life'. Once bare life is freed from *zoē* then the concept is less a universal or essentialized notion of subjectivity and is recast as a contingent position into which both citizens and non-citizens alike may be interpellated.

Second, leaving aside the complexity and open-ended nature of the 'bare life' thesis, the move to 'test' the empirical and/or historical 'accuracy' of Agamben's thought against some notion of lived 'reality' is an equally unstable ground. This line of critique is only made possible from the sort of empiricist position that allows certain claims about 'social reality' to be 'verified' or 'falsified' according to sufficient evidence. Such a position entirely bypasses the problematization of the concept of reality, the politics of interpretation and representation, and the relationship between power/knowledge as found in the poststructuralist tradition and in which Agamben's work is usually located. Perhaps more significantly, it also fails to engage Agamben on his own terms because, as the earlier discussion of paradigmatic analysis highlights, his method is not sociologically driven, but one that aims to 'make intelligible' structures of violence and exclusion on which political life is predicated. For this reason, Agamben should be treated as a 'political strategist' who seeks to identify patterns across a broad range of hitherto unconnected phenomena in order to construct a series of (polemical) diagnoses and interventions (De La Durantaye 2012). Read in these terms, Agamben's approach to paradigmatic analysis is reminiscent of Foucault's famous aphorism that 'knowledge is not for understanding – it is for cutting'. That is to say, the point of Agamben's work is not to offer 'better' understandings of contemporary phenomena, but to challenge existing frameworks of interpretation by revealing their limits and putting forward new sets of problematizations.

Third, the criticism that the lived experience of migrants in contemporary borderzones and camps globally challenges Agamben's characterization of the camp also warrants closer consideration. While some secondary works noted above have sought to apply Agamben's thesis to contemporary detention centres, this move is already called into question in his own insistence that the sovereign ban does not work in every space of confinement. For this reason, while critics have tended to draw on empirical evidence to 'disprove' that thesis rather than engage with Agamben on his own terms, the move to equate the concentration camps of the early twentieth century with contemporary spaces of detention is highly problematic, and one that I also seek to contest and develop an alternative engagement with in Chapter 4. Nevertheless, a more faithful interpretation of Agamben's notion of the camp—understood as the space that performatively opens up via the operation of the sovereign ban—offers an instructive mode of interpreting the phenomena of contemporary push-backs and abandonment at sea in the context of EUrope's contemporary border crisis.

Moreover, I will use these phenomena to argue that while some commentators rightly highlight the importance of recognizing the agency of some 'irregular' migrants in certain contexts, it is equally significant to note other situations in which the capacity for political contestation and resistance may be severely curtailed. To be clear, this is not to agree with the characterization that Agamben's work leaves no room for accounting for political struggles, acts of profanation, and moments where sovereign power may be challenged. Indeed, although Agamben does not use the terms 'resistance' or 'agency' in his work, at no point does he depict the operation of the sovereign ban as totalizing or inevitably successful: this would make his a structuralist—rather than a poststructuralist—account.[5] However, as I will go on to illustrate, depending on the specificities of particular circumstances it is politically important not to allow an equally abstract emphasis on the agency of 'irregular' migrants to gloss over or detract from the identification and diagnosis of the often-violent methods via which attempts are made to constrain their mobility.

Push-Backs and Abandonment in the EUropean Borderscape

'Irregular' boat activity on the Mediterranean Sea is a recent phenomenon, which arose as a result of the closure in 1991 of 'regular' channels of labour mobility into the EU (Guild and Carrera 2013). Of a total of 300 million people seeking to enter the EU via land, sea, and air borders in 2012, only a relatively small number—23,254 or approximately 7 per cent—sought to enter 'irregularly' via the Mediterranean and other sea border crossings (Guild and Carrera 2013). On the one hand, as François Crepeau, the UN Special Rapporteur for the Human Rights of Migrants has argued, most 'irregular' migrants in the EU enter legally and then overstay their visa and for this reason there is a 'disproportionate' policy and media focus on 'irregular' arrivals, particularly those on unseaworthy vessels crossing the Mediterranean (UN 2013a, 6; see also Mainwaring 2012). On the other hand, as Crepeau also notes, such arrivals—particularly at sea, but also on land—constitute a highly political site of encounter between EU border security authorities and 'irregular' migrants where some of the 'most of the egregious human rights abuses appear to take place' (UN 2013a, 6). Despite the fact that the Mediterranean is one of the busiest and most monitored stretches of water globally it has been referred to as the 'graveyard of the EU' (Human Rights Watch 2011a). Conditions on the Aegean are no less favourable and between August 2012 and May 2013 there were 101 documented cases of 'irregular' migrants drowning (Amnesty 2013, 3). During the same period an unknown number have also died in the Evros region as a result of drowning and hypothermia when trying to cross the river that separates Greece and Turkey—an unofficial cemetery for unidentified corpses has been established on the hillside just outside the village of Sidiro (Pro Asyl 2013, 89). It is precisely at this site of encounter—particularly in the twinned contexts of 'push-back' operations and the abandonment of 'irregular' vessels in distress at sea—that the space of the sovereign ban is opened up, the thanatopolitical drift of EUropean biopolitical bordering practices can be identified, and the force of the Agambenian diagnosis is revealed.

A substantial body of research presented by NGOs and brought before the European Court of Human Rights (ECtHR) points to the active interception of 'irregular' migrants on the Mediterranean (see, for example, Human Rights Watch 2009; PICUM 2010). These so-called 'push-back' operations—where 'irregular' vessels have been ordered by EU Member States and Frontex to return to third countries often despite requests for humanitarian assistance—have become an increasingly visible practice in the field of contemporary EU border security and migration management. According to a report published by the Platform for International Cooperation on Undocumented Migrants (PICUM), 2009 was a watershed in the 'indiscriminate deflection' of 'irregular' migrants (PICUM 2010, 54). The report claims that in May 2009 approximately 500 'irregular' migrants were diverted by Italian coastguard authorities back to Libya: 'never before in modern times had a European state summarily returned migrants in distress at sea to a country that does not even pretend to abide by international standards of humanitarian protection' (PICUM 2010, 58). The PICUM report also refers to a similar case one month later when on 21 June 2009 a German Super Puma helicopter—allegedly belonging to Frontex Operation Nautilus IV in Malta—picked up seventy-four 'irregular' migrants and handed them over to a Libyan vessel, which they claim marks 'the first forced return operation coordinated by Frontex on the high seas' (PICUM 2010, 58).[6] In a related context, research presented by other NGOs also reveals the practice of failing to respond to the distress signals of 'irregular' migrants and their vessels at sea, which may in certain circumstances be linked to push-back operations or arise independently of them. For example, in October 2012 a Frontex-commissioned airplane was reported by the Parliamentary Assembly of the Council of Europe (PACE 2013) to have crossed a boat in distress without offering any assistance and, as a direct result, it was alleged that fifty-six passengers died. Other research suggests that such acts of omission are commonplace, particularly on the Mediterranean, and have contributed significantly to the death tolls reported by the UNHCR (PACE 2012; Pro Asyl 2012a, 2013). Before considering in greater depth the phenomena of push-backs and acts of omission in terms of the operation of the sovereign ban and as forms of thanatopolitical bordering practices, it is first instructive to outline the legal and political background against which these practices take place.

Aside from general principles enshrining the right to life as found in Article 2 of the EU Charter of Fundamental Rights and Article 2 of the European Convention on Human Rights, a number of legal instruments apply to push-backs and failures to respond to distress calls at sea. Regarding the former, the international legal principle of *non-refoulement*—one of the cornerstones of the 1951 Geneva Convention and Protocol Relating to the Status of Refugees—stipulates that 'No Contracting Parties shall expel or return ("*refouler*") a refugee in any manner whatsoever to the frontiers of territories where his life or freedom would be threatened on account of his race, religion, nationality, membership of a particular social group or political opinion' (Article 33(1) UNCHR 1951). On this basis, and as concluded by the ECtHR in its 2012 ruling in the case of *Hirsi Jamaa and Others v Italy*, all EU Member States are obliged under international law to examine the personal circumstances of 'irregular' migrants arriving at their land, sea, and air borders if they wish to pursue an application for asylum.[7] Furthermore, as outlined in the EU Directive on Asylum Procedures (2005/85/EC), 'irregular' migrants are entitled to information about asylum procedures, access to legal and translation assistance, the ability to present their case to a competent authority, formal notification of the outcome, and the right to appeal a negative decision. Similarly, a number of international legal provisions—in the form of the 1979 International Convention on Maritime Search and Rescue (the SAR Convention) and 1982 United Nations Convention on the Law of the Sea (UNCLOS)—require all states to coordinate SAR Operations wherever distress at sea occurs. In this context, 'distress' is defined as 'a

61

situation wherein there is a reasonable certainty that a person, a vessel or other craft is threatened by grave and imminent danger and requires immediate assistance' (quoted in Fundamental Rights Agency 2013, 32). 'Rescue' is understood in terms of 'an operation to retrieve persons in distress, provide for their initial medical or other needs, and deliver them to a place of safety' (quoted in Fundamental Rights Agency 2013, 32). Furthermore, seeking to strengthen provisions for SAR within the territorial waters of EU Member States, a new set of regulations on maritime surveillance was also adopted by the European Council in April 2014. According to legal analysts, these regulations are designed to 'ensure that migrants are rescued from drowning wherever possible' providing that they are 'detected in time' (Peers 2014).

Despite these legal provisions, however, there remains a series of ambiguities surrounding the treatment of 'irregular' migrants at sea, which condition the possibility of persistent human rights abuse and illuminate the operation of the sovereign ban in the Agambenian sense. One lacuna in existing provisions is that EU Member States are currently not considered responsible for the human rights violations of third-country border security authorities during push-back operations (Fundamental Rights Agency 2013). This allows EU Member States to defer responsibility for the treatment of 'irregular' migrants—even under circumstances when they are directly funding third states to carry out their 'borderwork', to use Chris Rumford's (2009) phrase, and/or supporting these efforts by supplying vital equipment (Fundamental Rights Agency 2013, 46). Perhaps more significantly still, however, the legal status and human rights responsibilities of Frontex remain fundamentally ambiguous and reflect a logic of exceptionalism whereby the agency performatively claims to occupy a transcendent position vis-à-vis EU and international law. Because it is a coordinating agency and not a state, Frontex argues that it is permitted to push back 'irregular' vessels in coastal waters and hand 'irregular' migrants over to the authorities of third countries at its discretion and according to the security imperatives of individual circumstances 'on the ground'. Importantly, former Frontex Executive Director Ilkka Laitinen has claimed that 'Frontex is never in lead of joint border control operations, playing a mere coordinating role' and on his view 'it is the individual responsibility of member states to process applications of asylum seekers and to undertake rescue operations' (Tondini 2010). Thus, in response to the recommendation of the European Ombudsman P. Nikiforos Diamandouros in March 2012—that Frontex should adopt a mechanism to deal specifically with allegations of its own breaches of humanitarian standards—the agency maintained that as a coordinating body it had no such responsibility (Statewatch 2012). More recently, in an interview published in the Finnish newspaper *Fifi Voima*, Mr Laitinen argued that Frontex is not only legally incapable of violating human rights but also not responsible for responding to 'irregular' migrants' distress calls at sea (Migrants at Sea 2014). For this reason, legal experts have highlighted that despite the 2014 maritime surveillance mechanisms Frontex continues to claim exemption from SAR obligations faced by states (Peers 2014). As German MEP Ska Keller has noted, 'this leaves Frontex and the Member States participating in a Frontex operation with important loopholes for escaping the principle of *non-refoulement*' (Keller 2014). Put in stronger terms, Human Rights Watch has portrayed Frontex 'as a spectre-like coordinating manager as well as an actor with legal autonomy' (Human Rights Watch 2011b). Drawing these points together, the concern is that Frontex assumes the position of a temporary sovereign—above the law and unanswerable to anyone—whose decisions on the worthiness of protecting certain lives remain largely at the agency's own discretion. Returning to Agamben, it is precisely this extra-legal zone of indistinction that Frontex operates within and performatively produces—often in conjunction with Member States and authorized by a claim about the exceptionality of circumstances 'on the ground' and the security imperatives of the EU and Member States—that gives rise to the space of the sovereign ban and some of the most violent thanatopolitical effects of EUropean border security practices. As reported in NGO research, the recent experiences of 'irregular' migrants exposed unconditionally to the violence of the ban in the Evros region of the Greece–Turkey borderlands—described in 2011 by Frontex as the 'centre of gravity' of its operations (quoted in Migreurop 2014)—offer a powerful insight into this aspect of EUrope's border crisis.

Between 2008 and 2012, the Evros region of Greece—with a 203-km land border with Turkey to the north and a sea border with the Aegean to the south—became a major hub for the arrival of 'irregular' migrants to the EU in the context of population displacements arising from conflicts in Afghanistan and Syria (UNHCR cited in Pro Asyl 2012b, 5). In August 2012, amid growing pressure from the Austrian and German governments to act, Greek authorities launched Operation Aspida (Shield) in collaboration with Frontex. The deployment of 1,800 additional police officers together with the erection of a 12.5-km fence and the construction of five new detention centres in the region led to a decline in 'irregular' arrivals at the land border from approximately 6,500 in August to none by November (Pro Asyl 2013). As a direct consequence of the 'success' of these operations, however, 'irregular' migrants have since turned to alternative and significantly more dangerous routes via the Aegean. Despite the ruling of the ECtHR in the case of *Hirsi Jamaa and Others v Italy* several months earlier, interviews conducted by Pro Asyl reveal repeated push-back operations in which 'irregular' migrants seeking international protection have been 'left in life-threatening situations' on the sea in 'unseaworthy vessels' and even 'thrown into the water of the river Evros' (Pro Asyl 2013, x).

Further still, many of the 169 'irregular' migrants interviewed by Amnesty and Pro Asyl between 2012 and 2013 emphasize the inherent ambiguity of the situation they typically faced: it was fundamentally unclear to them whether calling emergency helpline numbers would lead to their rescue or death at the hands of EU border security officials. According to the Pro Asyl report, 'during push-back operations in the Aegean Sea, some... claim to have dialed the emergency number, and sent out distress signals from their boats, only to be pushed back when they were located by the Greek authorities' (Pro Asyl 2013, xi). Similarly, Amnesty interviewed twenty-eight 'irregular' migrants who had together experienced thirty-nine separate incidents of collective expulsion and 'described how they were first relieved to see Greek coastguard boats only to discover what they believed to be a rescue was in fact an operation to send them back to their point of departure' (Amnesty 2013, 11).

Push-back cases and acts of abandonment on the Mediterranean and Aegean seas are especially significant for the purposes of understanding the complexity and aporetic nature of the contemporary relationship between EU border security and humanitarianism. The above cases serve to illustrate the way in which the ostensibly 'positive' humanitarian policies and policies designed to optimize and enhance life discussed in Chapter 2 may suddenly take on a 'negative' and lethal set of characteristics that threaten, diminish, or indeed kill the very lives that the EU Commission's GAMM claims to protect. Many of those 'irregular' migrants who do survive their journey and encounters with EU border security practices have provided accounts of their experiences that testify to these thanatopolitical dynamics arising from the operation of the sovereign ban:

> I tried to look at their faces and remember them, but when I lifted my head one of them immediately attacked me with his baton screaming: 'Don't look at me!' They were dressed in black... (H. G. R., with his family, from Afghanistan, pushed back from Samos in July 2013, quoted in Pro Asyl 2013, 20).

A typical scenario according to research undertaken by Pro Asyl is one whereby 'irregular' vessels discovered in Greek waters are approached by an unidentifiable boat, often in the hours of darkness, and then dragged to Turkish waters where they are stranded. Testimonies illuminate the violent methods used to disable 'irregular' migrants who are often left without fuel or food and having had their passports and mobile phones 'confiscated' by various and often unidentifiable agents of sovereign power:

> They had a wooden stick with a small metal hook in one edge. With one movement they disconnected something like a small pipe or a wire from the engine, so it wouldn't work anymore (A. M., from Syria, pushed back from Chios in mid-August 2013, quoted in Pro Asyl 2013, 20).

They told us to lie on the ground facing down and they stepped on our back. One of the coastguards jumped in our dinghy and searched the women and touched their breasts. They were screaming in a terrifying way and they put their guns on people's faces (F. K. N., pushed back from Samos on 19 September 2013 while having launched a distress alert, quoted in Pro Asyl 2013, 20).

When they left us in the Turkish waters they made waves again and six of us—all men—fell into the sea . . . They didn't help, they just left (M. S., from Syria, pushed back from Lesvos on 8 September 2013, quoted in Pro Asyl 2013, 20).

An incident on the night of 25–26 October 2014 and reported to NGO 'Watch The Med' illustrates what many migrant activist groups consider an emerging norm in the Aegean Sea (Watch The Med 2014). In this episode, 'Mr D' claims to have witnessed an illegal push-back operation by the Greek coastguard, which left thirty-three passengers—all of whom were of Syrian nationality— stranded in Turkish waters. 'Mr D' describes the way in which his group left Cesme in Turkey on a rubber vessel with the intention of reaching the Greek island of Chios when they were intercepted. In the pitch black on the high seas 'Mr D' claims that the Greek authorities boarded their boat, siphoned the tank of engine fuel, and punctured the outer membrane rendering it unseaworthy: 'they wanted to see us drown'.

What these many examples highlight is that Foucault's concept of 'letting die' is arguably insufficient to the task of diagnosing the conditions under which 'irregular' migrants are routinely exposed to violence and the possibility of death.[8] It is not simply the case that EUropean border authorities 'let' migrants die: this implies a passivity that belies the active nature of attempts to abandon them as described above. While the existence of legal and political ambiguities surrounding the status and responsibilities of Frontex are significant in facilitating abandonment, it is important to note that the creation of zones of indistinction in which 'irregular' migrants are abandoned are the outcome of a series of performative acts undertaken by EU border security authorities: 'the thanatopolitical is . . . the end of communal protections and the death by exposure to those left without protection' (Campbell 2011, 93). These authorities' actions render their target populations unworthy of protection and therefore vulnerable to 'an unconditional capacity to be killed' (Agamben 1998, 85).

Furthermore, testimonials also highlight that it is the *materiality* of 'irregular' migrants' embodied encounters with those authorities that gives the sovereign ban its thanatopolitical charge at the level of the everyday.[9] Although Agamben notes that the sovereign ban has a 'substantial' character beyond merely a formal juridical-political logic, testimonies underscore the importance of this material dimension of abandonment. This dimension is otherwise underplayed when considered from the perspective of trying to understand techniques of governance on their own terms. From the perspective of 'irregular' migrants' embodied encounter with those techniques of governance, however, its significance is brought into stark relief. Indeed, it is important to note that the exposure of 'irregular' migrants to life-threatening conditions arising from the hostility of environments in which they are abandoned is intrinsic to the operation of the sovereign ban: the active use of these environments forms part of a broader biopolitical strategy of governance that attempts to police unwanted populations and render them immobile. In the situations described above, the inherent dangers of the physical context in which 'irregular' migrants are stranded is not an innocent or inert backdrop against which EUropean border politics play out, but rather an *active* part of the field of forces that enable spatial technologies of deterrence and attempts at border control: a point that is readily acknowledged as such by Frontex.[10] In this way, the material conditions of push-backs at sea—the lack of access to food and drinking water; the danger of strong winds, tides, and currents; and the generally inhospitable nature of a drifting, overcrowded vessel—are all imbued with 'agentic capacities', to borrow a term used by Diana Coole (2013). On this view, an anthropocentric understanding of agency gives way to an approach that sees the potential for 'energies and forces of transformation' across a broader range of inanimate, material entities (Coole 2013, 453; see also Lundborg and Vaughan-Williams 2015; Squire 2015). Thus, the very materiality of the Mediterranean and Aegean seas and their potentialities for shaping regimes of (im)mobility can be read as forming part of a wider assemblage of human and non-human forces that play a fundamental role in the contemporary performance and reproduction of EUrope's borders. Aspects of EUropean borderwork are in this sense effectively outsourced to non-human actors found in physical sites of thanatopolitical abandonment, which human agents of border security depend on in policing 'irregularity'. Moves to ensure the absence of assistance to 'irregular' migrants and their vessels in these circumstances are, nevertheless, acts with significant material, ethical, and political consequences. In these terms it is instructive to conceive of the operation of the sovereign ban precisely as an act of omission: a decision *not* to act is still a decision to act with potentially lethal implications.[11] The 'boat-left-to-die' incident with which this chapter opened is a particularly striking case of such an act of omission—about which more is known than usual due to the testimonial evidence of survivors—and epitomizes the material operation of the sovereign ban and the reliance of EUropean border security on the unconditional exposure of certain 'irregular' migrants to death at sea.

In conclusion, the experiences, particularly of the passengers on the 'boat-left-to-die', draw attention to a number of features of EUrope's border crisis that I want to underscore. This incident is by no means a singular one-off 'tragedy'

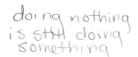

or the consequence of merely a passive neglect on behalf of EUropean border authorities, but the outcome of a more systemic set of biopolitical security problematics—some of which operate according to the logic of thanatopolitical abandonment as set out by Agamben. The case, among others, brings into sharp relief the way in which the sovereign ban operates via the suspension of EUropean and international legal conventions, which arise from a political 'decision' (in the Agambenian sense) on the status of the lives of some 'irregular' migrants as being unworthy of protection. The deaths of the sixty-three passengers aboard the dinghy unequivocally demonstrate that, under certain circumstances, the violence of EUropean border security practices renders particular lives more vulnerable to lethal conditions in which contestation, protest, and resistance—though possible in certain contexts— are nonetheless severely curtailed or even impossible in others. To reiterate, this argument is not to deny that these aspects are not unimportant at other sites within the field of EU border security and migration management or indeed to overlook the significant fact that, of the original group of seventy- two passengers, nine ultimately still survived.[12] However, to prioritize 'political agency' in abstract discussions about the nature of this field fails in my view to grasp what is at stake in the 'boat-left-to-die' case and others like it: such a position cannot offer either a diagnosis or a critique of the conditions of possibility for such border violence and 'irregular' migrants' habitual exposure to it. Indeed, the example of the 'boat-left-to-die' highlights the limitations of any position that offers no diagnostic insight into the 'agency' of thanatopolitical apparatuses of security in attempting to produce political subjectivities whose agentic capacities are deliberately and violently stymied. For this reason, to highlight 'ambivalence' as an overarching or even defining characteristic of EUropean border security and migration management is in the final analysis an equally impotent move. Giving special emphasis either to the 'agency' or 'ambivalence' of 'irregular' migrants does not scandalize nor inflict damage to the biopolitical apparatuses that all too often succeed in (re)producing their subjecthood and the EUropean border security project. Indeed, neither offers any commentary on the contemporary field of border security and migration management that border security authorities such as Frontex would find objectionable: it is because of a recognition that 'irregular' migrants have 'agency' that such populations are performatively identified and targeted by such authorities in the very first place. Rather, in concrete circumstances where 'irregular' migrants lives are quite literally put on the line, only a perspective that understands the thanatopolitical potential and lethal material workings and effects of the sovereign ban can begin to appreciate the stakes of what it might mean to engage in a critique of the condition of possibility for the violence of contemporary biopolitical border security practices in EUrope.

Notes

1. Prozorov (2013, 191) argues that conventionally Foucaultian biopolitics is 'understood as positive and productive', but that this is inadequate to address the power of death within that frame: 'the problematic of biopolitics may no longer be viewed in terms of a simple temporal succession from the dark age of sovereign negativity to the glorious age of positive power that makes life live'.

2. On the question of resistance and the potential for another politics in Agamben's earlier work see the debate between Edkins and Pin-Fat (2005) and Prozorov (2005), which I have offered a critical commentary on elsewhere (Vaughan-Williams 2009). For an assessment that includes some of Agamben's more recent texts see Prozorov (2014).

3. The formulation offered by Debrix and Barder (2012, 70) is helpful in this regard: 'The camp matters in contemporary geopolitics of exception or *as* the exception because it can, potentially, be actualized anywhere and at any moment. The camp is indeed exceptional because its geography is not fixed.' For these reasons, as they go on to argue, the virtuality of the camp does not reject materialist geographies, but helps to diagnose their instantiation.

4. For a more sympathetic reading of the implications of Agamben's work for an 'interlocking' account of class, race, and gender in the context of the 'war on terror' see Razack (2008) and Basham and Vaughan-Williams (2013).

5. For Agamben there is no simple or straightforward move outside the *attempt* of sovereign power to desubjectify, but he argues that it is, nevertheless, possible to identify a space at the interval between desubjectification and resubjectification where the potential for another politics may lie.

6. In an interview with Mr Ilkka Laitinen, former Frontex Executive Director, conducted by Dr Matteo Tondini on 12 May 2010, Mr Laitinen denied that the return operation took place in the 'Frontex operational area' and stated that 'generally, it must be noted that Frontex is never in lead of joint EU border control operations, playing merely a coordinating role...' (Tondini 2010).

7. On 23 February 2012 the Court found Italy in violation of the European Convention on Human Rights for intercepting 'irregular' migrants on the high seas within Malta's search and rescue zone, and sending them back to Libya without any opportunity to claim asylum. In the ruling of the case of *Hirsi Jamaa and Others v Italy*, which was the first case on the interception of 'irregular' migrants brought before the ECtHR, it was established that 'whenever states' agents exercise control and authority over an individual, then that state is obliged to safeguard that individual's rights and freedoms under Section 1 of the European Convention on Human Rights, even if the state is operating outside of its own territory' (Fundamental Rights Agency 2013, 40). The ruling also included a prohibition on the return of an individual to a country where their human rights are likely to be abused: 'States have to ensure disembarkation of those intercepted at sea at a place where they are not only physically safe but where their rights are respected. These include the right to an individual and fair assessment of any asylum claim' (PACE 2013, 10).

8. In the light of the 'boat-left-to-die' case it is difficult to agree with Rose's (2007, 70) assertion that 'While biopower, today, certainly has its circuits of exclusion, letting die is not making die. This is not a politics of death, though death suffuses and haunts it . . . it is a matter of the government of *life*.' Perhaps Rose's account is apposite to the task of analysing advanced liberal societies from the perspective of 'biological citizens', but this does not consider the biopolitical production of the 'non-citizen' as a constitutive outside those societies and citizens. Therefore, it would seem that a supplement is necessary in order to account for thanatopolitical potentiality within biopolitical governance.

9. For more on the need to identify and interrogate the materiality of contemporary bordering practices, albeit in different contexts and by drawing on various conceptual resources, see also Dodds (2013), Sundberg (2011), and Squire (2014).

10. The role that material forces play in shaping the context in which attempts are made to police 'irregular' migration is directly acknowledged by official documents produced by Frontex. Thus, for example, in the 'Africa-Frontex Intelligence Community Joint Report' (2013) references are made to the 'weather', 'sea currents', and 'prevailing winds' as factors in influencing both the pattern of 'irregular' migrants' movement and its detection (Frontex 2013, 20–2).

11. I am grateful to Andrew Neal for his observations on this point during discussions at the 2012 BISA Annual Conference, Edinburgh.

12. According to the Strik Report (PACE 2012, 22) five of the survivors—Dain Haile Gebre, Mahmmd Ahmed Ibrhaim, Kabbadi Asfao Dadi, Elias Mohammed, and Mariam Moussa Jamal—have been granted asylum in Italy, Norway, and Australia. The remaining four—Bilal Yacoub Idris, Ghirma Halefom, Abu Kurke Kebato, and Filmon Weldemichail Teklegergis—were all awaiting decisions on their asylum applications in EU Member States when the report was published.

4

Zoopolitical Borders

Introduction

Since the NATO-led bombing of Libya and the fall of Muammar Gaddafi in 2011, the municipal zoo in Tripoli has been closed to public visitors and put to a different use: it is now a migrant processing centre. While the capital city has twenty-two permanent processing centres, in recent years these have been reported to have exceeded their capacity and each day the zoo receives, on average, twenty 'irregular' migrants destined for the EU, typically from Ghana, Nigeria, and Chad (*The Guardian* 2013). According to local sources, the processing centre is on the edge of the grounds of the zoo—it has barred doors and windows, is sparsely furnished such that detainees sleep on the floor, and 'an ironic sticker, grazed by a gunshot hole, advertises a Libyan tourism company' (*Libya Herald* 2013). Libyan authorities—in receipt of €10 million for assistance in border control from the EU under the terms of the European Neighbourhood Policy (Amnesty 2013)—outsource the operation of the zoo to local private militias. The militias round up 'irregular' migrants suspected of attempting to leave for the EU on boats launched from nearby Gargaresh beach and bring them to the zoo for medical examinations to test for hepatitis C and HIV (NPR 2013). Research undertaken by NGOs suggests that human rights abuses are endemic not only in Tripoli zoo, but also across Libyan processing centres: 'They [the guards] don't even enter our room because they say that we smell and have illnesses. They constantly insult us, and call us: "You *donkey*, you *dog*". When we are moving in their way, they look disgusted and slap us...' (unnamed male detainee from the Gambia held in Tripoli, quoted in Amnesty 2013, 14, emphasis added).

While this scenario depicts several familiar characteristics of EUrope's border crisis considered in previous chapters, one aspect of the Libyan zoo-turned-processing centre and its wider significance remains less familiar: the fact that *humans* in Tripoli are (mis)placed in a *zoo*. *Prima facie* it might be suggested that the redesignation of this zoological space is merely a function of the chaotic asylum system in Libya and the short-term exigencies of overcrowding in processing centres established for that purpose (Garelli and Tazzioli 2013). Yet, a significant body of NGO research suggests that thousands of 'irregular' migrants are detained in zoo-like spaces not only in Libya, but also Morocco (Médicin Sans Frontières 2013) and southern EU Member States, including Italy, Cyprus, Greece, and Spain (Borderline Europe 2013). Perhaps more significantly still, as the analysis will go on to identify and investigate in greater detail, *animalization* is a powerful and recurring discourse—understood here as an intertextual assemblage of linguistic and material phenomena (Lundborg and Vaughan-Williams 2015)—that structures many 'irregular' migrants' testimonies of their embodied encounter with diverse aspects of EUropean border security at various sites—particularly, though not exclusively, in the context of contemporary spaces of detention. While some testimonies of that encounter feature political claims made in the name of a common *humanity* (Johnson 2013; Puggioni 2014), others are characterized by the reverse narrative of *dehumanization* (Borderline Europe 2013; Human Rights Watch 2011b; Médicin Sans Frontières 2013; Migreurop 2012; Pro Asyl 2012a, 2012b). These dynamics raise a number of questions pertinent to the investigation mounted in this book: what is the political and spatial significance of the animalization of 'irregular' migrants in the context of contemporary EUropean border security practices? How does the attempt to (re)produce animalized subjectivities in dehumanizing spaces create the conditions of possibility for particular forms of bordering? Where might we find apposite conceptual resources for understanding the work that the human/animal distinction does in shaping both techniques of governance and avenues for critique?

Several writers have already noted the prominence of animal metaphors and imagery in representations of 'irregular' migration at border sites globally. For example, Susan Coutin's (2005) study of the US–Mexico border refers to the way in which unauthorized Mexican border-crossers are commonly spoken of as *pollos* or 'chickens'. In the EUropean context, Shahram Khosravi (2007) hints at the political significance of these animalized representations when he draws a parallel between the traditional use of chickens as a sacrificial animal and the sacrificial logic of acts of border transgression. Also moving beyond a figurative connotation, Ruben Andersson (2014, 123) highlights the animalization of 'irregular' migrants in order to emphasize that there is a distinctive material and embodied dimension to the contemporary field of EU border controls, which he characterizes in terms of one marked by the interplay between 'police "hunters" and their elusive clandestine "prey"'. This work echoes the longer tradition of postcolonial thought in which the animalization of the colonized was recognized as a method for the maintenance of racial and juridical-political hierarchies between different 'species' of men (Fanon 2001; see also Feldman 2010, 126). By contrast, Dimitris Papadopoulos, Niamh Stephenson, and Vassilis Tsianos (2008, 216) draw on Gilles Deleuze and Félix Guattari's (2004) notion of 'becoming animal' to argue that animalization is a tactic that some 'irregular' migrants employ in order to 'claim their freedom of movement'.

Drawing on testimonial material that complicates the view offered by Papadopoulos et al., this chapter argues that the animalization of 'irregular' migrants constitutes a specific technology of power within the contemporary apparatus of EU border security that neither Foucaultian biopolitics (Chapter 2) nor Agambenian thanatopolitics (Chapter 3) can adequately grasp. The former works largely within an anthropocentric frame of understanding biopower as applying to the already given referent object of 'man-as-species'. As such, while Foucault is attentive to borders produced *within* the population in the form of racism, his account does not step back and consider the prior border between human and animal that makes 'man-as-species' possible in the first place. For this reason, Foucault's biopolitics is one that is ultimately inattentive to the politics of life and death as they relate to the operation of the human/animal distinction: it fails to appreciate Nicole Shukin's (2009, 10) pithy insight that 'the power to animalize humans first lies in the power to animalize the animal as non-human'. Agamben's lesser-known treatment of the 'anthropological machine'—most notably in *The Open* (2004)—offers some critical resources for interrogating the operation of the human/animal distinction in contemporary political life. Indeed, Agamben's account of the anthropological machine—more so than in his *homo sacer* thesis—contributes to a diagnosis of what is at stake in the attempt to produce animalized subjectivities in contemporary EUropean detention centres. However, as Allen Feldman (2010, 123), among others, has argued, Agamben's treatment of the human/animal distinction is, nevertheless, limited in respect of its tethering to the figure of *homo sacer*.

Drawing on Derrida's (2009) recent lectures published posthumously as *The Beast and the Sovereign: Part One*, I develop the notion of the 'zoopolitical border' in order to characterize both the bestial potentiality of contemporary EUropean border security and its reliance on the creation of spaces of confinement in which attempts are made to render otherwise unknown 'irregular' populations 'knowable' and, therefore, governable. By emphasizing the performative production of zoopolitical spaces—such as the Tripoli zoo-turned-processing centre—I argue that it is possible to open new avenues for critiquing the limits of humanitarian border security beyond the dominant rhetoric/reality frame. Such a move also responds to extant calls for the development of alternative border imaginaries apposite to the complexities of bordering practices in global politics in general (Johnson et al. 2011; Parker and

Vaughan-Williams et al. 2009, Parker and Vaughan-Williams 2012; Rumford 2006, 2009; Walker 2010), the further elaboration of the (post)biopolitical paradigm (Clough and Willse 2011; Debrix and Barder 2012; Wolfe 2012), and the exploration of how Derrida's zoopolitical treatment of the relationship between biopolitics, sovereignty, and the human/animal distinction might help 'inform a new, critical geography' (Rasmussen 2013, 1130). Crucially, however, the analysis departs from recent efforts to bring 'the animal' and animal–human relations back in to political geography and border-making (Philo and Wilbert 2000; Brown and Rasmussen 2010; Collard 2012; Sundberg 2011). Rather, I focus more specifically on how the zoopolitical logic identified by Derrida operates as the constitutive outside of humanitarian discourses, the application of human rights, and the citizen as the 'proper' human subject in spaces of animalization across EUrope.

Borderwork and Contemporary Spaces of Detention in EUrope

Against the backdrop of the militarization, offshoring, and outsourcing of EUropean border security practices and the emergence of neo-liberal 'migrant-centred' humanitarianism of the EU Commission's GAMM, the 'exceptional' practice of detention has become entrenched as a routine method of attempting to control 'irregular' mobility throughout the EUropean borderscape.[1] While the temporary incarceration of 'irregular' migrants seeking entry to the EU is not a new phenomenon, research undertaken by the UN and NGOs suggests that there has been a dramatic increase in the number of detainees, the range of sites used as detention centres, and the use of detention as a form of border security, particularly since the onset of population movements associated with the Arab Spring in 2011. According to the NGO 'Open Access Now!', in 2012 there were 600,000 'irregular' migrants detained while seeking entry to the EU. Spaces of detention vary considerably from large, clean, permanent, and professionally run processing centres to small, makeshift facilities where some of the most egregious human rights abuses take place (Pro Asyl 2012b). Centres may be visible landmarks with high perimeter walls or anonymous spaces invisible to the rest of society; located in urban centres or in rural backwaters; in EU Member States or neighbouring third countries; on land or at sea, as in the case of the Spanish NATO warship that is claimed to have detained more than 100 'irregular' migrants it 'rescued' in July 2011 (Migreurop 2011, 8). Therefore, while spaces of detention run through and connect diverse aspects of the EUropean borderscape, it is neither possible nor desirable to make empirical or conceptual generalizations about the nature of all detainees' experiences across every site of incarceration.

Under the terms of the 2008 EU Directive on Minimum Standards for the Reception of Asylum Seekers, the practice of detention should only be considered for use by Member States as an 'exceptional measure'. The Directive states that detention should not be used arbitrarily 'for the sole reason that [a person] is seeking international protection' and in all cases asylum seekers should be 'treated in a humane and dignified manner' (EU Council 2008). Article 8 asserts that Member States may resort to detaining those in search of international protection only 'when it proves necessary' and on the basis of 'an individual assessment of each case' if other less coercive options cannot be applied effectively. On this basis, Member States may apply in accordance with national legislation in order to detain a person for the following specific purposes:

(a) in order to determine, ascertain or verify his [sic] identity or nationality;
(b) in order to determine the elements on which his application for asylum is based which in other circumstances could be lost;
(c) in the context of a procedure, to decide on his right to enter the territory; and
(d) when protection of national security and public order so requires.

Furthermore, according to Article 9, detention should only be used as a 'temporary measure'—under certain circumstances and up to a maximum of eighteen months—in order to 'fulfill the administrative procedures required in order to obtain information' as set out in Article 8. Minimum standards on the conditions of detention are set out in Article 10 where it is established that detainees should not be kept in 'prison accommodation'; that only 'specialized detention facilities' should be used; that legal representatives and NGOs should have access; and that information should be shared using translation assistance where necessary.

Despite these legal provisions and the humanitarian commitments of the GAMM to ensuring the highest possible standards, however, a substantial body of research produced by NGOs demonstrates that many 'irregular' migrants' embodied experience of detention is one marked by violence. Between 2009 and 2013 a group of MEPs and MPs from national parliaments collaborated with the NGO 'Open Access Now!' and made annual visits to twenty-one detention centres in Belgium, Cyprus, Spain, France, Italy, and Lebanon. The 2013 report on parliamentary visits illustrates further the extent of variation in the conditions of detention (Open Access Now! 2013). For example, when compared with other NGO reports during the same period into facilities in Greece, Italy, and Libya, the conditions in Belgium, Cyprus, and France appear somewhat more favourable: facilities in the latter Member States were found generally not to be operating to capacity; at centres in Bruges, Belgium, and Nisou, Cyprus there are references to the provision of access to outside space; in Zona Franca it is reported that 'irregular' migrants have access to lawyers for up to eight hours per day and medical assistance between the hours of 08.00 and 22.00; and in Centre No. 3 in Mesnil-Amelot, France there are up to 120 'beds' available for detainees (Open Access Now! 2013). Nevertheless, the overall conclusion of the Open Access Now! report is that conditions have not improved and, while some facilities are markedly worse than others, 'detention conditions resemble those in the prison system and there are recurrent violations of human rights' (Open Access Now! 2013, 2).

Much of the NGO research on the use of detention as an instrument of border security in the EUropean context has focused on the experiences of 'irregular' migrants at the Greece–Turkey border, which was described in March 2012 as being EUrope's 'barn door' by Austrian Interior Minister Johanna Mikl Leitner (quoted in Pro Asyl 2013, v). Between 2008 and 2012 the Evros region of Greece—with a 203-km land border with Turkey to the north and a sea border with the Aegean to the south—became a major hub for the arrival of 'irregular' migrants to the EU (UNHCR cited in Pro Asyl 2012b, 5). In November 2010 the Greek government requested assistance from the EU Commission and Frontex deployed 175 guest officers recruited from twenty-six Member States under the auspices of the first RABIT operation. RABITs were first introduced in EU law by Regulation (EC) 863/2007 and allow for the deployment of a pool of experts from Member States in the face of 'urgent and exceptional migratory pressure'. Although RABIT simulation exercises have previously taken place in Portugal, Slovenia, Romania, and Moldova, the Evros deployment was the first 'real' test of these military-style task forces.

The 'success' of the Frontex mission led to the arrest of thousands of 'irregular' migrants facing deportation and/or awaiting decisions regarding their asylum application by the relevant police directorates (Council of Europe 2014; Human Rights Watch 2011b; Pro Asyl 2012b, 2013). Seeking to monitor the work of Frontex in the Evros region, several teams of researchers from various NGOs visited detention centres at Venna, Fylakio, Tychero, Feres, and Soufli (Council of Europe 2014; Human Rights Watch 2011b; Pro Asyl 2012b). Field research suggests that far from being a neutral and passive coordinator, Frontex has played an active role in implementing and enforcing EU immigration and asylum policies across these sites (Human Rights Watch 2011b, 11). In practice, Human Rights Watch researchers have found that Frontex personnel often make ad hoc decisions concerning asylum outcomes, including 'the apprehension of migrants and in making nationality-determination recommendations that [are] rubber-stamped by the Greek authorities' (Human Rights Watch 2011b, 38). Moreover, as highlighted by Pro Asyl, the registration process in detention facilities throughout the Evros region is often chaotic and with no access to translation services, which means that vital information may be recorded incorrectly: 'We saw cases where Afghans were registered as Algerians, Turks or Iranians, Algerians and Moroccans as Syrians, Sudanese as Nigerian, Iraqis as Syrians, Francophone Africans as Nigerian, Palestinians as Syrians' (Pro Asyl 2012b, 22). These errors have significant potential to impact on 'irregular' migrants' personal situations as they determine how lengthy the period of detention is likely to be and may ultimately lead to deportations back to the wrong country of origin: 'French speaking Africans, who've been identified and registered as Nigerians, can be deported to Nigeria' (Pro Asyl 2012b, 22).

Recently, as discussed in Chapter 3, many academic commentators have argued that 'irregular' migrants detained across EUrope should not be portrayed as passive victims of border security practices (Garelli and Tazzioli 2013; Johnson 2013; Puggioni 2014). Far removed from Agamben's paradigmatic figure of *homo sacer*, these writers have convincingly shown how many 'irregular' migrants in contemporary spaces of detention are politically active and protest against the conditions in which they often find themselves (see also Chapter 6). For this reason, critics of some secondary (mis)applications of Agamben's *homo sacer* thesis argue that it is both empirically inaccurate and politically dangerous to draw any parallels between the subject positions of the *Muselmänner* of the Nazi *lager* and that of detainees in migrant processing centres in EUrope today. Whereas the former are (in)famously depicted by Agamben in *Remnants of Auschwitz* (1999) as an undifferentiated mass of voiceless *homines sacri*, a number of scholars have sought to demonstrate the various methods through which many 'irregular' migrants resist their desubjectification.

In this context, the landmark case of *MSS v Greece and Belgium* is instructive because it illustrates that not all 'irregular' migrants are 'banned' from juridical-political structures and that some find ways of accessing them. An 'irregular' migrant known only as 'MSS' had worked as an interpreter for international troops in Kabul when he was forced to flee in 2008 from Afghanistan and travelled through Iran, Turkey, and then Greece, where he was arrested for 'illegal' entry. He continued on to Belgium, but under the Dublin Convention was returned to Greece as the Member State of original entry. On arrival, 'MSS' was incarcerated with twenty other detainees without food or toilet facilities at a prison located within the grounds of Athens airport. 'MSS' was subsequently released after three days and slept rough with other Afghan asylum seekers in the Greek capital where he filed a complaint to the ECtHR (Open Society 2011). In its verdict, the Court ruled against Greece and Belgium for 'inhuman and degrading treatment' in respect of their arrangements for the detention of asylum seekers—the first time in legal history that an EU Member State was found in breach of international humanitarian law. Moreover, the ruling was used by the ECtHR to further warn all EU national governments of the need to comply with international human rights legislation in respect of conditions of detention.

While the ECtHR ruling in *MSS* demonstrates 'irregular' migrants' ability to access the same juridical-political structures of protection as EU citizens *post*-detention, the work of Rafaella Puggioni (2014) has sought to emphasize that 'irregular' migrants also mount political contestation and resistance from *inside* spaces of detention. Drawing on publicly available detainees' testimonies, Puggioni asserts that migrant processing centres in EUrope are not only 'a space where the violence against the Other is acted and legitimized by sovereign power, but *also*... a space of dissent and contestation' (Puggioni 2014, 2). Whereas, on her reading, Agamben's emphasis on the totalizing nature of sovereign power 'makes *homo sacer*'s potential resistance against subjugation impossible', Puggioni (2014, 2) points to the contrasting everyday experiences of 'irregular' migrants incarcerated in Italy. As well as high-profile cases of several police officers, doctors, and lawyers protesting against the conditions inside Italian holding centres, Puggioni points to the occupation of buildings, hunger strikes, and bodily mutilations as examples of 'some of the modalities through which non-status migrants are contesting and resisting dominant politics inside the camp' (Puggioni 2014, 1). Puggioni argues that these should not be read as mere 'acts of desperation', but rather political acts 'which attempt to make use of all available gaps in the system for protesting, resisting, and uncovering camps' violent spatiality' (Puggioni 2014, 10). Echoing the work of Squire (2011), McNevin (2013), and Johnson (2013) discussed in Chapter 3, Puggioni's account stresses that 'irregular' migrants' use of the language and logic of human rights can be interpreted as a 'strong claim against the inconsistency, illegitimacy, and even illegality of the sovereign acts' (Puggioni 2014, 7). On her view, migrants' testimonies—including oral accounts given to NGO researchers and letters to local, national, and international authorities—should also themselves be read as acts of resistance in which a recurring theme is a 'strong desire to defend and reaffirm their *human* rights and their belonging to a common humanity' (Puggioni 2014, 10). Puggioni gives the example of the case of detainee Stefca Stefanova, who, in May 1999, wrote an open letter to local politicians in which he said: 'Who am I here? An animal, like all foreigners who are here in Italy without documents because they do not have the money to buy them' (quoted in Puggioni 2014, 10). Using such illustrations, Puggioni urges a conceptual approach to EUropean border security and migration management that recognizes the potential for the voice 'as a weapon against abuses' and the possibility of contesting a politics of exceptionalism (Puggioni 2014, 11).

To gain insight into how 'irregular' migrants encounter, perceive, and experience EU border security practices while in spaces of detention it is, indeed, instructive to turn to testimonial material, which offers a 'counter-archive' to 'official' narratives of EU border security and migration management produced by the Commission and its agencies (Shapiro 2012; see also Walters 2011, 152). However, testimonies of 'irregular' migrants across EUrope reveal a far more multidimensional picture of detention than Puggioni and others tend to imply. Without doubting the existence of practices of resistance in detention centres and their significance in challenging the notion that 'irregular' migrants are somehow always merely passive 'victims' of EUropean border security, the politics of contestation in Puggioni's terms is, nevertheless, somewhat difficult to discern in systematic research undertaken by NGOs in the Evros region of Greece. This may be because the ability to resist violent border security practices is particularly limited at certain sites in this specific region of the EUropean borderscape; or because moments of resistance are fleeting and perhaps difficult for researchers to observe or interviewees to testify to (Johnson 2013); or because NGOs choose not to highlight the issue in their reports for political strategic reasons (Fassin 2012); or some combination of these explanations.

While it is possible to find albeit infrequent references to hunger strikes, verbal protests, and attempted escape in 'irregular' migrants' testimonials presented by NGOs working in the Evros region, these events are typically accompanied with details of brutal repression at the hands of detention centre officials intended to quell protest and deter against future acts of insurrection:

> Some of my friends wanted to protest against the long detention period and they started a hunger strike. The police did not like it. They entered the cell and started beating them. Finally they were forced to accept the food to be put in the cell. The other refugees asked them to take it, so that the police stops the beatings (Soraya, from Somalia, 5 August 2010, Alexandroupolis, quoted in Pro Asyl 2012b, 25).

> We protested against the condition in our cell, the sewage water, the clogged toilet, and we asked to see the director. After a while, some police officers came and asked us to choose four representatives who would talk about our problems with the director. Two hours later they returned, injured. They told us that the police took them out into the yard, next to the parking lot, and beat them up (H. M., from Afghanistan, 15 April, 2011, Fylakio, quoted in Pro Asyl 2012b, 78).

> Once I tried to run away. They caught me after five minutes. They beat me after that. They beat me a lot on my neck, legs, and head. They kicked me. For hours they tied up my hands. They tied my hands to the bars for hours. And they threw water on me. It was in Soufli (unnamed sixteen-year-old boy caught after trying to escape from Soufli Border Police Station, quoted in Human Rights Watch 2011b).

In a report on conditions of detention throughout the Evros region, the Council of Europe (2014, 13) refers to the persistence of 'physical ill-treatment of persons detained in police and border guard stations'. As well as accounts of border security officials' brutality against detainees, NGO field research also indicates that the overcrowded conditions, lack of personal space, and competition for food, water, and 'luxuries' such as bars of soap means that conflict also often breaks out *among* detainees, thus prompting further cycles of violence:

> There was a fight between Afghan and Algerian inmates for a place to sleep. The police took us out of the cell and dragged me to the doctor's room and began beat me with clubs. They took seven of us in the room with the telephones, took off our t-shirts and handcuffed us. We were kept there from 22.00 til 12.00 with no food and clothes on, just our underwear (H. M., from Afghanistan, 15 April, 2011, Fylakio, quoted in Pro Asyl 2012b, 76).

> Since I was detained, they gave only two soaps to our cell – with literally 80 persons. We ended up fighting for the soaps... (M. S., from Iran, 20 December, 2011, Fylakio, quoted in Pro Asyl 2012b, 36).

> I am afraid of the others, because they are fighting for a place to sleep, for the meals, for the toilets (S. A., from Iraq, 19 December, 2010, Soufli, quoted in Pro Asyl 2012b, 34).

Thus, while Puggioni and others are doubtless correct to highlight the political militancy of some 'irregular' migrants in certain circumstances—and, indeed, the very act of giving testimony and bearing witness can itself be conceptualized as a form of protest against border violence—it is also important not to overlook contexts in which the possibilities for contestation are minimal and deliberately curtailed through violent means. Instead of depicting politically active subjects who are able to make their voices heard through the 'normal' juridical-political channels—as in *MSS*—testimonials from many 'irregular' migrants incarcerated in the Evros region are more commonly characterized by accounts of a violent culture of 'brutality, despair, and dehumanization' (Pro Asyl 2012b, 3; see also Amnesty 2013; Human Rights Watch 2011b; Pro Asyl 2012a). Furthermore, while Mezzadra and Neilson (2013, 132) argue that the purpose of contemporary detention centres across EUrope 'serves less as a means of excluding migrants than of regulating the time and speed of their movements into labor markets', an emphasis on economic factors alone does not allow for a critique of the embodied violence experienced and narrated by detainees beyond the 'rhetoric' versus 'reality' bind. Nevertheless, although testimonials presented by NGOs do not regularly tell of flashes of resistance against EUropean border security authorities, neither do they reveal the sort of unconditional exposure to death that Agamben (1998) argues is central to the operation of the sovereign ban. Rather, I want to argue that it is possible to identify in these narratives a different technology of power at work, which demands alternative conceptual resources to those commonly available in critical border and migration studies.

Critical Infrastructure, Dehumanization, Animalization

According to Pro Asyl (2012b), Tychero detention centre in the Evros region—a former warehouse with high windows and poor ventilation that has been turned into a makeshift processing facility—accommodates an average of 180 people in two cells. Each detainee is effectively allocated an area amounting to 40 cm^2 of personal space. Under these conditions it is only possible for detainees to sleep sitting in an upright position. The extent of overcrowding means that the toilets are not separated off and often detainees are left with no choice but to sleep in this area: 'If a detainee . . . has to urinate, police guards would guard him/her to the fields or he/she had to urinate through the bars into the corridor' (Pro Asyl 2012b, 30). During winter, temperatures at the facility regularly fall to −10 degrees Celsius and in the summer there is no cooling method. Food is offered to detainees twice a day, but local vendors are also encouraged to visit the facility because the standard portion sizes are often insufficient for adults. There is only one card-operated public telephone, which detainees can use if they purchase a card for €4 that lasts for several minutes only. Similar conditions can be found at Feres, where an average of eighty-five detainees share two cells with no daylight; at Soufli where an average of 170 detainees share one cell and are forced to sleep in sewage (Farsana from Afghanistan, August 2010, quoted in Pro Asyl 2012b, 34); and at Fylakio where detainees speak of not eating in order to avoid having to use the toilets (M. S. from Iran, 20 December 2011, quoted in Pro Asyl 2012b, 37).

While the question of the formal juridical-political status of 'irregular' migrants has been the subject of extensive debate in the extant academic literature, what comes through most strikingly from the testimonies of 'irregular' migrants' detained in the Evros region are protests about the everyday *material* aspects of their incarceration. In particular, it is the systematic denial of access to basic forms of critical infrastructure networks—water, food, medicine, sanitation, electricity, communications, and so on—that many detainees frequently emphasize in their accounts of detention:

> I am originally from a land at war, but I never saw suffering like I see here . . . There is no electricity and no water. We drink from the urinal (unnamed Iraqi male, quoted in Human Rights Watch, 2011b).

> You cannot imagine how dirty and difficult it is for me here. It is not possible to shower; it is really difficult. I don't know what will happen. I don't sleep at night. I just sit on a mattress (unnamed fifty-year-old woman from Georgia detained for twelve days in Feres police station, quoted in Human Rights Watch, 2011b).

> We don't have any clothes. The toilet is broken. The sewage comes out. There's a very bad smell. If a person comes here, 100 per cent he will get sick. There are no adults in our cell. The youngest boy is twelve years old . . . We're children, but we're

treated badly (unnamed fourteen-year-old Afghan boy detained for forty-three days in Fylakio detention centre, quoted in Human Rights Watch, 2011b).

Actually, detention here is a form of torture . . . We have no access to the outside world, meaning we do not have any newspapers, radio or TV. We don't know what is happening outside. We are deprived of our right to information (S. Q., from Iran, 14 October 2011, Feres, quoted in Pro Asyl 2012b, 48).

On the one hand, this strong emphasis on the material conditions of detention echoes the nature and effects of biopolitical abandonment also spoken of by 'irregular' migrants pushed back and stranded at sea (see Chapter 3). Like the passengers in the 'boat-left-to-die' incident, the detainees above all testify to the embodied impact of the hostility of the environment in which they are stranded: at both sites, EUropean borderwork relies on rendering individuals effectively stranded from vital networks and exploits the agentic capacities of the physical contexts in which they are abandoned in an attempt to control 'irregular' mobility (see also Sundberg 2011; Squire 2014). Moreover, both are sites of biopolitical bordering practices precisely because the *bodies* of 'irregular' populations—their basic needs and vulnerabilities—are targeted and managed by EUropean border security authorities and their proxies.

On the other hand, however, unlike the experiences of those aboard the 'boat-left-to-die', the testimonies presented here clearly demonstrate that, despite the often violent conditions in which 'irregular' migrants are incarcerated, contemporary detention spaces do not operate by mediating the border between life and death. Indeed, in the specific context of detention we are not dealing with the same kind of thanatopolitical bordering practices as witnessed in the case of push-backs and acts of omission on the Mediterranean and Aegean seas. For this reason, to repeat, Puggioni (2014) and others are correct to insist on the inadequacies and dangers of drawing parallels between the experiences of detainees in contemporary detention centres across EUrope and those of *Muselmänner* in the Nazi death camps. While the latter represented a subject position that is exposed unconditionally to death, the same cannot be said of the former and, indeed, Agamben has warned about mistakenly reading the operation of the sovereign ban into situations of mere confinement (Agamben 1998, 28). Therefore, I want to suggest that an alternative frame within the horizon of biopolitics is necessary in order to understand the spatial technologies of power bound up in contemporary spaces of detention.

In this regard, the work of Andrew Lakoff and Stephen Collier (2010) is an instructive starting point because they note the intrinsic and yet otherwise overlooked relationship between political subjects' physical access to critical infrastructure networks and broader questions of political community and sovereign power. According to Lakoff and Collier (2010), connectivity to water, electricity, and other critical infrastructure forms an intrinsic part of what it means to be a 'human' political subject that is included in any given political community. To some extent, the 'communal' aspect of that very community is predicated upon collective access to and mutual dependence on these normally invisible material networks. Moreover, such networks are intrinsically linked both to the health, vitality, and survival of populations and the maintenance and reproduction of particular ways of living: in short, the conditions deemed necessary to belong to 'humanity' today. Equally, communities' reliance on these systems is also a shared vulnerability from the effects of its potential breakdown. Pushing this line of analysis further it is, therefore, also the case that differential access to critical infrastructure constitutes a fundamentally biopolitical problematic. Those subjects who are granted access to such networks are performatively produced as being included in certain political communities, whereas those who are cut off are excluded and effectively abandoned. From the perspective of populations produced as 'irregular', such abandonment is one that operates at the level of everyday embodied experience and, as we shall go on to see, often threatens the very 'humanity' of those excluded.[2]

Applying these insights to the context of contemporary spaces of detention, 'irregular' migrants' testimonies demand better conceptual acknowledgement of the role that access to and denial from material critical infrastructure networks play in the drawing and maintenance of EUropean border security. Read via the insights of Lakoff and Collier (2010), practices of detention (re)produce borders between 'regular' citizen-subjects, who are connected to vital networks necessary to support (a particular modern, liberal, EUropean understanding of) 'human' life; and those deemed to be 'irregular', who are perceived to be potential threats to EUropean security, rendered immobile, and disconnected from those networks in spaces designed to support their abandonment. Indeed, what arguably characterizes the specificity of detention spaces from the perspective of incarcerated populations—and yet is hardly ever understood as such—is precisely the temporary abandonment of those deemed to be 'risky' from those networks. Via their abandonment from critical infrastructure, detainees are produced as 'needy' and 'vulnerable' subjects perpetually in need of assistance from and, therefore, at the mercy of temporary sovereigns whose role is to gather information pending a decision on 'irregular' migrants' immediate future. Moreover, it is against the inability of detained migrants to access these critical infrastructure networks that the identity of the modern, liberal EU citizen-subject is (re)produced. In contrast to the view that the exclusion of 'irregular' migrants does not animate EUrope's border crisis (Mezzadra and Neilson 2013, 132), the lived reality of the latter as a 'proper', 'civilized', and 'worthy' 'regular' subject depends precisely upon that of the 'improper', 'uncivilized', and 'unworthy' 'irregular' migrant cut off from EUropean political community. Further still, it is as a result of this form of biopolitical abandonment that the status of 'irregular' migrants as a form of political subjectivity that is somehow *less than human* is produced in concrete terms. Given the systematic denial of access to critical infrastructure networks necessary to be 'human', the narrated experience of many detainees is that they gradually acquire a status that becomes more akin to an 'animalized' figure.

Many current and former detainees do not speak of 'protection', 'empowerment', or other terms associated with the GAMM in their encounter with EU border security authorities, but of diverse practices that challenge their sense of belonging to humanity in various ways. For example, interviewees at Fylakio detention centre talked to researchers from Pro Asyl about the fundamentally depersonalizing experience of incarceration. On arrival, individual belongings are not tagged with names but are simply thrown onto piles of anonymous possessions. Old trucks are used as makeshift storage units and upon their release 'irregular' migrants can no longer find their property: 'One by one the ex-detainees entered the yard, which was filled with bags. No names, no numbers, no registration. They searched the piled [sic] of personal belongings: "F" could not find her Asthma medicaments; "H" desperately searched for his documents without a reasonable chance to find even his bag; "A" lost the contact phone numbers of all his relatives' (Pro Asyl 2012b, 37).

More commonly still, throughout the testimonies of detainees and ex-detainees is a powerful discourse not only of dehumanization. Far from an exceptional case, the opening example of the Tripoli zoo-turned-processing centre is arguably symptomatic of a more pervasive and yet under-examined feature of detention in the field of EUropean border security as experienced by some 'irregular' migrants: their animalization. The direct usage of animalized language, imagery, and metaphors by detainees to describe their embodied experiences of EU border security practices is a key and yet otherwise unexamined feature of many of their narratives:

They are aggressive in Fylakio...The police don't look at us as humans but as animals. They don't care. They just throw the food inside the cell and they don't care if people kill one another over the food. Those who are stronger eat. The others don't (unnamed adult migrant from Georgia described conditions inside Fylakio detention centre, quoted in Human Rights Watch, 2011b).

In four months, I had been given soap twice, and never shampoo nor toothpaste. I didn't cut my nails in all the time. When I asked the police for a scissor, they replied 'Eat them!' We had not enough food and we had to eat on the floor like animals. We were always sitting in the dark. We couldn't go out...The situation was devastating (A. T. M., from Afghanistan, 11 October 2011, quoted in Pro Asyl 2012b, 43).

They brought us to the place with the big tree. It's where they bring everyone they push back to Turkey. It is a place for animals, not humans. A stable. There is a wooden hut of maybe 12 x 3 meters. It might be used for keeping the police dogs (R., from Afghanistan, with his elderly mother, pushed back from Evros in September 2012, interviewed in Athens, 6 January 2013, quoted in Pro Asyl 2013, 33).

Beyond the immediate context of detention spaces in the Greece–Turkey borderlands, testimonies gathered from a range of NGOs working across EUrope—especially in southern Mediterranean and North African states—reveal that the same discourse of animalization is a potent and recurring theme in 'irregular' migrants' accounts of their encounter with EUropean border security: 'M' from Morocco, interviewed by Pro Asyl in Patras on 3 April 2012, refers to being chased around by security officials at the port 'as if I were a cat' (Pro Asyl 2012a, 21); Marie, thirty years old and interviewed in March 2013 by Médicin Sans Frontières in Morocco, testifies that militias providing outsourced border security for the EU 'have sex with you like a dog, morning, noon and night' (Médicin Sans Frontières 2013, 20); 'Mr A', detained in Otopeni, Romania and interviewed by Migreurop on 13 and 14 June 2012, describes being forced to eat 'food dropped on the floor' as if he was an animal (Migreurop 2012); and an unnamed interviewee in Rome, who agreed to speak to Borderline Europe as part of their field research in 2013, said of conditions there: 'We are in a zoo. Every cage has two rooms. The cages have barriers almost 5–6 meters high. We are left there like savage beasts' (Borderline Europe 2013, 24).

This discourse of animalization ostensibly stands in radical contrast with notions of humanitarian border security and 'migrant-centredness', which seemingly adds weight to the prominent argument that there is a 'gap' between policies on the one hand and practices on the ground on the other. However, the reading advanced here is that the discourse of animalization is not simply a metaphor used by 'irregular' migrants as a linguistic device, but rather an onto-political account of the material conditions in which their struggles with EUropean border security authorities take place. Indeed, the manner in which testimonies highlight what it means to be 'kept' in zoos and zoo-like spaces that are not befitting of contemporary understandings of what it means to be 'human' points to the way in which, far from a discourse of 'freedom' (Papadopoulos et al. 2008, 216), animalization operates in the field of EUropean border security relations as a specific technology of power. In turn, this raises a number of hitherto unaddressed questions: why might the animalization of 'irregular' migrants assist in the task of policing and (re)producing the borders of EUrope as a sovereign political community? How are we to understand the nature of the biopolitical relationship between the human/animal distinction, sovereign power, and bordering practices? Ultimately, I want to argue that it is a mistake to see the discourses of animalization and humanitarianism as in any way contradictory: as the work of Franz Fanon (2001) among others in the postcolonial tradition has already shown, the former is a necessary condition of possibility for the latter.[3] Further still, discourses of animalization expose the limits not only of humanitarian-based critique, but also of Foucaultian biopolitics and Agambenian thanatopolitics.

Derrida's Zoopolitics and the Bestial Potential of Border Security

In seeking to address the questions above, I want to suggest that it is helpful to return initially to the work of Agamben as one of few theorists who has considered the salience of the human/animal distinction under biopolitical conditions. To some extent the figure of *homo sacer* already gestures towards the political salience of the becoming animal of the human subject. In his discussion of the medieval ban, for example, Agamben traces references to the bandit in Germanic and Anglo-Saxon sources as the 'wolf-man': 'what had to remain in the collective unconscious as a monstrous hybrid of human and animal, divided between the forest and the city—the werewolf—is, therefore, in its origin the figure of the man who had been banned from the city' (Agamben 1998, 105). Agamben argues that it is significant that the figure of the bandit—the subject of the medieval ban—was not straightforwardly 'man' nor 'animal', but a 'wolf-man': 'the life of the bandit, like that of the sacred man, is not a piece of animal nature without any relation to law and the city' (Agamben 1998, 105). On the contrary, and further underscoring the reading of 'bare life' presented in Chapter 3, Agamben posits the life of the bandit as that which occupies 'a threshold of indistinction and of passage between animal and man': neither the simple natural life of *zoē*, nor the politically qualified life of *bios*: 'the bandit is the life of the werewolf . . . who is precisely neither *man* nor *beast*, and who dwells paradoxically within both while belonging to neither' (Agamben 1998, 105). But while these obscure passages of Agamben's *homo sacer* thesis offer some potential for understanding the hybrid subject position of the bandit caught between man and animal in medieval law, his overall focus, nevertheless, remains centred on the question of the mediation of the border between life and death, rather than that between the human and animal (or how the two thresholds interrelate in the context of contemporary biopolitics and thanatopolitical drift).[4]

Elsewhere in Agamben's work, however, it is possible to find other critical resources for investigating what is at stake in the prior mediation of the human/animal distinction under biopolitical conditions. In *The Open* (2004a), Agamben offers an extended discussion of the concept of 'man' not as an essential form of life, but rather as the product of a series of 'ceaseless divisions and caesurae' (Agamben 2004a, 16). For Agamben, the condition of possibility for the very notion of man is a prior separation between human and animal that 'passes first of all as a mobile border within living man' (Agamben 2004a, 15–16). That is to say, the foundation of man is predicated upon a separation between human and animal: 'It is possible to oppose man to other living things, and at the same time to organize the complex—and not always edifying—economy of relations between men and animals, only because something like animal life has been separated within man, only because his distance and proximity to the animal have been measured and recognized first of all in the closest and most intimate place' (Agamben 2004a, 16). On this basis, man is merely a category that humans have invented via their own self-knowledge: 'man is the animal that must recognize itself to be human' (Agamben 2004a, 26).

With this decentred approach to 'man', Agamben reads the allied concept of humanity as an 'anthropological machine' that produces the 'divisions and caesurae' necessary for 'man's' self-reproduction: '[humanity] is not a clearly defined species nor a substance; it is, rather, a machine or device for producing the recognition of the human' (Agamben 2004a, 26). Agamben identifies two historically contingent logics of the anthropological machine, which he connects with modernity. The first operated according to the inclusion of an outside and the humanization of the animal: 'the man-ape, the *enfant sauvage* or *Homo ferus*, but also and above all the slave, the barbarian, and the foreigner, as figures of an animal in human form' (Agamben 2004a, 37). By contrast, the modern post-Darwinian operation works to produce an outside by excluding an inside via the animalization of the human—as in the case of what Agamben calls the figure of the 'neo-mort'. Nevertheless, the humanization of the animal and the animalization of the human are part of the same structure: at the heart of both machines is 'neither an animal life nor a human life, but only a life that is separated and excluded from itself – only a *bare life*' (Agamben 2004a, 38).

In today's context, Agamben argues that what is most urgent for political analysis is, therefore, not the issue of the practical application of human rights, but rather the prior question of which forms of life are produced by the anthropological machine as being worthy of counting as 'human' in the first place: 'In our culture, the decisive political conflict, which governs every other conflict, is that between the animality and the humanity of man. That is to say, in its origin Western politics is also biopolitics' (Agamben 2004a, 80). Furthermore, it is precisely in the name of attempting to halt the anthropological machine that Agamben seeks to understand the way in which it works: 'To render inoperative the machine that governs our conception of man will therefore mean no longer to seek new—more effective or more authentic—articulations, but rather to show the central emptiness, the hiatus that—within man—separates man and animal, and to risk ourselves in this emptiness' (Agamben 2004a, 92).

In this commentary, Agamben pushes the anthropocentric limits of the Foucaultian account of biopolitics in order to consider the prior work that the human/animal distinction does in conditioning the possibility of drawing further distinctions within the category of the human—in other words, what Foucault referred to as 'state racism' (see also Shukin 2009). For this reason, Agamben's account is potentially helpful for understanding what R. B. J. Walker has outlined as the need for political analysts to better understand not only the politics of bordering practices in contemporary political life, but also the ways in which certain borders enable others to be drawn and reproduced (Walker 2010). Agamben's discussion of the human/animal distinction and the anthropological machine in *The Open* begins to address the issue of what is at stake in the contemporary animalization of 'irregular' migrants in the context of contemporary spaces of detention across EUrope. However, as a number of critics have already pointed out, Agamben's move to reconnect this operation back to his *homo sacer* thesis is ultimately a reductive one, which limits the scope of his investigations into the relationship between animalization, sovereignty, and biopolitics.[5]

In his series of lectures published posthumously as *The Beast and the Sovereign: Volume 1* (2009), Derrida connects his earlier treatments of terrorism, autoimmunity, and rogue states with the question of the animal (Derrida 2008; see also Calarco 2008; Rasmussen 2013; and Wolfe 2012). He shows how the negotiation of the human/animal distinction is—and always has been—central to the conceptualization and operationalization of sovereign power. Before considering this argument and its potential implications for understanding the contemporary animalization of 'irregular' migrants in EUrope today in greater depth, it is first necessary to note Derrida's general approach to the question of the animal.

Like Agamben (2004a), Derrida (2008) argues that the human/animal distinction is not a stable trans-historical given, but rather a binary opposition that is often used in a simplistic and reductive way in order to performatively categorize different forms of life. The distinction is not a 'given' because, against the Heideggerian view, there is nothing that is essentially 'proper' to either 'human' or 'animal'. Instead, the term 'animal' is one that the 'human' has invented not only to define itself against, but also to inscribe a hierarchy such that the human is a form of life whose priority is perpetually reassured. Derrida thus coins the term *'animot'* to emphasize that the animal is nothing other than 'an appellation that men have instituted, a name they have given themselves the right and authority to give to the living other' (Derrida 2008, 23). That *'animot'* sounds like the plural *'animaux'* in French serves to underline the violence that is done to the multiple forms of non-human life that the singular concept of 'animal' necessarily produces (Derrida 2008, 31). Crucially, for Derrida it is impossible to understand what is at stake in the activity of sovereign power—the decision over life and death—without a prior appreciation of its fundamental relationship with the human/animal distinction and the onto-political work that this distinction performs. It is in this context that his lecture series arguably moves beyond the insights established by Agamben in *The Open*.

Developing his earlier theory of sovereignty in *Rogues* (2005) as the reason of the strongest, Derrida argues that the first move of sovereign power is to posit animality as the other against which reason is defined. This move to identify and exclude the animal in its various forms as the non-human other reveals the violent foundations on which notions of 'human' sovereign political community are founded: 'the worst, the cruelest, the most inhuman violence has been unleashed against living beings, beasts or humans, and humans in particular who precisely were not accorded the dignity of being fellows' (Derrida 2009, 108). For this reason, as Cary Wolfe has pointed out, while 'thou shalt not kill' purports to be a universal maxim, it applies only to forms of life that fall within the 'proper' frame of human protection, however that is defined historically and culturally (Wolfe 2012, 9). In keeping with the logic of deconstruction, however, Derrida also seeks to demonstrate how animality is not *external* but rather *intrinsic* to the activity of sovereign power: this operation fundamentally relies upon that which it attempts to exclude. This is because, according to Derrida, in seeking to perpetually identify and exclude animality, sovereign power necessarily acquires the very bestial characteristics it purports to be different and separate from. The animal, the 'improper being', is excluded from the political and this gives the human its 'proper' identity in the polis. Yet, the practices through which sovereignty mediates the borders between the proper/improper, political/apolitical, and human/animal are often inhuman: the sovereign is 'the most brutal beast who respects nothing' (Derrida 2009, 19). In this context, the line between man and animal, the zoological threshold that sovereignty polices and depends on, auto-deconstructs. It is precisely this move to exclude the animal and yet its perpetual haunting and reappearance in the figure and activity of sovereign power that Derrida draws upon in order to mount a critique of biopolitics as found in both Foucault and Agamben.

According to Derrida, both Greek words for life—*zoē* and *bios*—are fundamentally related to the zoological and biological question of the nature and location of the limit between animal and man (Derrida 2009, 309). However, as we have already seen, this limit is not natural but constitutes a threshold that is intrinsically political because it is bound up with questions of belonging, exclusion, and, therefore, sovereignty. As with all thresholds, furthermore, it is not secure, but open to the other and, therefore, fundamentally deconstructible. On this basis, Derrida challenges the notion—originally taken from Aristotle—that a rigorous separation can be made between *zoē* and *bios* in the first place. Rather, *zoē* the simple act of living associated with 'animal' life is always already contaminated by *bios* because, as shown above, sovereign power is not free from the inhumanity it purports to be distinct from. For this reason, Derrida argues that we cannot speak straightforwardly of a modern 'entry' of *zoē* into *bios* as per the Foucaultian frame: if these terms, fundamental for life, have always coexisted then it does not make any sense to think of one as historically being absorbed by the other. Moreover, the same line of critique applies to the Agambenian formulation because if—as Derrida (2009, 316) puts it—the 'differentiation [between the two terms] has never been secure' then it makes little sense to refer to a zone of indistinction between them: such a zone would only make sense on the basis of a prior distinction.

On the Derridean reading, the search for a point when biopolitics came into existence is a futile search for an origin: such a move glosses over a host of unexamined and unanswerable questions about who has founded modern politics and on the basis of what founding event (Derrida 2009, 326). Derrida does not deny that there are no novel or historically contingent aspects of political life and neither does he dismiss the salience of the concept of bio-power *tout court*. Rather, he argues that biopower 'is an arch-ancient thing and bound up with the very idea of sovereignty', which in turn means that it cannot be analysed outside the series of bestial moves that seek to identify and exclude animality (Derrida 2009, 330). These are a potentially significant set of reflections because, in effect, Derrida argues that the question of the animal is central to and yet remains obscured from the biopolitical frame as paradig-matically set out by Foucault and developed by Agamben: he suggests that ultimately both remain trapped within an anthropocentric starting point for understanding life and its attempted capture. For this reason, the term that Derrida prefers to use in place of biopolitics in order to grasp the mediation of the threshold between human and animal that is central to sovereignty is 'zoopower'. On this view, the 'human' is always already a product of the zoopower that separates him/her from the animal that he/she is supposed not to be. This formulation is most clearly expressed in Derrida's reading of Aristotle for whom 'man is that living being who is taken by politics: he is a political living being, and essentially so. In other words, he is zoopolitical, that's his essential definition, that's what is proper to him' (Derrida 2009, 349).

Derrida's 'zoopolitical critique' speaks to several existing research agendas in critical political geography—and the interdisciplinary fields of posthuman and postbiopolitical studies more generally—that seek to decentre the human subject as a stable ontological given. In one direction, the move to interrogate the prior zoopolitical borders that condition the possibility of what Foucault referred to as 'state racism' among humans paves the way for an understanding of biopolitics in the context of a 'newly expanded community of the living' (Wolfe 2012, 105). This move chimes with recent efforts to recover 'the animal' and animal–human relations in political geographical studies. For example, Chris Philo and Chris Wilbert (2000), inspired partly by Bruno Latour's Actor-Network-Theory (ANT) approach, have sought to move away from older zoogeographies designed to 'map the distributions of animals' towards an exploration of the ways in which 'humans are always, and have always been, enmeshed in social relations with animals' such that it is 'impossible to recognize a pure "human" society' (Philo and Wilbert 2000, 4, 15). Michael Brown and Claire Rasmussen (2010) illustrate what this might entail more concretely in their study of rural bestiality, specifically the case of Kenneth Pinyan who in 2005 died from a perforated colon following intercourse with a male horse, and ways in which challenging 'human exceptionalism' queers our understanding of the sexual politics of spatiality. Similarly, Rosemary Collard's (2012, 32) exploration of the encounters and spatial entanglements in cougar–human relations in the context of Vancouver Island reveals 'the struggles over power and life between . . . residents, their pets, livestock, and cougars'. Yet, importantly, Derrida's zoopolitical critique is not simply about bringing non-human animals back into political geography and related fields. The analytical and ethical-political risk is that this move on its own merely works to reinscribe the human/animal distinction such that the latter is reprivileged over the former. This ultimately works within rather than deconstructs the human/animal binary and thereby maintains the very zoopolitical logic that Derrida is so critical of. Such a problem is evident, for example, when Brown and Rasmussen argue: 'Bestiality requires a consideration of sexual activity along a continuum of activities involving bodies and pleasures, including the range of bodies and pleasures *we* encounter in *our* relationships with animals' (2010, 159 emphasis added). Stressing the political importance of human–animal relations, while potentially significant as an initial step, does not necessarily challenge the prior zoopolitical threshold that gives rise to this assumed separation between 'us' and 'them' in the first place.

In a different direction, to move towards a conclusion, I want to suggest that Derrida's zoopolitical critique helps to better understand what is at stake in animalization as a technology of power that attempts to produce and secure spaces of sovereign political community in the name of humanity. Derrida's insight that the border between the human and the animal is the site at which sovereign power operates offers an alternative conceptual ground for rereading the animalized imagery in 'irregular' migrants' testimonies as indicative of something more than merely figurative or metaphoric wordplay. Instead, reminiscent of Fanon's (2001, 27) account of the colonial attempt to produce the native as a sub-species, the material conditions of certain detention spaces and their animalizing effects can be read as a symptom of the zoopower that seeks to (re)produce sovereign lines of distinction between the 'proper' life of the 'regular' citizen-subject whose humanity is assured and the 'improper' life of the 'irregular' migrant whose belonging to humanity is habitually called into question. In this regard, it is not only that the former is made possible by and given meaning in contradistinction to the latter, but also that, as Ilana Feldman and Miriam Ticktin (2010, 19) have put it, 'the unhuman also provides the constitutive ground on which humanity is enacted'. Indeed, reflecting the fundamentally ambiguous nature of the EU Commission's GAMM and humanitarian border security more generally, the freedom of movement and the protection of the lives of trusted 'regular' travellers is logically and substantively dependent on the production and containment of untrusted 'irregular' migrants across EUropean space. Beyond simply a difference between the 'rhetoric' of the EU's neo-liberal humanitarianism on the one hand and the violent 'realities' of detention on the other, however, Derrida offers critical resources for diagnosing how the animalization of 'irregular' migrants reveals the bestial potential of contemporary EU border security practices under the rubric of humanitarianism and, in turn, how these depend on and reproduce prior zoopolitical distinctions and spaces.

Moreover, it is arguably the zoo—perhaps more so than the camp—that acts as the paradigmatic figure for understanding the specific technology of the animalization of 'irregular' migrants in EUrope today. While the camp and the zoo share certain common characteristics—particularly when Agamben's treatment of the former is read topologically rather than topographically (Debrix 2013)—the latter is, in effect, the condition of possibility for the former. That is to say, the camp as an exceptional space always already presupposes the prior zoopolitical border drawn between humans and animals. While Derrida observes that, like the camp, 'zoos are about restricting the movements of living beings' (Derrida 2009, 298), this is not the only historical and political function of the latter (see also Philo and Wilbert 2000. 13). Importantly, Derrida charts how the zoo in Europe transformed in the nineteenth century from a menagerie solely for the amusement of the sovereign to a space designed for the production of knowledge about the characteristics of different species (Derrida 2009, 283). This reading of the zoo as a paradigmatic space for the purpose of acquiring knowledge of the otherwise unknown other helps to explain the way in which—far from the thanatopolitical designs of the Nazi *lager*—contemporary spaces of detention are geared towards producing as much information about 'irregular' populations as possible. While detention centres throughout the EUropean borderscape no doubt function in part 'to regulate the time and speed of migrations' for the purposes of controlling labour markets (Mezzadra and Neilson 2013, 149), a distinctive characteristic of contemporary detention centres is that they are also spaces that enable the production of knowledge about 'irregular' migrants: this allows for their transformation from 'unknowable' and, therefore, 'risky' populations into 'knowable' and, therefore, governable subjects (Garelli and Tazzioli 2013; see also Ticktin 2011). Thus, for example, while migrant health-care programmes have been rolled out across the Evros region, NGO Euro Surveillance found that medical examinations were designed for the short-term purposes of 'disease surveillance' rather than longer-term health care as follow-up treatment for chronic illnesses is not offered (European Surveillance 2011, 4): a practice mirrored in the testing for hepatitis C and HIV in the opening case of Tripoli zoo (see also Chapter 5).

Finally, the insights of Derrida's zoopolitical critique demand a keener awareness and interrogation of the operation of the human/animal threshold not only in contemporary border security policies and practices, but also in the context of critical responses to them. This is particularly significant when considering difficult questions about the possibility for resistance, contestation, and other modes of critique of the animalization of 'irregular' migrants. While it may be too hasty to dismiss human rights as a weapon at the disposal of what Foucault (2000) famously referred to as 'all members of the community of the governed', any response reliant upon 're-humanization' runs a risk of inhabiting and thereby reproducing the very zoopolitical logic upon which the violence of contemporary EUropean border politics rests: abstract notions of 'the human' always already rely on those excluded from that frame (Wolfe 2012). This is why, on the Derridean view, the neo-liberal humanitarian discourse of 'migrant-centredness' is not only insufficient to the task of mounting an effective critique, but is in part constitutive of the very problem that it purports to address and overcome. For this reason, the humanitarianism of the EU Commission's GAMM is not strictly at odds with the dehumanizing practices that it claims to restrain because it also works within rather than deconstructs the human/animal distinction that Derrida has shown sovereign power to rely on. Ultimately, the Derridean position offers no easy way out of this conundrum and characteristically of deconstruction, it certainly does not lend itself towards a clear political programme (Fagan 2013).[6] The zoopolitical threshold cannot be redrawn more inclusively or democratically and yet it is never stable and always haunted by its constitutive outsides.[7] What we are left with, therefore, is a legacy of thought that urges perpetual identification and deconstruction of the zoopolitical categories and spaces through which sovereign power attempts to reproduce itself: an endless work. At the very least, this diagnosis provides an alternative basis for the critique not only of the bestial potential of contemporary EU border security policies and practices that render many 'irregular' migrants animalized in zoos, but also to the specific spatial technologies of power in detention spaces and the possible limitations of humanitarian discourses purporting to curb the violent excesses of dehumanization.

Notes

1. According to UN Special Rapporteur François Crepeau: 'The systematic detention of "irregular" migrants has come to be viewed as a legitimate tool in the context of EU migration management, despite the lack of any evidence that detention serves as a deterrent' (UN 2013a, 12).
2. In broad terms, these lines of critique are, of course, not new and echo Franz Fanon's phenomenological method of rendering visible the materiality of the colonized people's town. Indeed, there are obvious parallels between the content of the 'irregular' migrants' testimonies presented here and Fanon's description of the conditions in which 'the native' was 'kept': 'It is a world without spaciousness; men live there on top of each other, and their huts are built on top of the other. The native town is a hungry town, starved of bread, of meat, of shoes, of coal, of light' (Fanon 2001, 30).
3. Fanon argues that the Manichaeism of the colonized world 'dehumanizes the native, or to speak plainly it turns him into an animal. In fact, the terms the settler uses when he mentions the native are zoological terms' (Fanon 2001, 33). In other words, the 'humanity' of the colonizer is dependent on the 'animalization' of the colonized.
4. This point relates to an emerging critique of the anthropocentrism of biopolitical theory more generally—see, for example, Shukin (2009).
5. Thus, for example, Feldman (2010, 123) writes that in Agamben's thought 'life is already partitioned, commensurated, and politicized in being made to appear as a substrate, and as the replicating code and subjugated topography for sovereign power... which is why animality diversely resurfaces in Agamben as pretext, waste product, and effluvia and as a conditioning and conditioned divergence that is both an invasive threat and a locus of punishment'. For other extended critiques of Agamben's limited approach in this regard see the works of Calarco (2008) and Wolfe (2012).
6. While Agamben's position is no clearer, some interlocutors have associated it—in contrast to the Derridean stance—with a refusal of the law and human rights (see Calarco 2008). In his commentary on Derrida's autobiographical encounter with his own cat (Derrida 2008), Feldman argues that one political response to zoopolitics is nakedness: 'Nakedness both decenters humanity and is a heightening of animality, the raising into visibility of the deferred animal biographics of the culturally and politically constructed human' (Feldman 2010, 136).
7. This deconstructive move ultimately signals a departure in Derrida's line of critique of the zoopolitical threshold from Fanon's depiction of the Manichaeism of the colonial world.

5

Immunitary Borders

Introduction

In April 2012 Andreas Loverdos, then Greek Minister of Health and Social Solidarity, described 'irregular' migrant populations living in Athens as a 'hygiene bomb' and announced the introduction of mandatory health examinations for all new arrivals (Pro Asyl 2012a, 11). Legislative change in Greece under Amendment 4075/11.04.2012 has allowed for the detention of 'irregular' migrants if they are deemed by immigration authorities to pose a threat to public health security for a period of up to ninety days or a maximum of 180 pending deportation (Open Access Now! 2013). Individuals may be detained on the grounds that they are suspected of suffering from an infectious disease, belonging to groups with infectious diseases, or living in conditions that do not meet the minimum standards of hygiene (Human Rights Watch 2012). On arrest, 'irregular' migrants are required to undergo a series of medical tests involving both a questionnaire about their medical histories and an invasive clinical examination: screenings are typically carried out for TB, hepatitis B, Crimean–Congo haemorrhagic fever, and syphilis. While these practices have been enshrined legally since 2012, a number of health initiatives have run previously in Greek detention centres, particularly in the Evros region, and with partial funding from the EU. For example, a five-month project coordinated by the Hellenic Centre for Disease Prevention and Control (HCDPC) was implemented from March 2011 entitled 'Healthcare and psychosocial support activities for third country nationals that may require international protection in the area of Evros – Greece'. The stated aim of the programme was to improve access to medical and psychosocial support to detainees and the services at the University Hospital of Alexandroupolis (European Surveillance 2011, 2). With 80 per cent funding from the EU and the remainder from Greek authorities, the support consisted of seven doctors, eight nurses, five psychologists, three social workers, and a number of translators working across the region (European Surveillance 2011, 4). Seeking to monitor the impact of the HCDPC initiative and the public health situation in the Evros region more generally, a joint mission was launched in April 2011 by the European Centre for Disease Protection (ECDP) and the World Health Organization (WHO). On the one hand, their findings were broadly supportive of the initiative, which they claimed 'has greatly improved access to healthcare including psychosocial support for migrants' (European Surveillance 2011, 5). On the other hand, however, the joint ECDP–WHO report also expressed a concern that many of the measures introduced as part of the initiative were designed for the short-term security-orientated purposes of 'disease surveillance' rather than to support the long-term health care and well-being of individuals because follow-up treatment was not offered (European Surveillance 2011, 4). It is therefore ultimately ambiguous whether the measures introduced temporarily by the HCDPC initiative and then made permanent under the terms of the 2012 Amendment are to be welcomed or questioned from the point of view of 'irregular' migrants who encounter these humanitarian border security practices: the promise of 'better' access to a limited form of health care is accompanied by intrusive knowledge-production practices that render otherwise 'unknown' populations 'knowable' and, therefore, 'manageable' via medicalized responses.

The ambiguities surrounding the health initiatives in Greek detention centres echo a number of contexts already considered in this book whereby EUropean humanitarian border security practices are fundamentally aporetic in terms of their character and performative effects. Whether it is the unstable subject position of the 'irregular' migrant as *both* a security threat *and* threatened life in need of saving in the EU Commission's GAMM, the uncertainty about whether calling helplines on the Mediterranean will lead to rescue or push-back operations, or the lack of clarity surrounding detention as both a site of enhanced access to medical attention and dehumanization, each of these examples points to the potential for thanatopolitical and zoopolitical drift within contemporary biopolitical bordering practices. How are we to interpret these seemingly contradictory dynamics and understand what the deeper stakes are politically without lapsing into a totalizing or deterministic account? Existing conceptual resources in critical border and migration studies are not particularly well equipped to address this question. As discussed previously, the literature is to a large extent beset by a theoretical impasse concerning the tendency for perspectives either to prioritize border control or the movement and political agency of 'irregular' migrants (McNevin 2013; Squire 2011). While, as preceding chapters have already discussed, both positions offer insights into various aspects of the field of contemporary EUropean border security and migration management, they are equally limited in capturing the paradoxical logic whereby humanitarian bordering practices designed to enhance and optimize the lives of 'irregular' migrants potentially end up killing or dehumanizing the very people that they claim to protect. On this basis, an alternative approach to conceptualizing EUrope's border crisis is a pressing necessity: one that does not flinch from addressing the thanatopolitical and zoopolitical spatial technologies of power explored in Chapters 3 and 4 respectively; nor one that fails to recognize the more 'vitalist' dimensions and fundamental contingencies of biopolitical governance at play. Rather, when viewed from the perspective of the *encounter* between EUropean border security and 'irregular' migrants—instead of apparatuses of attempted control on the one hand *or* 'irregular' migrants on the other hand—a far more complex picture emerges, which is summed up in the example of the Greek migrant health initiative.

While some commentators have sought to investigate and draw out this ambiguity largely in empirically grounded terms (McNevin 2013), I aim to offer an alternative—albeit complementary—conceptually driven approach by returning to debates within (post)biopolitical theory. In particular, I seek to explore the otherwise underutilized work of Roberto Esposito (2008, 2010, 2011, 2012a, 2012b, 2013) for developing new border imaginaries in view of the concrete practices and experiences of 'irregular' migrants considered in earlier chapters. I argue that Esposito is instructive in the crucial task of understanding how the dichotomous terms of existing debates set up a false 'choice' between interpreting contemporary biopolitical conditions—and their effects in structuring the field of contemporary border security and 'irregular' migration—as *either* essentially 'vitalist' *or* 'thanatopolitical'. Esposito claims that this bifurcation within contemporary biopolitical theory and its applications stems from prior unresolved ambiguities found within Foucault's paradigmatic account of biopolitics, as outlined in Chapter 2. Via the introduction of the concept of immunity, Esposito deconstructs the vitalist/thanatopolitical dichotomy by showing that these poles do not simply reflect divergent schools of thought about the nature of biopolitics, but rather represent deeper contradictory dynamics immanent within biopolitical forms of governance.[1] As well as an exegesis of the steps in this argument, I focus in particular on the spatial-ontological devices found in Esposito's thought and examine their implications for developing new understandings of the concept of the border. I argue that Esposito's work offers critical resources not only for retheorizing security relations in terms of the immunitary logic of protection, but also for rethinking the border precisely as a biopolitical immune system that seeks to defend the life of the body politic such that 'society' and 'the border' become indistinguishable. The problem, however, is that the immunitary features of border security always already run a risk of stimulating excessive—and sometimes lethal—*auto*immune defensive mechanisms that may threaten the lives that it is ostensibly designed to protect. In this way, I suggest that Esposito offers an alternative perspective that can be used to conceptualize contemporary EUropean border security practices as neither intrinsically 'good' nor 'bad', but precisely as a biopolitical immunitary mechanism with ambivalent potential. Returning to the opening example of the Greek health initiative, Esposito's work on immunity and biopolitical forms of immunization also helps to diagnose the political significance of the growing connection between EUropean border security and discourses of public health. Beyond the Greek case, I point to several contexts across the EUropean borderscape where the 'problem' of 'irregular' migration is framed as a medical issue requiring a series of therapeutic interventions. I use these examples as further illustrations of the role of the immunitary paradigm in shaping contemporary bordering practices and symptoms of what a number of scholars have termed more generically as the 'medicalization of security' (Elbe 2010; Howell 2011; Nunes 2013). Drawing these empirical and conceptual strands together, the chapter as a whole, therefore, seeks to outline and explore a further technology of power illuminated by Esposito's contribution to biopolitical theory and illustrated in the medicalization of EUropean border security and migration management: immunitary borders.

Life, Politics, and Immunity in Esposito

Running throughout Esposito's oeuvre is an attempt to address a central problematic in contemporary biopolitics that can be considered a deeper undercurrent to the more specific line of enquiry explored in this book; namely: 'Why does a politics of life always risk being reversed into a work of death?' (Esposito 2008, 8). In *Bíos: Biopolitics and Philosophy* (2008), *Immunitas: The Protection and Negation of Life* (2011), and *Terms of the Political* (2013), Esposito illustrates this general problematic with several examples. One of these is the case of the 'humanitarian' aerial bombardment of Afghanistan in November 2001 by the US and its allies as part of 'Operation Enduring Freedom'. In this case the same allied airplanes dropped both bombs and food parcels on the same local populations and across the same territories. What this illustrates, according to Esposito, is an 'acute oxymoron' whereby under the logic of humanitarianism such bombardments are 'destined to kill and protect the same people' (Esposito 2008, 4). Moreover, he attributes this 'oxymoron' not to the changing nature of warfare per se, but rather to 'the much more radical transformation of the idea of *humanitas* that subtends it' (Esposito 2008, 4). Indeed, once *humanitas* is 'reduced to its pure vital substance', Esposito argues that 'the humanity of man remains necessarily exposed to what both saves and annihilates it' (Esposito 2008, 4). With this example and others—which are strongly reminiscent of the ambiguities surrounding humanitarian border security practices in the EUropean context explored thus far—Esposito shows that there is more at stake in the convergence between the declared intention to preserve life and the production of death than extant explanations around 'tragedies', 'mistakes', and/or notions of the difference between 'rhetoric' and 'reality' can accommodate (Esposito 2008, 4). Rather, for Esposito the case of humanitarian bombardments of Afghanistan reflects a central *aporia* that is internal to contemporary biopolitical forms of governance and its attendant crises.

Esposito articulates the central problematic with which his work on biopolitics grapples in terms of the duality between the protection and negation of life: 'Why does a power that functions by insuring, protecting, and augmenting life express such potential for death?' (Esposito 2008, 39). As such, Esposito declares a common set of interests with Foucault, who, though not the first theorist to use the term 'biopolitics' (Lemke 2011), offered a novel formulation of the relationship between politics and life precisely as a *problem* or site of investigation, as discussed in Chapter 2. For Foucault, as most notably articulated in *The History of Sexuality: Volume 1* and the series of lectures published as *Society Must Be Defended*, the intersection of the two is a complex site whereby one dimension is 'simultaneously the matrix and provisional outcome of the other' (Esposito 2008, 30). However, while both Foucault and Esposito see the slide towards death—or 'thanatopolitical drift'—as the central 'enigma' of biopolitics, the latter argues that the former ultimately 'hesitated' in addressing this question (Esposito 2008, 8).

On Esposito's reading, the roots of contemporary debate about the seemingly competing 'thanatopolitical' and 'vitalist' strands of biopolitics can be traced back to a prior oscillation in Foucault's writings. The first is the so-called 'negative' dimension, which, as explored via Agamben in Chapter 3 and to some extent Derrida's notion of zoopolitics in Chapter 4, focuses on forms of subjectification and gives primacy to power *over* life. The second, in a more 'positive' sense, refers to an absolute power *of* life over attempts at capturing it, associated with the work of Antonio Negri (1993, 2004, 2008) and the tradition of autonomous Marxist thought (see Chapter 6).[2] According to Esposito, however, neither strand can ultimately be given primacy in the context of Foucaultian thought as a whole. The former runs counter to Foucault's broader philosophy of history (and to this we might add his conception of the relationship between power and resistance). In equally problematic terms, the latter fails to adequately account for the frequent reinscription of death under contemporary biopolitical conditions: 'If life is stronger than the power that besieges it, if its resistance doesn't allow it to bow to the pressure of power, then how do we account for the outcome obtained in modernity of the mass production of death?' (Esposito 2008, 39). Consequently, Esposito argues that Foucault's characterization of biopolitics pulls simultaneously in two opposing directions—towards thanatopolitical and vitalist poles—and ultimately remains locked within this *aporia* without exploring it as such. In order to address this problem in Foucault's work, Esposito (2008, 45) claims that the missing link in conceptualizing the relationship between politics and life is the concept of immunization.

As Esposito (2011, 2012b) explains, immunity is a term that is central to both juridical-political and bio-medical traditions of thought: in the context of the former it relates to a safeguard that exempts a subject from the law; in the case of the latter it refers to the ability of an organism to respond to disease. What is common to the meaning and practice of immunity in both lexicons is that it amounts to 'a protective response in the face of a risk' (Esposito 2011, 1). The principle of immunity operates by using precisely that which it seeks to oppose in order to develop resistance against it. But, while in non-lethal doses this operation may be successful in protecting life, beyond a certain threshold there comes a point when the immune system comes to threaten what it is supposed to protect:

> In social immunization, life is guarded in a form that negates what is life's most intense shared meaning. Yet a truly fatal leap occurs when this immunitary turn in biopolitics intersects with the trajectory of nationalism, and then racism. (Esposito 2013, 71)

On this basis, thinking in terms of immunity acts as a point of contact between the otherwise divergent thanatopolitical and vitalist strands of biopolitics—found initially in Foucault and taken further in separate directions by Agamben and Negri, respectively—and brings them into relation with each other: 'It is only immunization that lays bare the lethal paradox that pushes the protection of life over into its potential negation' (Esposito 2008, 116). As we shall see, Esposito argues that immunization occupies the blind spot in the Foucaultian account. He argues that it acts as a specific 'interpretive category' that helps us to better understand how the thanatopolitical and vitalist impulses of biopolitics are not separate and contradictory, but intimately connected and constitutive of a single protective device (Esposito 2011, 1). In order to unpack this dense yet elaborate argument—and before we can consider its implications for rethinking contemporary EUropean border security and migration management in the context of the current crisis—it is first necessary to trace Esposito's development of the 'immunitary paradigm' and then to examine in greater detail how this reorientates the relationship between politics and life in biopolitical thought.

The Immunitary Paradigm

Esposito (2011) identifies two interrelated strands to the etymology of immunization and the emergence of what he calls the 'immunitary paradigm': the juridical-political; and the bio-medical. According to Esposito, immunity first takes on historical significance in the context of legal under-standings of community. This connection is important to grasp because community and immunity are inextricably intertwined in Esposito's thought as a whole. Moreover, in order to fully appreciate the latter term it is instruct-ive to first consider his attempt to reconceptualize the former.

In *Communitas* (2010), Esposito argues for the need to rethink the concept of community in political philosophy in such a way that avoids reducing it to an object. He seeks to move away from what he considers to be the dominant method of approaching community: as a collection of preformed sovereign individuals each with a property—'an attribute, a definition, a predicate that qualifies them as belonging to the same totality' (Esposito 2010, 2). Instead, Esposito returns to the Latin root of community—*munus*, meaning the law of reciprocal giving or donation—in order to propose an alternative ground and lexicon to reconceptualize both community and subjectivity. The notion of *munus* connotes the mutual reciprocity that is characteristic of community and this constitutes an empty spot around which it forms: *communitas* is 'the totality of persons united not by a "property" but precisely by an obligation or debt; not by an "addition" . . . but by a "subtraction" . . . by a lack, a limit that is configured by an onus' (Esposito 2010, 6). With this emphasis on *munus*, therefore, Esposito is able to offer a diagnosis of what community is with reference to a negative quality: not a 'property' or 'possession'—such as a national identity, for example—but rather 'a debt, a pledge, a gift that is to be given' (Esposito 2010, 6). In turn, this eliminates a prior view of the subject as dependent on having positive qualities: 'the subjects of community are united by an "obligation", in the sense that we say "I owe *you* something", but not "you owe *me* something"' (Esposito 2010, 6). What defines *communitas*, then, is precisely the void that is produced by this radical decentring of the subject.

The upshot of Esposito's reconceptualization of community is that the *munus* around which it is forged poses a radical and inescapable threat to the self-identity of the individual: 'That which everyone fears in the *munus*, which is both "hospitable" and "hostile" . . . is the violent loss of borders, which awarding identity to him, ensures his subsistence' (Esposito 2010, 8). This threat to individuality is given by the condition of our very being-in-common—'the constitutive danger *of* our co-living' as humans (Esposito 2010, 8)—which, in turn, is said by Esposito to animate immunization in response as the central motif of the modern political lexicon:

> Modern individuals truly become that, the perfectly individual, the 'absolute' individual, bordered in such a way that they are isolated and protected, but only if they are freed in advance from the 'debt' that binds them one to the other; if

they are released from, exonerated, or relieved of that contact, which threatens their identity, exposing them to possible conflict with their neighbor, exposing them to the contagion of the relation with others. (Esposito 2010, 13)

At base, the function of immunity then is to protect the self-identity of the individual against the fundamental risk that it will be jeopardized or even lost as a result of exposure to others in the context of being together in the community: 'If community is so threatening to the individual integrity of the subjects that it puts into relation, nothing else remains for us except to "immunize us" beforehand and, in so doing, to negate the very same foundations of community' (Esposito 2010, 11). As an immunitary device, the modern subject is conceived of in this schema as a particular form of protection against that risk of dissolution in the face of *communitas*: 'Separated from the world of objects and master of itself, the subject closes itself off inside a circle, one that is exclusive and exclusionary, which safeguards it against a potentially hostile outside world' (Esposito 2012b, 258). Furthermore, it is necessary for the identity of the self to be protected because the very idea of community—required for the mitigation of social disorder and conflict—is precisely founded around this 'lack of the one':

> More than the defensive apparatus superimposed on the community, immunization is its internal mechanism . . . ; the fold that in some way separates community from itself, sheltering it from unbearable excess. The differential margin that prevents community from coinciding with itself takes on the deep semantic intensity of its own concept. To survive, the community, every community, is forced to introject the negative modality of its opposite, even if the opposite remains precisely a lacking and contrasting mode of being of the community itself. (Esposito 2011, 52)

Against this backdrop, it is possible to better understand the way in which *communitas* and *immunitas* are fundamentally inseparable across Esposito's work: 'If *communitas* is that relation, which in binding its members to an obligation of reciprocal donation, jeopardizes individual identity, *immunitas* is the condition of dispensation from such an obligation and therefore the defence against the appropriating features of *communitas*' (Esposito 2008, 50). Indeed, this interconnection is highlighted by the meaning of *immunitas*, which derives from the *munus* or 'office' it lacks: in literal terms, immunity refers to someone who performs no office in the context of the community at large (Esposito 2011, 5). The subject who is 'immune' does not have any obligations or duties according to the law of reciprocal giving and exchange in *communitas*, but is 'disencumbered, exonerated, exempted . . . from the *pensum* of paying tributes or performing services for others' (Esposito 2011, 5). Thus, to enjoy immunity is to occupy a privileged subject position: one that is excepted from mutual obligations with others. On this reading, immunity is precisely an uncommon or non-communal form of subjectivity: 'whoever is immune ... places himself or herself outside the community' (Esposito 2011, 6). For these reasons, immunity and community are not cast as opposites by Esposito, but as relational terms within a field of force: two 'blocks of meaning', which alternate in their prevalence vis-à-vis each other (Esposito 2012b, 256).

Though initially found in the juridical-political context, Esposito explores the way in which, from the eighteenth century onwards, immunity played an increasingly important role in the development of bio-medical knowledge and formed a crucial point of intersection between the two strands. In the bio-medical context, the idea of immunity as a self-defence mechanism refers most commonly to 'the refractoriness of an organism to the danger of contracting a dangerous disease' (Esposito 2011, 7). The increasing spread of major epidemics in sixteenth- and seventeenth-century Europe—particularly syphilis and the plague between 1536 and 1546—formed the backdrop against which new theories of the communication of disease via contamination arose (Esposito 2011, 121). In the later half of the eighteenth century, Edward Jenner's discovery of a vaccination against smallpox was, among others, a significant milestone in the emergence of the idea of an *acquired* as opposed to a *natural* form of immunity in organisms: 'The basic idea came into play ... that an attenuated form of infection could protect against a more virulent form of the same type' (Esposito 2011, 7). From Jenner's discovery a theory of immunization developed that non-lethal quantities of a virus can produce antibodies necessary for the neutralization of otherwise deadly pathogens.

As the discussion will go on to explore in greater depth, Esposito traces the gradual intertwining of the juridical-political and bio-medical lexicons of immunity. In particular, he argues that the rethinking of the relationship between disease and health in dialectical rather than oppositional terms gradually filtered into political theoretical discussions of the state organism and the idea that 'nothing reinforces the host body politic better than an ill that has been dominated and turned against itself' (Esposito 2011, 124). Esposito shows that from the early nineteenth century, medical metaphors were not only employed in legal-political discourses; the vocabulary of the latter was also employed in the former—as illustrated, for example, in the Malthusian theory of population growth (Esposito 2011, 127). On Esposito's account, this process has since intensified such that not only have the medical and legal-political fields been brought into closer contact, but also that the immunitary paradigm has become increasingly generalized throughout Western societies at large:

> The threshold of awareness with regard to risk has differed over time ... The more human beings, as well as ideas, languages, and technologies communicate and are bound up with one another, the more necessary preventative immunization as a counterweight becomes. (Esposito 2013, 60)

For Esposito, the paradigm of immunity, therefore, constitutes much more than merely a formal interpretive category: it is a *dispositif* in the Foucaultian sense of the term and as such has material substance and effects (Esposito 2013, 59). Not least, Esposito seeks to identify and interrogate the ways in which the mutual implication of politics and medicalized terms has been manifested via a range of 'legitimising practices aimed at defensive, or pre-emptive, strikes against real and imaginary enemies' (Esposito 2012b, 259).

Immunity, Biopolitics, Modernity

The immunitary paradigm enables Esposito to put forward a novel response to the problem of the historicity of biopolitics. Within extant (post)biopolitical theory it is possible to identify a division in this context that to a large extent maps onto the bifurcation between 'vitalist' and 'thanatopolitical' strands. Thus, for example, Negri emphasizes the idea that biopolitics is a modern phenomenon associated with the eclipse of sovereign power, whereas Agamben treats biopolitics as arch-ancient and coexistent with sovereignty. This ambiguity surrounding the temporality of biopolitics is again one that Esposito traces back to Foucault's paradigmatic account, which he argues incorporates two contradictory periodizations. By contrast, Esposito's innovation is to argue that what the paradigm of immunity does methodologically is to 'insert biopolitics into a historically determined grid' (Esposito 2008, 52). It is instructive to consider Esposito's particular philosophy of history because this further elucidates how he uses the paradigm of immunity and helps to contextualize the basis for some of his claims about the contemporary nature of biopolitical governance, which in turn inform my treatment of the crisis of contemporary EUropean border security.

According to Esposito, life did not 'enter' the sphere of the political at any given historical juncture: both have always already been connected to each other because 'life . . . has always constituted the material frame within which politics is necessarily inscribed' (Esposito 2013, 69). Moreover, life and politics are inescapably interrelated because of immunization:

> Rather than being superimposed or juxtaposed in an external form, that subjects one to the domination of the other, in the immunitary paradigm, *bios* and *nomos*, life and politics, emerge as the two constitutive elements of a single, indivisible whole that assumes meaning from their interrelation. Not simply the relation that joins life to power, *immunity is the power to preserve life*. (Esposito 2008, 46)

Esposito emphasizes that the societal need to protect life is not a new phenomenon and he argues that it is possible to find ample evidence of what we now think of as biopolitical apparatuses at work in the ancient world, for example in the context of the agrarian politics of the ancient empires, the politics of hygiene and sanitation in Rome, and (in biopolitics' more 'negative' or thanatopolitical guise) forms of slavery and other exclusions (Esposito 2008, 52; 2013, 69). However, whereas biopower was largely orientated around collective subjectivities in the ancient world, Esposito argues that what was essentially missing was 'the intrinsic immunitarian connotations' associated with modern forms of biopolitics (Esposito 2008, 52). The preservation or optimization of life as such—a central feature in the Foucaultian account of biopolitical conditions today—was not the chief political criterion of those ancient and medieval societies.

What changed under modern conditions, according to Esposito, was that the weakening of transcendence as the 'symbolic shell protecting human experience' created the need for alternative methods of self-protection (Esposito 2013, 70). For this reason, Esposito turns the idea of modernity as a period of human history on its head and argues that 'what we call modernity' is in fact 'nothing more than the language that allowed us to give the most effective answers to a series of requests for self-protection that sprang forth from the very foundations of life' (Esposito 2013, 70). He argues that in Hobbes we find the articulation of the Leviathan as a paradigmatic response to the biopolitical question of how to protect 'human life from the dangers of violent extinction' (Esposito 2013, 70).[3] While this era constituted what Esposito characterizes as a 'first modernity', the period from the late eighteenth century is marked out as a 'second' phase because it is in this context that, as Foucault had investigated with reference to the increased weight given to public health, demography, and urban life, we find an intensification of the biopoliticization of social relations (Esposito 2013, 70–1).

In other words, biopolitical apparatuses have gradually taken on increased significance in the modern age precisely as a result of the possibilities opened up by new forms of knowledge associated with the development of the paradigm of immunization:

> That politics has always in some way been preoccupied with defending life doesn't detract from the fact that beginning from a certain moment that coincides exactly with the origins of modernity, such a self-defensive requirement was identified not only and simply as a given, but as both a problem and a strategic option. (Esposito 2008, 54)

Again, this is not to say that historically societies have not always been concerned in different ways with the issue of self-protection, but that 'it is only in the modern ones that immunization constitutes its most intimate essence' (Esposito 2008, 55). In this way, the emergence of immunitary thinking can be thought of as a kind of supplement that altered the nature of the relationship between life and politics such that the latter became called upon to keep the former safe 'precisely by immunizing it from the dangers of extinction threatening it' (Esposito 2011, 112).

Autoimmunity, Thanatopolitics, Zoopolitics

While the immunitary protection of life is central to the operation of late modern biopolitics, a central plank of Esposito's overall argument is also that beyond a certain threshold efforts to protect life may end up destroying it in the form of an *auto*immune crisis. This is a crucial step that Esposito makes because it is precisely in the potential for autoimmunity that the ambivalence of biopolitical governance ultimately lies. Put differently, it is in this context that Esposito locates immunity/autoimmunity as the fulcrum around which 'vitalist' and 'thanatopolitical' (and 'zoopolitical') dimensions of biopower hinge. As we shall see, this helps to understand how both dimensions do not run in parallel, but are in fact conjoined as part of the same mechanism. It also forms the basis of an explanation as to why humanitarian border security practices have the capacity to both protect 'irregular' migrants and expose them to lethal or dehumanizing conditions.

With the 'politicization of life and the biologization of politics' at the beginning of the twentieth century, Esposito argues that we not only witness the movement of life into 'the heart of the political game', but also the process through which 'this biopolitical vector is turned into its thanatopolitical opposite' and efforts to enhance life may end up, in fact, causing death (Esposito 2013, 71). According to Esposito, nowhere is this more apparent historically than at the intersection of biopolitics, immunitary protection, and racism under Nazism, which on his view 'signals the apex of this thanatopolitical drift' (Esposito 2013, 73). Esposito acknowledges that it was Foucault who offered the first biopolitical interpretation of Nazism via racism. As a category, racism in Foucault's account works to separate the lives of those deemed to be worthy of living from those deemed not to be (see Chapter 2). In this way, racism authorizes the deaths of the latter in order to secure and enhance the lives of the former (Esposito 2008, 110). Such a logic can be identified in the Nazi commitment to the preservation and enhancement of (a particular understanding of) the 'German race', which rendered other races—most notably the Jews—as contaminants of a supposedly pure organic body in need of a 'radical cure' (Esposito 2008, 10). However, while Esposito embraces this well-known Foucaultian account as a starting point, he argues that it is ultimately limited in its ability to acknowledge the radical extent to which under Nazism the power to kill was distributed throughout German society: 'Its absolute newness lies in the fact that anyone, directly or indirectly, can legitimately kill everyone else' (Esposito 2008, 111).

This is an important point for countering any impression that in Esposito's work we somehow find a sensationalist or hyperbolic account of contemporary forms of biopolitical governance and thanatopolitical drift. Rather, it is in *this* totalizing context that Esposito identifies the historical specificity and irreducibility of Nazism as the most violent and transparent confluence of the biopolitical protection and thanatopolitical negation of life: 'The supreme strengthening of the life of a race that pretends to be pure is paid for by the large-scale production of death: first that of others, and, finally, in the moment of defeat, of their own' (Esposito 2013, 73). Moreover, it is only via the (auto)immunitary *dispositif* that Esposito argues we are able fully to grasp the otherwise paradoxical nature of the way in which both 'killing and healing' occupied the same discursive terrain in such radicalized and generalized terms (Esposito 2008, 116). Under Nazism the medical profession became intimately involved in the incidence of mass homicide because the German body politic as a whole came to be problematized as a single patient in need of therapeutic intervention:

> The thesis that emerges is that between this therapeutic attitude and the thanatological frame in which it is inscribed isn't a simple contradiction, but rather a profound connection; to the degree the doctors were obsessively preoccupied with the health of the German body, they made a deadly incision, in the specifically surgical sense of the expression, in its body. In short, and although it may seem paradoxical, it was in order to perform their therapeutic mission that they turned themselves into the executioners of those they considered either nonessential or harmful to improving public health. (Esposito 2011, 115)

Using Nazism as the extreme point of an underlying potentiality, Esposito argues that when the protection of life is framed in gradually more racist terms and the protective apparatus become excessively aggressive an *auto*immune crisis begins to emerge whereby all life—external enemies, internal enemies, and finally the self—is ultimately submitted to the 'regime of death' (Esposito 2013, 74; 2008, 111).

Nevertheless, it is important to underscore that while for Esposito the potential for the drift towards thanatopolitics is always already inherent within the immunitary paradigm, his work does not see Nazism as in any way inevitable. On his view, biopolitics and Nazism are related to each other, but they are not synonymous and the latter is not straightforwardly a product of the former. Rather, Esposito characterizes Nazism as having taken biopolitics to its logical extreme: 'Nazism is the paroxysmal and degenerated product of a certain kind of biopolitics' (Esposito 2013, 75). As such, on his view Nazism's principle of enhancing life only through death constituted a radical break from modern biopolitics. Indeed, the treatment of the Jews, in particular, as parasites, bacteria, and other forms of 'animal' life means that for

Esposito what we saw in Nazism was, in fact, beyond the limits of what can be understood as biopolitics: 'In this sense, Nazism wasn't even a proper biopolitics, but more literally a *zoopolitics*, one expressed directly at human animals' (Esposito 2008, 117).

Here, Esposito draws attention to the operation of the zoopolitical threshold in the idea that the task of Nazism was to save the German people—and the West more generally—from what its leaders deemed to be the 'degeneration' of that population towards the 'non-man in man and therefore the man-animal' (Esposito 2008, 119). However, it is significant to note that for Esposito the specific form of zoopolitics associated with Nazism exceeded the limits of the animalization of the human, as discussed via Derrida in Chapter 4. This is because, paradoxically, one of the peculiar features of Nazism was that the regime actually prohibited any form of cruelty towards animals, 'in particular reference to cold, heat, and to the inoculation of pathenogenic germs' (Esposito 2008, 130). Instead, Esposito argues that the Third Reich did not 'bestialize man', as such. Rather, more accurately it 'anthropologized the animal' such that the definition of the *anthropos* came to include animals of inferior species: 'He who was the object of persecution and extreme violence wasn't simply an animal (which was respected and protected as such by one of the most advanced pieces of legislation of the entire world), but was an *animal-man*: man in the animal and the animal in the man' (Esposito 2008, 130). In this way, Esposito conjoins thanatopolitical and zoopolitical drift as part of the same autoimmune potentiality within biopolitical forms of governance while underscoring the distinctiveness of Nazism and its elements of discontinuity with modern biopolitics.

Risk, Security, and Contemporary (Auto)Immune Biopolitics

While Esposito argues that the specific operation of Nazi zoopolitics was 'the most terrifying form of historical realization of biopolitics', he also claims that the former did not somehow mark the passing of the latter (Esposito 2008, 146). Despite Nazism, Esposito claims that the current period in global politics is one in which the logic of (auto)immunization has not disappeared, but is, in fact, operating at worryingly high levels. In support of this argument he points to what he considers to be several symptoms of a crisis of excessive immunitary defence in contemporary biopolitical life.

Esposito draws attention to the way in which current biopolitical dynamics turn around the perception of risk. Although he acknowledges that the prospect of the 'contamination' of the body politic is an arch-ancient fear, Esposito argues that in more recent years the perception of risk and immunitary efforts to respond to it have intensified: 'what frightens us today is not contamination *per se*...as much as its uncontrolled and unstoppable diffusion throughout all the productive nerve centres of our lives' (Esposito 2011, 2–3). In this context, Esposito claims that there has been a 'contagion drift' whereby the need for immunization has now become 'the linchpin around which our social systems rotate' (Esposito 2011, 2). As such, we have witnessed the entrenchment of a tautology whereby 'instead of adapting the protection to the actual level of risk', contemporary forms of societal immunization seek to 'adapt the perception of risk to the growing need for protection' (Esposito 2011, 16).

Central to the intensification of the perception of risk and efforts to mitigate it, on Esposito's view, is the role of technology, which has come to redefine the relationship between politics and life, and the very way that immunitary processes operate. Esposito draws on the work of Donna Haraway in order to conceptualize the changing material conditions that, with the proliferation of bionic, electronic, and information technology, today demand a new paradigm of interpretation for understanding not only the relationship between politics and life, but also the governance of life and the very nature of the immunitary paradigm itself. Whereas Foucault took the human body as a unitary figure, Esposito draws on Haraway's 'material semiotic' reinterpretation of that body as a 'complex field inscribed by sociocultural codes represented by the hybrid figure of the cyborg, equally divided between man and machine' (Esposito 2011, 147). On this interpretation, the subject can no longer be thought of as coterminous with itself such that today we find a radical restructuring of the 'individual' body as a result of the manifold technologies that now inhabit and permeate it:

> While up to a certain point human beings projected themselves into the world, and then also into the universe, now it is the world, in all its components—natural and artificial, material and electronic, chemical and telematics—which penetrates us in a form that eliminates the separation between inside and outside, front and back, surface and depth: no longer content merely to besiege us from the outside, technique has now taken up residence in our very limbs. (Esposito 2011, 147)

Under late modern conditions whereby a heightened sense of risk has led to the neurotic drive for security throughout society, Esposito argues that once again protection has itself become a major risk (Esposito 2011, 16). Internationally, he points to the onset of an 'autoimmune' crisis whereby 'the risk from which the protection is meant to defend is actually created by the protection itself' (Esposito 2011, 141). This is most apparent in the context of the global 'war against terrorism' and, in particular, the 'obsessive search for security' associated with Western governments' response to the perceived risk of terrorism (Esposito 2008, 147). In this context, the emergence of and commitment to preventative forms of warfare can be considered a key symptom of the intensity of current conditions because it 'constitutes the most acute point of this autoimmunitary turn of contemporary biopolitics, in the sense that here, in the self-confuting figure of a war fought precisely to avoid war, the negative of the immunitary procedure doubles back on itself until it covers the entire frame' (Esposito 2008, 147).[4] Both Western secularism and Islamic extremism can be considered 'immunitary obsessions' according to this view: the latter seeks to protect its imagined purity from being contaminated by the former; the former seeks to protect its privileged wealth and power from the latter and the rest of the world (Esposito 2013, 62). As oppositional political monotheisms, Esposito claims that both represent the most violent aspect of an immunitary logic via the 'exponential multiplication of the same risks that would like to be avoided, or at least reduced, through instruments that are instead destined to reproduce them more intensely' (Esposito 2008, 147).

Esposito's diagnosis of the (auto)immunitary features of contemporary global politics and his prognosis of further potential thanatopolitical (and zoopolitical) drift in the context of the ongoing war against terrorism appear to lead inexorably towards a somewhat bleak picture in terms of the possibility for political contestation and the emergence of alternative border imaginaries. Indeed, *prima facie*, many of the critiques commonly (though not unproblematically) made of Agamben in this regard might be said to apply equally to Esposito's overall outlook: for this reason it might be argued the latter runs the risk of falling back into the very totalizing and depoliticizing trap that his work has purported to avoid. However, whereas the 'affirmative' dimension of biopolitics in Agamben's work is at best implicit and often hard if not impossible to find in some secondary engagements, by contrast Esposito has sought to emphasize that thanatopolitical drift is *not* the automatic corollary of biopolitics and that the destruction of life in an autoimmune fashion is far from the inevitable outcome of modernity.[5] The question of what a more affirmative biopolitics might look like from Esposito's perspective and what the implications would be for rethinking EUropean border security are core themes that are expanded upon in greater detail in Chapter 6. Before that, however, it is instructive in the context of the preceding discussion to consider briefly the basis on which Esposito seeks to rework biopolitics in a more affirmative direction from within.

Reworking Biopolitics From Within

In the quest for an affirmative biopolitics, Esposito (2012b, 270) argues that it is a mistake to 'imagine' that 'the keys' might be 'found in the diametrical opposite of the thanatopolitical dispositifs'. Rather, his search for a politics that is 'no longer *over* life, but *of* life' is one that is mounted from *within* the context of the thanatopolitical (zoopolitical, even) potentiality of the (auto)immunitary frame (Esposito 2008, 157, emphasis added; see also Esposito 2013, 77; 2012b, 270). In *Bíos* (2008) and elsewhere (Esposito 2012b), Esposito illustrates the guiding logic of his approach by drawing out the three principal immunitary *dispositifs* of Nazism and then showing how, one by one, they can be rethought and displaced on their own terms.

The first *dispositif* that Esposito identifies is the 'absolute normativization of life', which relates to the emergence of a norm of 'an anticipatory logic about life only being managed via death so that there becomes "no way out" of the thanatopolitical cycle' (Esposito 2008, 140). The second is the 'double enclosure of the body' whereby the biology of the individual body is seen as pure, coincidental with itself, and the basis of 'the ultimate truth' for the body politic (Esposito 2008, 141). Finally, the suppression of birth in advance of its emergence via practices of sterilization works to nullify life and instantiate the privileged position of death in social and political organization. He argues that all three dimensions are inherent to the thanatopolitics and zoopolitics of Nazism.

In response, Esposito seeks to 'turn inside out' these immunitary *dispositifs* (Esposito 2008, 156). Here, it is argued that the works of classical political theorists such as Hobbes, Kant, Schmitt, and Kelsen do not help in the task of rethinking biopolitics along more affirmative lines because they either work inside or outside the thanatopolitical frame without engaging directly with and challenging its essential tenets. Instead, Esposito finds more promise in Spinoza and ultimately Deleuze—thinkers whom he argues substitute 'a logic of presupposition with one of reciprocal immanence' (Esposito 2008, 185). With its alternative emphasis on becoming and the vitalism of life, Esposito claims that a Spinozist view introduces 'a powerful semantic in the juridical norm against the immunitary normativization of life that is able to push beyond its usual definition' (Esposito 2008, 191). Such an outlook is taken further by Deleuze most notably in *Pure Immanence: Essays on A Life* (2005) where, instead of imprisoning life within its own *bios* and thanatopolitical impulse, a primacy is afforded to the singularity of life—'as that of the newborn, who is similar to all the others, but different from each of them for the tonality of the voice, the intensity of a smile, the sparkle of a tear' (Esposito 2008, 193).

From Esposito's Spinozist-Deleuzian perspective, the first move in response to the threefold immunitary *dispositif* of Nazism is to oppose the normativization of life precisely via the vitalization of that norm. The Nazi separation between norm and life does not make any sense from the Spinozist-Deleuzian heritage of thought 'because they are part of a single dimension in continuous becoming' (Esposito 2008, 185). By contrast, on this view the norm becomes not one of transcendental capture and thanatopolitics, but rather 'the immanent impulse of life' (Esposito 2008, 194). This position also challenges the figure of the racially purified body (of the individual and body politic) that requires immunization in the first place, because it attempts to rethink the location of politics not as the individual body but in terms of the more radical idea of the multiplicity of flesh (Campbell 2008, xxxiii). The figure of flesh is understood to be more radical for rethinking politics because, emerging from Christian, phenomenological, and twentieth-century art, Esposito sees it has having more 'disruptive force' than the body: 'Flesh is the body that doesn't completely coincide with itself... that isn't unified beforehand in an organic form, and that is not led by a head... No. Flesh is constitutively plural, multiple, and deformed' (Esposito and Campbell 2008, 52). Finally, birth is reconfigured from a process that reproduces the national body politic to one that repeatedly multiplies difference in such a way that evades capture. For Esposito, the vitalism of Spinoza and Deleuze offers the basis for rethinking subjectivity and difference as not residing at the level of the individual person, but rather in the radical opening of human community at that of the *impersonal* (Campbell 2011, 73). Indeed, it is in the very commitment to a norm of life that refers to 'the potentiality of life's becoming' in the context of an impersonal singularity of being that ultimately, he argues, we can 'glimpse... the figure of an *affirmative* biopolitics' (Esposito 2008, 194, emphasis added).

With this emphasis on the affirmative potentiality of biopolitics, Esposito offers a contrasting picture of the thanatopolitics that is often though not uncontroversially associated with Agamben. By contrast, with his deconstruction of the terms of the thanatopolitical *dispositif* and turn to the vitalism of Spinoza and Deleuze, we arguably see in Esposito more of a systematic attempt to consider what is at stake in the attempt to rethink biopolitics in an affirmative direction from within. Where Esposito leaves us overall then is a sense in which while thanatopolitical and affirmative potentiality is always already inscribed within biopolitics because of its immunitary nature, there is no predetermined *telos* in either a 'positive' or 'negative' direction: 'Whether its [biopolitics] meaning will again be disowned in a politics of death or affirmed in a politics of life will depend on the mode in which contemporary thought will follow its traces' (Esposito 2008, 194). What an affirmative biopolitics entails—and what the implications for rethinking EUropean border security and migration management in response to the current crisis might involve—are key themes picked up and explored further in the final chapter. The immediate task is to clarify how the immunitary paradigm offers the basis for reconceptualizing the border in contemporary political life.

Reconceptualizing EUrope's Borders as an Immune System

Having investigated some of Esposito's key ideas the discussion now turns to consider the important and yet otherwise hitherto overlooked connection between the immunitary paradigm and the question of borders. I focus on the spatial-ontological devices that Esposito uses—particularly the work that lines, limits, and thresholds perform in his analysis—and also on how these contribute to an expansion of the vocabulary available to critical border and migration studies. Inspired by Esposito's oeuvre, I argue that the very notion of 'border security' can be rethought as performing an immunitary function: that the nature and location of the immunitary function of bordering practices has, nevertheless, changed over time and continues to diversify and become more complex; and that Esposito's thought offers a distinctive set of critical resources for diagnosing the contemporary EUropean problematization of 'irregular' migration as a security risk, the increasing tendency for this problematization to be allied with discourses of public health, and the potential of bordering practices to both protect and negate the very same lives.

The Immunitary Function of Borders

For Esposito, the relationship between life, politics, and immunity is fundamentally characterized by the concept of the border not as a given, but as a site of enquiry: 'Whether the danger that lies in wait is a disease threatening the individual body, a violent intrusion into the body politic, or a deviant message entering the body electronic, what remains constant is the place where the threat is located, always on the border between the inside and the outside, between the self and the other, the individual and the common' (Esposito 2011, 2). The importance of the concept of the border to Esposito is immediately apparent in his discussion of the etymology of *immunitas*, which is understood as a form of protective response to the perceived 'threat' of common life immanent to all forms of community: 'Common life is what breaks the identity-making boundaries of individuals, exposing them to alteration—and thus potential conflict—from others' (Esposito 2011, 22). In this context, immunity is said to reinstate the borders of the self that are otherwise threatened by excessive communal bonds and the encounter with and exposure to the other: 'One can say that generally *immunitas*, to the degree it protects the one who bears it from risky contact with those who lack it, restores its own borders that were jeopardized by the common' (Esposito 2008, 50).

As Vanessa Lemm (2013, 4) has argued, social immunization can be thought of precisely as a sort of 'frontier, a dividing line, a term or limit . . . that protects individual life from the demands of the community'. Added to this, we can say that the logic of immunity works at two border sites that nevertheless become increasingly interrelated in Esposito's account of *immunitas*: internally, between individuals and the community that threatens their very identity; and externally, between the body politic and its outside. But while *immunitas* has always functioned as a border concept, its nature and location is not presented as a trans-historical given in Esposito's work. Rather, his genealogy of biopolitics demonstrates how developments in knowledge of epidemiology came to influence and shape dominant juridical-political understandings of the border, which has been renegotiated, redrawn, and reproduced in the light of developments in the immunitary paradigm as a whole—developments that have also affected the ways in which risk is perceived and 'known'. For example, Esposito discusses how, against the backdrop of the epidemics of the sixteenth century, new ideas about how to combat the risk of infection in the human body gave rise both to alternative spatial arrangements in Europe's cities and novel conceptualizations of the external borders of the body politic in juridical-political discourses.

The old medieval model of protection against disease entailed a spatial logic of quarantine whereby those infected with leprosy and the plague would typically be kept beyond the walls of the city. However, new knowledge about how infectious germs breed meant that instead of banishing those with disease *outside* of cities, new spatial techniques were adopted in order to distribute and isolate diseased bodies *throughout* urban space and thereby better control the risk of infections spreading: 'All the urbanization that developed in Europe starting in the middle of the eighteenth century took on the appearance of a dense network of fences between places, zones, and territories protected by boundaries established according to political and administrative rules that went well beyond sanitary needs' (Esposito 2011, 140). This involved the creation of zones for the management of bodies—in 'ports, prisons, factories, hospitals, cemeteries'—which enabled further spatial sub-divisions 'based on the need for both medical and social surveillance' (Esposito 2011, 139). In this way, Esposito traces the arrival of an immunity framework that sought to *combine* therapeutic practices and the striation of space in an attempt to produce social order.

Esposito also points to the parallel connections that were developed between immunitary thinking in medicine and references to the state of health of the body politic *as a whole* in juridical-political discourse. This engendered new discourses about the *external* borders of political community as reflected in 'the images of besieged cities, fortified castles, and territories surrounded by potential invaders that filled the pages of English, French, and Italian political treatises' of that period (Esposito 2011, 123). The prevalence of disease necessitated the development of new 'immunitary barriers, protection and apparatuses aimed at reducing, if not eliminating, the porosity of external borders to contaminating toxic germs' (Esposito 2011, 123). However, this classical mode of *preventing* movement and keeping threats *outside* the body politic later gave way in the eighteenth century to another type of border thinking—one that focused instead on the pre-emptive biopolitical attempt to save, enhance, develop, and protect the life of the population via public

113

health initiatives. For these reasons, the border was no longer to be found straightforwardly at the outer-edges of cities or states, but rather throughout society at large. This is because, as Esposito sees it, the immunitary intention of biopolitics is 'to delay the passage from life to death as long as possible' in order that the 'inevitable deaths of individuals' will not come to threaten the security or continuity of the body politic (Esposito 2011, 115).

Pulling these strands together, the figure of the immune system running throughout Esposito's thought is therefore more than merely a *metaphor* for rethinking the border as a protective membrane because developments in medical science came to influence and shape border thinking and practices. Moreover, what started effectively as two separate border sites—one internal to society in the context of the management of urban space and the other designed to protect the body politic as a whole from external threats—gradually became conjoined as part of one biopolitical immune system. With the perception of the proliferation of risk, the concomitant need for increasingly sophisticated forms of immunization, and the role of technology changing the nature and governance of life, Esposito's diagnosis lends itself towards a radical reconfiguration of the contemporary conceptualization of the border. Although he does not present it explicitly in these terms, using his thought the border can be reconfigured precisely as a biopolitical immune system that is no longer an 'exteriority' of the body politic, but in fact *coextensive with it* so that 'the border' and 'society' become increasingly indistinguishable: 'the nerve centre through which the governance of life runs' (Esposito 2011, 150). Indeed, Esposito's discussion of the contemporary paradigm of biopolitical immunity helps us to rethink the border precisely as a mobile therapeutic device that is designed to intervene whenever necessary in order to 'recognize, incorporate, and . . . neutralize' risks wherever they may be deemed to exist (Esposito 2011, 160). It is for this reason that the border as a biopolitical immune system has become of central strategic importance in societies today.

Here, we are no longer dealing with a straightforward inside/outside topological relation as conventional theories of the border assume (Bigo 2001; Parker and Vaughan-Williams et al. 2009, Parker and Vaughan-Williams 2012; Salter 2012). Instead, the border as a biopolitical immune system is marked by a far more complex and multifaceted topology: 'Evil must be thwarted, but not by keeping it as a distance from one's borders; rather, it is included inside them. The dialectical figure that thus emerges is that of exclusionary inclusion or exclusion by inclusion. The body defeats a poison not by expelling it outside the organism, but by making it somehow part of the body' (Esposito 2011, 8). The border-as-immune system is thus an unusual spatial-ontological figure in Esposito's thought because it both instantiates and disrupts the inside/outside binary that is usually associated with the concept of the border (Walker 1993). Significantly, biopolitical immunitary protection does not straightforwardly involve 'a strategy of frontal opposition'—which would entail a reversion to a more conventional inside/outside topology associated with the older model of quarantine and banishment outside the city walls—but rather a more sophisticated spatial manoeuvre that consists of 'outflanking and neutralizing' the perceived risk *from within* (Esposito 2011, 8). Such a move involves the co-option of the unknown other not in a gesture of Kantian cosmopolitan hospitality (Vaughan-Williams 2007; see also Chapter 6), but with the effect of neutralizing the risk that they are perceived to pose. In this way, the biopolitical border as an immune mechanism 'reproduces in a controlled form exactly what it is meant to protect us from' (Esposito 2011, 7).

But while in this capacity the border remains a kind of defensive immunitary membrane—designed to act as a 'protective response in the face of a risk' (Esposito 2011, 1)—at the same time, Esposito's thought paves the way for an understanding of how this protective dimension also has a capacity for thanatopolitical and zoopolitical impulses in the name of preserving life on humanitarian grounds. In *Immunitas*, this is most evident in his discussion of the ways in which the contemporary biopolitical immune system is undergoing a series of transformations along increasingly militarized lines: 'The immune system mechanism takes on the character of an out-and-out war: the stakes are the control and ultimately the survival of the body in the face of the foreign invaders who seek first to occupy it and then destroy it' (Esposito 2011, 154). Although the roots of this aggressive militarism lie in seventeenth-century political treatises on the defence of the body politic from the *outside*, Esposito argues that these characteristics have now been reinforced and given added impetus by the task of identifying infiltrators *within* the body politic. On Esposito's view, the problem with this quasi-militarization of the immune system is twofold. First, too much faith has been placed in contemporary immunitary systems for the purposes of security: 'Contrary to what these war games suggest, there is no such thing as an apparatus or device that can ever, even potentially, grant us some form of immortality' (Esposito 2011, 159). Second, as we have already seen, the immune system is ultimately driven by a negative force, which can all too readily back fire and produce an 'over-active defense' that 'in seeking to strike at the enemy also causes harm to itself' (Esposito 2011, 163). In this way, the bordering practices of liberal democratic polities such as the EU have the potential to acquire a destructive logic—both in terms of the symbolic suicide of negating values supposedly at the heart of those societies and by posing risks to the very lives that they are designed to protect through increasingly aggressive degrees of combat. For this reason, the contemporary border as a biopolitical immune system has a distinctively *pharmakotic* character: one that holds dual potential to be both the poison and remedy in the face of diverse perceived risks (Derrida 1981).

115

'Irregular' Migration as Contagion

What are the implications of Esposito's thought for reconceptualizing EUropean border security and migration management, and diagnosing the contemporary crisis? At base, we see in Esposito's work not only an attempt to move biopolitical analyses of contemporary bordering practices away from the metaphor of the line, but also from an exclusive association with thanatopolitical drift. Unlike Agamben's account, which portrays the border essentially in terms of a sovereign cut between different lives, for Esposito (2011, 139) 'the purpose of biopolitics is not to distinguish life along a line that sacrifices one part of it to the violent domination of the other'. On the one hand, it is important to underscore that Esposito's diagnosis retains the capacity to recognize that 'this possibility can never be ruled out' (Esposito 2011, 139). Indeed, his assessment of many of the thanatopolitical features of contemporary global politics would suggest that this is a dimension of the work that certain bordering practices do perform. For this reason, his approach is compatible with a reckoning of sites of biopolitical abandonment in the context of push-back operations and acts of omission at sea, as well as in spaces of detention in which a particular zoopolitical logic can be seen to be at work. On the other hand, however, Esposito puts forward a more nuanced view that also embraces the more vitalist life-preserving aspect of Foucault's biopolitics, namely the 'attempt to save [life], protect it, develop it as a whole' (Esposito 2011, 139). Nevertheless, where Esposito departs from the vitalism of Negri and the tradition of autonomous Marxist thought is in the context of his supplementary argument that the 'positive' dimension within biopolitics always already 'involves the use of an instrument that is bound to it by the negative, as if the very doubling that life experiences of itself through the political imperative that "makes it live" contained something that internally contradicted it' (Esposito 2011, 139). What Esposito furnishes us with, then, is a complex diagnosis of the ontology of the border as a biopolitical immune system that is coexistent with society and one that has both thanatopolitical and affirmative potential. On this reading, some of the most egregious human rights abuses in the context of EUrope's border crisis—as explored in previous chapters—are carried out in the name of humanitarian border security not simply because of a failure to implement the GAMM 'in practice', but because of an autoimmune disorder whereby excessive and increasingly militarized forms of defence have ended up threatening populations they are supposed to protect.

Reconceptualizing EUropean border security practices as a biopolitical immune system offers a powerful diagnosis for why 'irregular' mobility—primarily of people, but also potentially of capital, services, and goods—is problematized as a security risk to Member States' identity, economy, and welfare. The immunitary paradigm can be seen at work in the problematization of 'irregular' migration, in particular, as an existential threat to the health and integrity of the body politic—a degenerative contagion deemed to constitute a 'biological risk' to both populations and territories (Esposito 2008, 4). Indeed, this is one reading of the health initiatives in Greek detention centres discussed at the opening of this chapter. Alongside 'official' elite speech acts describing 'irregular' populations in Greece as 'a ticking time bomb for public health' (Human Rights Watch 2012), NGO research illuminates the routine treatment of 'irregular' migrants as a potential contagion at the level of the everyday. In some contexts, this takes the form of micro-level practices that otherwise remain invisible to public scrutiny: such as the way in which, upon release from detention centres in the Evros region, 'irregular' migrants take buses to Athens that have seats covered in plastic and are driven by police officers wearing surgical gloves (Pro Asyl 2012b, 37).[6] In other contexts, the attempt to sanitize the health risk with which 'irregular' populations have become associated is publicly visible: video footage captured on a mobile phone showing naked detainees being sprayed with disinfectant on arrival at the *Centro di Primo Soccorso e Accoglienza* in Lampedusa was aired on the Rai 2 evening news programme in Italy on 16 December 2013 (AGSI 2013).

The convergence of border security and the medicalization of 'irregular' migrants—particularly in spaces of detention—further emphasizes the ambivalent and often contradictory nature of the dynamics that characterize EUrope's border crisis. There is no doubt that the health of 'irregular' migrants in detention is an acute issue, which is often made worse as a result of the dehumanizing conditions in which they are kept. Some of the most common problems experienced include skin infections, gastrointestinal problems, upper respiratory tract infections, musculoskeletal disorders, and psychological complaints (Amnesty 2013). Thus, in a 2013 report on parliamentary visits to spaces of detention across EUrope, the NGO Open Access Now! concludes with the following assessment:

> Detention conditions, isolation, obstacles to access to medical care, constant uncertainty and idleness cause permanent psychological harm to detainees. In most countries, there are no systems to offer psychological support to migrants. Their despondency and hopelessness are often remarked upon by medical staff who, where they are present, have very limited means. The frequency of acts of desperate protest, such as self-mutilation . . . hunger strikes and suicide attempts are testimony to the irredeemable psychiatric impact of detention on these vulnerable persons. (Open Access Now! 2013)

While the growing humanitarian emphasis on addressing these issues may lead to welcome outcomes for certain individuals in detention, the biopolitical move to enhance and optimize the lives of 'irregular' populations is, of course, not a straightforward, innocent, or apolitical one (Fassin 2012; Feldman and Ticktin 2010; Ticktin 2011). Irrespective of whether the 'intention' of health initiatives lies in favour of the well-being of detainees or disease surveillance, the increasing tendency for EUropean border security to be framed in terms of a public health issue is itself a highly significant and political phenomenon. As Stefan Elbe (2010) has highlighted, the definition of social issues as medical problems gives rise to new methods for gathering knowledge about and, therefore, managing both individual bodies and populations deemed to be risky. Elbe refers to this process as the 'medicalization of security', which enables new forms of biopolitical governance and surveillance techniques to emerge via therapeutic interventions that would be otherwise difficult to justify (Elbe 2010, 23). Such a process also leads to changing conceptions of what (in)security must mean: from 'military capabilities and hostile intentions of states' to 'the proliferation of medical conditions brought about by the rapid spread of potentially lethal infectious diseases brought within the population' (Elbe 2010, 30). Moreover, as part of this general logic whereby 'the body becomes the battlefield of the twenty-first century' and 'states will . . . ever more resemble enormous hospitals' (Elbe 2010, 166, 179), Alison Howell (2011) points to the increasing role of the 'psy' disciplines in the government of 'irregular' populations. Howell argues that the problematization of individuals and entire populations as sufferers of mental health disorders requiring medicalized interventions in the name of security is an area of particular concern because it justifies their exclusion from the rest of 'normal' society. In the context of Howell's discussion of the US Naval Base in Guantánamo Bay, Cuba, she shows that in drawing on the language of mental health, authorities simultaneously presented detainees as security threats and the US as benevolent 'carers'. Ironically, Howell argues that humanitarian discourses ostensibly critical of the US detention facilities also end up reproducing the same pathologizing logic: in referring to detainees as 'psychologically impaired victims', NGOs also deny their political agency (Howell 2011, 65). Although, for reasons discussed in Chapter 3, there are very considerable difficulties in drawing parallels between contemporary spaces of detention across the EUropean borderscape and the facility at Guantánamo Bay, it is nevertheless striking that a similar logic of pathologization structures EU authorities' health initiatives in detention centres and NGO discourses surrounding the mental health needs of 'irregular' populations.

In conclusion, the paradigm of immunity offers a series of coordinates for understanding the relationship between what João Nunes (2013) calls the 'health imaginary', practices of security, and contemporary biopolitical bordering practices. Esposito argues that the pathologization of the other—the foreign body perceived to threaten the body politic—is central to the logic of immunization: 'what is important is inhibiting, preventing, and fighting the spread of contagion wherever it presents itself, using whatever means necessary' (Esposito 2013, 60). While, as we have already seen, the roots of this model are to be found in the coming together of medical and juridical-political discourses of immunity over the course of several centuries, on Esposito's view this imaginary has today taken on several distinctive characteristics in relation to current border crises:

> The more the 'self' tends to make itself 'global', the more the self must struggle to include inside from what is outside; the more the self tries to introject every form of negativity, the more negativity is reproduced. It was precisely the breaking down of the great real and symbolic Berlin Wall that caused so many small walls to go up and that transformed and perverted the very idea of community into a besieged fortress. What matters most is limiting an excess of circulation and therefore of potential contamination. (Esposito 2013, 60)

The problem, as illustrated in the discussion above and elsewhere in this book, is that when viewed in the context of the paradigm of immunity, 'irregular' migrants are always already framed as the kind of contagion that requires ever more aggressive border control and for this reason Esposito argues that 'everywhere we look, new walls, new blockades, and new dividing lines are erected against something that threatens, or at least seems to, our biological, social, and environmental identity' (Esposito 2013, 59). In this context, biopolitical border security practices designed to protect, enhance, and save lives often end up abandoning, dehumanizing, and killing those very lives as a symptom of the autoimmune crisis that Esposito warns against. Having presented Esposito's work as offering grounds for a reworking of the nature of contemporary EUropean bordering practices, the final chapter now turns to explore what it might mean to develop a more affirmative border politics from within the horizon of biopolitical thought: whether such a move is possible in view of the immunitary paradigm; and what its ethical-political implications might be for critical border and migration studies.

Notes

1. Vanessa Lemm (2013) presents Esposito's work more generally as bridging biopolitical and deconstructive approaches.
2. For more on the relationship between Agamben, Negri, and Esposito see also Campbell (2008) and Esposito and Campbell (2008).
3. Esposito (2008, 59) argues that sovereignty can be thought of as a 'meta-immunity *dispositif*'.
4. In this context there are obvious similarities with Jacques Derrida's conception of the autoimmune crisis in the wake of the attacks on 11 September 2001. However,

while Esposito concurs with the thrust of Derrida's analysis of the lethal breakdown of the West's immune system, the former seeks to distinguish himself from the latter in several key respects (see Esposito and Campbell 2008, 52–3). First, Esposito claims that Derrida conflates autoimmunity with immunity. Second, this is because Derrida does not make the connection that Esposito draws between community, immunity, and biopolitics. Third, for Esposito, the consequence of these first two points is that Derrida is finally unable to see the potential for an affirmative biopolitics emerging within the immunitary paradigm. These differences and their implications for the possibility of a more affirmative border politics are the subject of more detailed discussion in Chapter 6.

5. While it is possible to identify moments of a more affirmative biopolitics in Agambenian thought when taken as a whole—particularly in *The Coming Community* (1993)—the reception of his *Homo Sacer* tetralogy suggests that this aspect remains somewhat implicit within his oeuvre. For a rereading of the affirmative potential within Agamben's oeuvre beyond the *Homo Sacer* tetralogy see Prozorov (2014).

6. Similarly, the Council of Europe's (2014, 20) report into the immigration estate in Greece makes reference to the way in which police officers commonly 'wear masks and gloves when interacting with detainees' and yet no long-term health provision is in place.

6

Affirmative Borders

Introduction

Melilla, September 2013—more than 300 'irregular' migrants, reported to be from Senegal, Mali, Côte d'Ivoire, Guinea, and Cameroon, attempt to scale the 6 m-high fence between the Spanish exclave and Moroccan sovereign territory. Up to a 100 make it to the other side. Frontex reports injuries to six Spanish border officials attempting to stop them (Frontex 2013, 21).

Komotini pre-departure centre, Greece, 23 November 2013—detainees stage a protest against conditions at the centre, initially by refusing to eat their breakfast. Mattresses are then carried out into the courtyard of the centre and burnt. Windows are smashed and pieces of iron from dismantled bedsteads are used as weapons against the police. Over the course of the day the uprising gathers momentum and up to 400 of the 500 'irregular' migrants are involved. Authorities throw stones, fire gunshots, and use tear gas to quell the insurrection and return detainees to their cells (PICUM 2012; Council of Europe 2014, 39).

Hamburg, May 2013—300 'irregular' migrants from sub-Saharan Africa organize a demonstration on the streets of the city. They were seasonal workers in Libya, but had to flee due to the outbreak of conflict. Seeking refuge in churches and mosques, they demand the right to stay in Germany (Statewatch 2014).

Brussels airport, 15 February 2014—an attempt is made to forcibly deport a female 'irregular' migrant on board a Brussels Airlines airplane bound for Kinshasa. She refuses to comply and is detained in her seat by twelve border security personnel. In protest, five passengers on the flight, including a Belgium MEP, go to her assistance. During the incident it is alleged that a police official used excessive force and the Minister of the Interior announces a formal investigation (PICUM 2014).

What is common to these moments and sites of encounter is an important reminder that contemporary EUropean border security and migration management practices are only ever *attempts* at controlling the movement and lives of 'irregular' migrants. EUropean border security is not a totalizing and inevitably 'successful' regime of capture and control: it breaks down, is challenged, and leads to unintended outcomes. As scholarship in critical border and migration studies has sought to emphasize and illustrate, it is both empirically inaccurate and politically problematic to portray 'irregular' migrants in a generalized and abstract way as mute, undifferentiated, and unable to contest the diverse attempts to produce 'them' as 'knowable' and, therefore, better 'governable' subjects. Many scholars, as discussed in Chapter 3, explore the 'excess' between logics of EUropean border security and migration management on the one hand and the lived embodied experiences of (those labelled as) 'irregular' migrants on the other, in terms of the imperceptible politics of 'escape' (Papadopoulos et al. 2008), 'agency' (Johnson 2013; Mainwaring 2012; Squire 2011), 'ambivalence' (McNevin 2013), 'appropriation' (Scheel 2014), and/or 'resistance' (Nyers 2013; Stierl 2014). But while these dimensions are of paramount significance in any sociological account of EUrope's border crisis, the argument developed in this study as a whole is that the potential for thanatopolitical and zoopolitical drift—and the relationship between this drift and the possibility of resistance and another border politics—is still in need of greater *conceptual* diagnosis. Indeed, the position developed here is that only by recognizing and tackling head-on the violent potentiality of biopolitical bordering practices is it possible to begin to sketch what a more affirmative approach in critical border and migration studies might look like: to prioritize escape, agency, and resistance *without* this prior diagnostic work risks ignoring or cushioning these dynamics in an anti-politics of wishful thinking.

One of the prominent positions in critical border and migration studies posited as an alternative to the so-called 'control'-biased or thanatopolitical paradigm is that associated with the post-Marxist AoM perspective (Papadopoulos et al. 2008; see also Mezzadra and Neilson 2013). *Prima facie* this outlook might be said to offer a more 'affirmative' approach by rereading 'migration as a constituent creative force which fuels social, cultural and economic transformations' (Papadopoulos et al. 2008, xviii). However, the impetus to evacuate the contemporary thanatopolitical and zoopolitical potentiality of biopolitical borders renders this approach somewhat inadequate to the task of engaging critically with the violence that characterizes EUrope's border crisis, which is ultimately left unchallenged. In *Escape Routes*, to take one prominent example of the AoM approach, Papadopoulos et al. (2008, xiv–v) acknowledge that contemporary constellations of border power operate by 'rendering populations the object of biopolitical control', but they argue that this is an inadequate diagnosis on its own. On their view, such a problematization is doubly deficient because it airbrushes 'people's escape, flight, subversion, refusal, sabotage' and other social struggles out of the frame, and fails to appreciate that such acts are *ontologically prior* to attempted control: 'Escape comes first! People's efforts to escape can force the reorganization of control itself; regimes of control must respond to the new situations created by escape' (Papadopoulos et al. 2008, xv). Famously, the hallmark of the AoM approach—undergirded by Negri's post-Marxist vitalist rendering of the biopolitical paradigm—is the argument that escape is temporally prior to and thus the chief animating force of control.[1]

Yet, as explored in Chapters 3 and 4 in particular, to emphasize the primacy of movement and to assume that flight will always disrupt control understates the 'agency' of border security authorities and the violent methods through which some 'irregular' migrants are abandoned and left to die at sea or animalized in contemporary spaces of detention: these dimensions remain understated in the AoM approach. Such a move to reprioritize escape is equally if not more problematic than prioritizing control because it recycles rather than displaces the operating binary opposition that is itself limiting and in need of critique.[2] What we are left with, then, is something of an intellectual and practical impasse, which is often presented in zero-sum terms as a simple interpretive 'choice' between privileging borders over migration, control over escape, closure over openness, violence over agency, and death over life, rather than seeing these as being mutually constitutive. The aim of this chapter as a whole, therefore, is to attempt a deconstruction of this tired and totalizing frame in order to break through the current impasse and ultimately to rethink the border not only as a site of thanatopolitical and zoopolitical potential, but affirmatively as a site of encounter with the other and a politically productive if, nonetheless, risky (and also potentially violent) opening to the common.[3]

Must biopolitical border security practices always result in death and/or animalization? Are humanitarian discourses sufficient for critiquing contemporary biopolitical forms of border violence? Is a more affirmative approach to borders possible within the biopolitical frame? I believe that these are some of the most pressing 'big picture' questions facing critical migration and border studies today and, yet, it is difficult to see how the popular sociological turn to empirical practice alone—with its focus on detailed accounts of disparate border sites and struggles—has the necessary diagnostic tools in order to step back and attempt to address what is at stake in these and related issues. Running somewhat against the grain of current scholarship, I wish to suggest that *in addition to* the sociological turn there is a need for and value in adopting a more critical-philosophical approach that challenges dominant frameworks of understanding and creates alternative problematizations for judgement and action.

In order to respond to this task while avoiding the trap of perpetuating the dichotomies above, this chapter advocates a return to critical resources found in contemporary (post)biopolitical theory. This is because the impasse reached in debates between 'border control' versus 'migrant agency' mirrors the bifurcation between 'negative/ thanatopolitical' versus 'positive/vitalist' strands of thought within the (post)biopolitical paradigm.[4] This tension, as we have already seen, is found originally in Foucault's paradigmatic account of biopolitics and carried over to the work of Agamben and Negri, respectively: the former translates into a focus on border control and the latter on the autonomy of migration. What Esposito's thought has attempted to do is to deconstruct the 'negative/positive' dichotomy and search instead for an affirmative biopolitics that refuses to gloss over the potentiality for thanatopolitical and zoopolitical drift. But while Esposito gets us so far, the analysis proposes a closer engagement between his work and Derridean deconstruction. In particular, I argue that Derrida's figures of autoimmunity and hostipitality are potentially affirmative—as well as thanatopolitical—technologies of power, which hold significant promise for reconceptualizing an alternative approach to contemporary EUropean border security and migration management under biopolitical conditions.

Departing from extant normative arguments about the future of border security in the EUropean context and beyond, I do not argue for the abandonment, overcoming, or negation of borders. The discourse of 'open borders' is a prevalent rhetorical position commonly arrived at in both academic and non-academic literatures that are critical of contemporary border-related violence, but it is one that I want to suggest ultimately reproduces the impasse referred to above. Rather, I seek to shift the contours of the conceptual debate in order to raise different questions and develop new openings for critical border and migration studies in an affirmative direction. The upshot of this deconstructive (post)biopolitical position is a call for biopolitical borders to be rethought, reworked, and reappropriated—troubled, left trembling, and reorientated towards a different heading—rather than simply dismantled, overcome, or rejected.[5] Only on the basis of a fuller understanding of the logic of biopolitical border security practices can we begin to comprehend what is at stake in the attempt to resist and/or, in some sense, move beyond their thanatopolitical and zoopolitical potentiality: this is the overriding motivation of the chapter and of the broader investigation.

Affirmative Biopolitics

In his recent reflections on the historical trajectory of Italian political philosophy, Esposito argues that the question of what an 'affirmative biopolitics' might look like is recognized in this tradition to be 'one of the most urgent tasks of contemporary thought' (Esposito 2012b, 269). At the same time, however, he also acknowledges that this is not an easy task because of the difficulties of 'translating paradigms with a philosophical provenance into concrete options and operational initiatives' (Esposito 2012b, 270). Aligning his theoretical approach to biopolitics alongside—rather than somehow in opposition against—'militant activism', Esposito sees the possibility of a radical praxis in alternative philosophical work: a form of 'thought in action—designed even beyond its intentions, to produce definite consequences external to it' (Esposito 2012b, 263). In searching for an alternative and affirmative biopolitics, Esposito advocates a renewed focus on the 'conceptual grammar' used in (post)biopolitical thought and 'in which we remain caught' (Esposito 2012b, 270). It is in this spirit that the following discussion proceeds.

Rethinking the Conceptual Grammars of Biopolitics

Esposito seeks to distinguish his affirmative approach to biopolitics from that of the autonomous Marxist perspective chiefly associated with the work of Negri.[6] As is well known, Negri (2008), in both his own texts and those co-written with Michael Hardt (Hardt and Negri 2001, 2004), has developed a critical materialist engagement with the Foucaultian biopolitical paradigm: one that seeks to re-establish the role of production. On Hardt and Negri's view, Foucault is hampered by the remnants of a structuralist epistemology that 'fails to grasp . . . the real dynamics of production in biopolitical society' (Hardt and Negri 2001, 28). To summarize, Negri argues that if biopolitics is fundamentally about the imprinting of power on life from the eighteenth century onwards, then it is also the case that during the same period life itself became imbued with power understood as the capacity to act and produce. For this reason, Negri asks critically of the Foucaultian view: 'Should we think of biopolitics as an ensemble of biopowers that derive from the activity of government or, on the contrary, can we say that, to the extent that power has invested the whole of life, thus life too becomes a power?' (Negri 2008, 72). In this context, Negri's distinction between constituent power (*potenza*) on the one hand and constituted power (*potere*) on the other hand is also significant: the former relates to the labour power and creative capacities of the multitude, which is posited as being in a perpetual struggle with the latter—understood in terms of the forces of capital—and its sovereign powers of appropriation. While political thought—arguably including that of Foucault—has historically focused on the dominance of constituted power, Negri has drawn critical attention to the capacity of the constituent power of the multitude understood as 'a multiplicity of subjects' (Negri 2004, 112) to challenge this depoliticization: 'the multitude embodies a mechanism that seeks to represent desire and to transform the world' (Negri 2004, 112). Such a position reflects Negri's vitalist belief, deriving from the tradition of political

125

thought stretching from Spinoza to Deleuze, that the intrinsic power of life as manifested in the multitude will always thwart, outsmart, and escape the thanatopolitical drift associated with constituted power (Muhle 2014).

To some extent, as we saw in Chapter 5, Esposito's turn to the Spinozist-Deleuzian embrace of a vitalist approach to life means that he shares common ground with Negri (1993, 2004, 2008) and Hardt and Negri (2001, 2004). For all these thinkers, as Vanessa Lemm (2013, 8) has insightfully argued, 'life is a matter of placing things in common, of opening communication between opposites': a disposition that identifies, interrogates, and attempts to in some sense move beyond the work that diverse borders, distinctions, and categorizations perform in contemporary political life. This particular (and political) disposition can be contrasted with totalitarian forms of thought, which operate instead via the sovereign inscription of distinctions and divisions that seek to cut things and people off from each other. Yet, Esposito's diagnosis of the immunitary paradigm and the precarious ways in which it contains the potential for both the preservation and negation of life means that his work arguably offers a more sophisticated and politically grounded assessment of the possibility for an affirmative biopolitics than that found in the rather more naked vitalism of Negri and works inspired by it in critical border and migration studies. According to Timothy Campbell (2008, xxxvi), what troubles Esposito about the overall position adopted by Negri and also in his work with Hardt is a tendency towards 'categorical (or historical) amnesia vis-à-vis modernity's negative inflection of biopolitics'. Moreover, as Maria Muhle (2014, 93) has highlighted from a Foucaultian perspective, any attempt to anchor the possibility of resistance or escape from biopolitics on the basis of a conceptualization of life that 'transcends its inscription into a power mechanism' is one that is destined to fail. This is because the 'normativity of life' is not something that is 'exterior to these strategies of power' and, therefore, cannot be read as offering a position from 'outside of power' (Muhle 2014, 93).[7] Thus, Esposito (2008, 2) argues that in imagining that 'biopolitics can contribute to the reconstruction of a revolutionary horizon in the heart of empire', Negri 'absolutely accentuates the moment of resistance to power, in opposition to the letter of the Foucauldian text'.

Elsewhere, Esposito (2012b, 234) has also drawn attention to what he considers to be a greater flaw in Negri's attempt to mount a more productive engagement with biopolitical conditions using the concept of constituent power. In one direction, Esposito points out that in order to rescue constituent power completely from constituted power as an original energy it is necessary for Negri to distinguish the former from sovereignty: 'To avoid slipping into constituted power, in order to remain what it is, constituent power cannot assume a subjective connotation that defines it in sovereign terms' (Esposito 2012b, 234). On Esposito's reading, however, this is precisely what Negri's thought ultimately relies upon via its valorization of the sovereign subject: 'without a subject who embodies it, the constituent power is incapable of producing politics' (Esposito 2012b, 234). On this basis, Esposito's conclusion is that Negri does, in fact, not offer the grounds for an affirmative horizon of thought, but ends up perpetuating the very appropriation of constituent power by constituted power that he purports to challenge. Instead, Esposito argues that what is necessary is a reconceptualization of the subject outside of the Schmittian theological paradigm associated with sovereignty (Schmitt 2005). His response over a series of recent texts via the paradigm of immunity is to rethink subjectivity not in terms of a substance that can be captured, but rather as a radical form of relationality 'and nothing else, which is always both singular and plural, and therefore, irreducible to a presupposed entity' (Esposito 2012b, 256).

With Esposito's urge to rethink the 'conceptual grammars' of biopolitics in mind, the following discussion picks up where Chapter 5 left off by attempting to understand in greater detail his articulation of a more affirmative biopolitical register of thought and action. While the previous chapter set the scene in terms of Esposito's general treatment of the immunitary paradigm and the need to rework biopolitics from within the context of thanato-political *dispositifs*, the subsequent analysis focuses on the affirmative potential that in recent years he has found in two related grammars: the subversive dimensions of *communitas* as an opening onto the common; and the impersonal as an alternative register to that of the modern sovereign subject. Ultimately, I want to suggest that both pave the way for rethinking in a more affirmative direction not only the concepts of community and subjectivity, but also contemporary border security and migration management under biopolitical conditions.

The Subversive Potentiality of Communitas

Throughout his works, Esposito mounts a search for what Lemm (2013, 10) refers to as an 'affirmative biopolitics of community', which is predicated upon what Esposito considers to be the politically subversive potentiality of *communitas*. Whereas, according to Esposito, the history of Western thought has treated community as the identity or property belonging to a group of individual subjects, Esposito seeks to rethink the term around its Latin root *munus*, meaning burden or obligation. As discussed in Chapter 5, Esposito reconceptualizes community not as the aggregate of predefined sovereign individual subjects, but rather in terms of the mutual debt and reciprocity entailed by the *munus*. In this context, immunization refers to an exception from the common *munus*, which characterizes the work of the modern subject as a category of thought: 'a logical mode of preventive protection against the self-dissolutive risk of "being in common"' (Esposito 2012b, 258).

An immunitary device par excellence, the modern subject works to mitigate the threat of the common and that of disorder. From the eighteenth century onwards, as we have also already seen, Esposito identifies the intensification of the intersection between juridical-political and bio-medical lexicons and the expression of politics in increasingly medicalized terms: a paradigm that is manifested via the problematization of the body politic—as with the individual human body—as a battlefield (Esposito 2012b, 259). For Esposito, the modern community-immunity-subjectivity triad thus constitutes a 'vicious circle'. In *Communitas* (2010), he poses the core (biopolitical) questions: 'How are we to fight the immunization of life without making it do death's work? How are we to break down the wall of the individual while at the same time saving the singular gift that the individual carries?' (Esposito 2010, 19). Esposito argues that any attempt to address these questions while retaining the logic of *immunitas* is destined to further perpetuate the kind of violent closures that he is critical of and seeks to move away from: 'Once identified, be it with a people, a territory, or an essence, the community is walled in within itself and thus separated from the outside' (Esposito 2010, 16). For this reason, he urges a move to deconstruct the triad on the terrain of the 'open and plural form of *communitas*' (Esposito 2013, 65).

Esposito's affirmative biopolitical strategy involves rereading *communitas* and the productive vulnerability and openness that it poses: 'it is precisely the ... indissolvable, albeit negative, relation with *communitas* that opens for me the possibility of a positive ... reconversion of the ... immunitary *dispositif*' (Esposito 2008, 6). As Campbell (2008, xxx) succinctly puts it, Esposito ultimately finds the prospect for an affirmative biopolitics in 'an openness to what is held in common with others'. Instead of immunizing against the threat of the *munus*—a 'risk-minimizing activity' that, in Lemke's words (2014, 73), 'seeks to defend an established identity and to define the borderlines that separate the community from strangers'—Esposito's affirmative thought advocates an alternative post-immunitary politics: one that embraces and negotiates this risk. While the modern political paradigm has viewed the subtraction of subjectivity by *communitas*—the exposure of individual members 'to a propensity that forces them to open their own individual boundaries'—to be a negative, Esposito (2010, 138) uses this exposure of the self to the other as the ground for an affirmative biopolitics.

In broad terms, Esposito mobilizes the concept of *communitas* to rethink the fundaments of community as an encounter between the self and what lies outside of the self (Esposito 2013, 61). Via exposure to others he claims that individual subjects undergo a change—not necessarily a loss—in their bordered self-identity: 'the relation that makes them no longer individual subjects because it closes them from their identity with a line, which traversing them, alters them: it is the "with", the "between", and the threshold where they meet in a point of contact that brings them into relation with others to the degree to which it separates them from themselves' (Esposito 2010, 139). Thus, towards the end of *Communitas*, Esposito frames the exposure of the self to others—in the context of an understanding that community 'always consists of others'—as a potentially productive opening, but one that is not easy, comfortable, and nor without its intrinsic threats: '*Communitas* doesn't keep us warm, and it doesn't protect us; on the contrary, it exposes us to the most extreme of risks: that of losing, along with our individuality, the borders that guarantee its inviolability with respect to the other; of suddenly falling into the nothing of the thing' (Esposito 2010, 140). Such exposure is risky precisely because, as we see in this excerpt, the very borders of the notion of the self are at stake. Yet, it is in this direction—one that does not seek to abandon the border between self and other *tout court*, but one that sees the border as being a potentially productive site precisely because of the self's always already vulnerable relationship with the other—that Esposito's affirmative biopolitical thought ultimately leads.

An illustration of how Esposito envisages the subversive—as opposed to the immunitary—potentiality of *communitas* as an affirmative biopolitical logic can be glimpsed in his treatment of the figure of the immune system as a response to and negotiation with what is common to all living beings. As discussed in Chapter 5, Esposito's use of the immune system is more than merely a metaphorical device: historical developments in medical science have come to influence juridical-political thought and the management of urban space. A protective shield designed to 'recognize, incorporate, and . . . neutralize' risks wherever and whenever they appear, the biopolitical immune system is not at the exterior of, but is, in fact, coextensive with the body politic (Esposito 2011, 160). In this context, Esposito's search for an affirmative biopolitics is not one that would advocate the abandonment of society's immune system, however, which he argues would lead to the 'explosion' and 'death' of any community (Esposito 2012b, 261; 2008, 6). Rather, Esposito's work advocates the reconceptualization, reorientation, and reappropriation of the biopolitical immune system in society towards a radically different end. Specifically, Esposito (2012b, 261) claims that the historical and contemporary entanglement between the paradigm of immunity and excessive military aggression means that the biopolitical immune system today has become envisaged narrowly and problematically in terms of 'a defence barrier against the outside'. What is required on his view is a disaggregation of the biopolitical immune system from this militaristic and defensive mode of thought and a recovery of the immanent potentiality of the same immune system to allow for an opening up towards the common: 'Far from constituting an impenetrable armour set in place to protect our identity, [the immune system] proves instead to be its epicenter of continuous modification, as well as a filter for contact and communication with the surrounding environment' (Esposito 2012b, 261).

For Esposito, this is not utopic because, despite the vigour with which contemporary biopolitical apparatuses of security operate, the total immunization of society would never be possible: 'the common can never be entirely exorcised' (Esposito 2012b, 262). Furthermore, pointing towards organ transplants and pregnancy as already existing examples of a different use of the same immunitary paradigm, Esposito argues that there is nothing inevitable about the figure of the immune system as an excessively defensive and militaristic posture, as described above (Esposito 2012b, 261). Esposito points towards the way in which during pregnancy the mother's immune system effectively immunizes itself against the possibility of excessive immunization, which would otherwise lead to the rejection of the foetus. Though a foreign body, the foetus is not only hosted but also allowed to develop and actively supported inside the mother's body precisely because of the potentiality of the immune system to be open—as well as defensive—in relation to what lies outside or beyond it. With this example, as Campbell (2008, xxx) explains, Esposito finds an affirmative or non-thanatopolitical use of the figure of the immune system. This gives an indication of the direction in which Esposito's affirmative biopolitical thought travels more generally: 'From this angle we begin to get a glimpse of the "common"—in other words, the positively contaminating—side of what is also intended as immune' (Esposito 2012b, 262). In other words, it is by reappropriating the immune system and redirecting it—rather than destroying it—that Esposito seeks to rework the biopolitical conditions of the present from within.

While to date this aspect of Esposito's thought remains the least developed, it is nevertheless clear that the reconceptualization of the immune system along more affirmative lines is central to his overarching political project. In *Living Thought* (2012), Esposito argues that any counter-movement to contemporary thanatopolitical (and zoopolitical) drift involves the expansion of 'the protective function of the immune system from the restricted sphere of the individual to the unlimited space of the entire world—itself conceived as a massive living body' (Esposito 2012b, 262). What this involves in concrete terms is again somewhat elusive in his existing oeuvre, but Esposito suggests that a first step would be to deconstruct the dominant modern conception of the individualistic subject as the basis for political thought and action under biopolitical conditions: 'When the most destructive tendencies reflect one another and redouble in the same mad dash toward massacre, the only possibility that remains is to shatter the mirror in which the self is reflected without seeing anything but itself, or to break the spell' (Esposito 2013, 65). It is, therefore, not the individual sovereign subject—already caught in the register of thanatopolitics—upon which Esposito builds his affirmative biopolitics, but rather 'the world in common, with all its vital and inexhaustible potency' (Esposito 2012b, 262). Beginning with this radical exposure to *communitas* amounts to what Esposito has termed an 'impersonal politics' and this related grammatical shift further assists in the task of understanding the ethical-political implications of his affirmative biopolitical approach and its differentiation from that of Negri's.

Impersonal Politics

Esposito's search for an affirmative biopolitics sees promise in the radical opening of human community to the *im*personal. One way of better grasping what a political philosophy of the impersonal looks like is via Esposito's critique of human rights as a discourse based around the person. This critique is also helpful for any attempt to diagnose the complicity of seemingly 'progressive' discourses of humanitarianism in contemporary thanatopolitical and zoopolitical drift associated with EUrope's border crisis. In *Third Person: Politics of Life and the Philosophy of the Impersonal* (2012), Esposito highlights the paradox that alongside the rise in humanitarian discourses since the 1948 Declaration of Human Rights, the twentieth and twenty-first centuries have witnessed some of the most egregious human rights abuses:

> Despite the rising rhetoric of humanitarian commitment, human life remains largely outside the protection of the law; so much so that one could easily argue that, even in the context of an increasing juridification of society, no right is more disregarded than the right to life for millions of human beings who are condemned to death from starvation, disease, and war. How is this possible where the human being is thought of as a person? (Esposito 2012a, 73)

While a common critique, as discussed in previous chapters, is one that focuses on the selective application of human rights 'in practice', Esposito moves the discussion beyond that of 'rhetoric' versus 'reality' by advancing a different and altogether more provocative hypothesis: that 'the essential failure of human rights, their inability to restore the broken connection between rights and life, does not take place *in spite* of the affirmation of the ideology of the person but rather *because* of it' (Esposito 2012a, 5, emphasis added). In other words, the 'disturbing' element of this hypothesis, as Esposito puts it, is the possibility that violence persists globally not merely because the concept of personhood on which human rights rest is too delimited in its scope and application, but rather due its very extension as an ideology (Esposito 2012a, 5).

Across several interventions, Esposito (2012a, 2012b) has advanced a critique of the limits of human rights discourses and the particular view of personhood or subjectivity that underpins them, which is an important precursor to his introduction of a politics of the impersonal as an alternative biopolitical grammar. In this context, he argues that the concept of the person has come to problematically represent the human being and has acquired the status of a universal value. While Esposito acknowledges that there are significant contemporary debates about the precise threshold that defines 'personhood'—conception, a particular embryonic stage, the moment of birth, and so on—he claims that it is, nevertheless, a universal category that is ascribed an important legal status. Indeed, for Esposito, personhood and the legal subject are mutually inseparable: human rights only apply to the 'closed space' of the person and 'conversely . . . to be a person means to enjoy these rights in and of themselves' (Esposito 2012a, 3). In particular, he suggests that the concept of person has developed universal appeal because it bridges the terms 'citizens' and 'humans', which are otherwise in tension: 'personhood is seen as the only semantic field that can possibly overlap the two spheres of law and humanity' (Esposito 2012a, 3). Yet, despite the ostensible appeal and apolitical character of the category of personhood and the notion of human rights carried by it, Esposito argues that this concept is a highly problematic construct because it is both enabled by and itself performatively enacts a series of intrinsically political exclusions: the category of person across time is based on 'determining thresholds, and shifting functions, between not only different species of living beings but also within the human race itself' (Esposito 2012b, 276). Thus, with reference to examples of the infant, the disabled adult, and the insane—to which we might add the figure of the 'irregular' migrant—Esposito argues that 'not all human beings are [always treated as] persons' (Esposito 2012a, 13).

Echoing Agamben's (2004a) treatment of the 'anthropological machine' and Derrida's notion of the 'zoopolitical threshold' discussed in Chapter 4, Esposito sees the prior border between human and animal within 'man' as a central site around which the category of personhood has developed in both juridical-political and biomedical thought. He notes that before developments in early eighteenth-century biology, the political-philosophical concept of personhood was understood largely in terms of 'a rational subject capable of self-determination' as part of a community of other sovereign individuals. However, Esposito (2012a, 6) points to the emergence of Bichat's theory of a double biological layer within every human being—'one vegetative and unconscious, and the other cerebral and relational'—as a seminal challenge to the traditional notion of the rational subject: 'From this moment on, the role of politics—*now inevitably biopolitics*—will no longer be to define the relationship between human beings as much as to identify the precise point at which the frontier is located between what is human and what, inside the human itself, is other than human' (Esposito 2012a, 24, emphasis added). Esposito traces the influence of Bichat's theory in Philosophy and Sociology via Schopenhauer and Comte, respectively, and the concomitant impact at the turn of the nineteenth and twentieth centuries of the dual-life principle for biopolitical understandings of the human as a species: 'The animal thus became a point of division within humanity, between the species of people who were separated by their relation to life—and thus to death, since the easy life of some turned out to be directly proportional to the forced death of others' (Esposito 2012a, 7).

The paradigmatic importance of Bichat's dual-life theory is that it gave rise to what Esposito considers to now be an enduring biopolitical assumption that modern personhood is intrinsically split between a rational self-determining subject as a 'site of legal imputation' on the one hand and a 'vital substratum', an 'animal' layer, or 'corporeal area subject to its control' on the other hand (Esposito 2012a, 147). With this separation he argues that it is possible for biopolitical cuts to be made within populations on the basis that some human beings are considered not to be able or worthy of controlling the latter dimension, which in turn opens up the possibility for external sovereign control: 'The personhood-deciding machine marks the final differ-ence between what must live and what can be legitimately cast to death' (Esposito 2012a, 13). As Lemm (2013, 5–6) explains, the category of the person is permitted by and itself reproduces a double separation: 'It first divides human life into a personal life and an animal life and, second, the category draws a dividing line with the human individual, separating out an irrational part that needs to be dominated and ruled over by a rational part.' Put differently, there is an inherent potential for (some) humans to be treated as 'less than' persons and thereby subordinated to others: 'authentic persons—unlike human beings who have only partial or no claim to this title—are those who have full control over their animal part' (Esposito 2012b, 273). Esposito illustrates this point with reference to the treatment of slaves, the threshold between 'a type of human being who is completely human, and another bordering on the regime of things' is one that is not stable, but historically contingent and politically constructed (Esposito 2012b, 273).

For these reasons, Esposito prefers to think not in terms of the stable category of personhood, but rather via the notion of the *dispositif* of the person in order to highlight that it is both a performative outcome and has performative effects. More than this, however, the *dispositif* of the person—along with the regime of rights that it supports—must be understood on Esposito's account precisely as an immunitary device (Lemm 2013, 5). To be a 'proper' person implies the ability to rule over oneself and herein lies the thanatopolitical potentiality of personhood as an immunitary device: the use of the category of the person always already implies a reification of 'the impersonal layer from which it distances itself' (Esposito 2013, 6). Thus, Esposito argues that what characterized the Nazi era was precisely a claim to 'the right to act decisively on the biological continuum of the species to rescue it from its incipient degeneration' such that the living substrate itself became 'the object of a political decision' (Esposito 2012a, 59). This move placed certain people outside of the law as non-persons and yet Esposito remarks that despite this logic the post-World War II response to Nazi atrocities was, nevertheless, to resort to human rights, the juridical-political subject, and the very form of personhood that they had been denied—and which had allowed for their desubjectification—in the first place.

Esposito argues that the twentieth-century human rights regime not only failed to identify and grapple with the key issues at stake, but also ended up unwittingly reproducing the conditions of possibility for the very 'crimes against humanity' that it was designed to combat. This is because the juridical-political mechanism of human rights is 'inclusive through exclusion', which is to say that it always already operates upon the basis of 'the prior assumption of a boundary between what lies inside and what remains outside its sphere of action' (Esposito 2012a, 69). Esposito notes that the basic problem with rights, as already discussed by Arendt (1951), is that the law only applies to those who are already included in the political community in which it is effective. The language of the person does not overcome the intrinsic problem to which human rights discourses are posited as the solution: 'To the extent that this language identifies, inside the human, an extracorporeal core defined in terms of will and reason, it necessarily ends up thrusting the body into animal or vegetal dimensions, putting it in direct contact with the sphere of things' (Esposito 2012a, 91). Thus, Esposito considers the tragedy of human rights-based responses to Nazism as the worst excesses of the *dispositif* of the person to be that 'the thanatopolitical powers that imagined that they were opposing it [were] actually enhancing its coercive power' (Esposito 2012a, 149).

In response to this diagnosis, Esposito calls for a deconstruction of the immunitary *dispositif* of the person and a move towards a philosophy of the 'impersonal'. This figure, he argues, offers an alternative ground on the basis of which life is not thought of as a property or an object of politics, but, as we saw fleetingly in Chapter 5, immanently as *a* life:

> If life should not be posited after the subjects that embody it from one time to the next, it should not be presupposed before them, either. Rather, it should be thought of as the living substance of their infinite singularity. If life is essentially substance ...and not simply an attribute, or, worse, a property of those who are its bearers, or of anyone else who claims it, this means that it cannot be conceived independently from them, whether in theological or scientific terms. (Esposito 2012b, 277)

Again, borrowing from Deleuze—this time his work with Guattari (Deleuze and Guattari 2004)—Esposito (2012a, 150) argues for a refusal to define life in relation to anything, but to conceptualize it as a radical singularity. Drawing on Deleuze and Guattari's chapter 'Becoming animal' in *A Thousand Plateaus*, Esposito (2012a, 150) claims that only life thought of as 'multiplicity, plurality, assemblage, with what surrounds us and with what always dwells inside us' can act as the basis for another non-immunitary politics. According to this immanent approach, that which is common to all living beings is not personal, but *im*personal: 'Life itself . . . is the term that would seem to sum up the entire theory of the impersonal, extending it into a form that is still indeterminate and, for this very reason, bursting with unexpressed potential' (Esposito 2012a, 147).

If the category of personhood has acted as a biopolitical border *within* humanity that, in turn, conditions the possibility for other borders to be drawn, then Esposito invests in the impersonal as a potential site of refusal of that immunitary logic. He draws on the work of Simone Weil who argued that if *rights* belong to the sphere of the person and its attendant exclusions then *justice* is aligned not with the personal but the impersonal. Weil's thought is located more generally by Esposito within the context of a broader philosophical tradition—including Benveniste, Kojeve, Levinas, and Blanchot (to which we might also add Derrida)—that he characterizes as engaging with the third person as an alternative figure for (re)thinking ethical-political relationality. In this tradition the third person is in effect a 'non-personal person': it is a mode of thought that 'refers to something, or even to someone, but to a someone who is not recognizable as this specific person, either because it does not refer to anyone at all or because it can be extended to anyone' (Esposito 2012a, 107). Inspired particularly by Benveniste's study of personal pronouns, Esposito argues that the third person—unlike the first or second person—does not have personal connotations despite being related to the logic of personhood:

> Of course the impersonal lies outside the horizon of the person, but not in a place that is unrelated to it: the impersonal is situated, rather, at the confines of the personal; on the lines of resistance, to be exact, which cut through its territory, thus preventing, or at least opposing, the functioning of its exclusionary *dispositif*. The impersonal is a shifting border: that critical margin, one might say, that separates the semantics of the person from its natural effect of separation; that blocks its reifying outcome. (Esposito 2012a, 14)

In this way, Esposito sees critical potential in the impersonal as the basis for reconceptualizing life beyond the exclusionary and immunitary *dispositif* of personhood and in favour of the common. This vitalist move towards the impersonal is potentially a radical one beyond the person at the heart of the present juridical-political order and with potentially far-reaching implications. To offer an illustration pertinent to the study of EUrope's border crisis, an impersonal politics is one that would refuse the contemporary biopolitical identification and management of populations based upon risk profiling, which in essence is an immunitary device that seeks to (re)produce and capture 'the person'. Indeed, the shift to the impersonal implies a rejection of the urge to 'better' categorize in order to 'know' and therefore 'govern' individuals and populations more 'efficiently': these are characteristics of a politics that contains violent thanatopolitical and zoopolitical potentiality. In contrast to mass surveillance, therefore, the grammar of the impersonal is suggestive of an opening onto what is common to life and hence what evades identity-based capture of this sort. What such an outlook might involve in concrete terms is always going to be highly suggestive as Esposito's own caveats imply, but it gestures towards the need to recalibrate the border as an immune system so that EUrope is once again able to confront—and allow itself to be confronted by—those whom it otherwise seeks to immunize itself against. Perhaps one reason why images of the so-called 'migrant ghost ship' that was abandoned by smugglers and left to drift onto Italian shores in January 2015 were considered so shocking by the mainstream media is that EUrope has largely insulated itself from exposure to what it has in common with those who fall outside an idealized image of itself (BBC News 2015). By contrast, the arrival of cargo boats carrying several hundred 'irregular' migrants at the ports of EU Member States force an encounter between EU citizens and non-EU citizens that is otherwise 'offshored' and 'outsourced': one of the possible upshots of Esposito's work is that diverse attempts to recover this encounter might act as a more politically engaged form of critique of the contemporary thanatopolitical and zoopolitical potentiality of EUropean border security practices than humanitarian logics that have already been co-opted. This is because, at the very least, the recovery of such an encounter appeals to the impersonal connection that deconstructs otherwise sedimented identity-based differences between 'EU citizens' on the one hand and 'irregular' migrants on the other hand, and forces open the ethical and political question of what kind of political community 'EUrope' seeks to be. However, while potentially productive in these terms, the denouement of Esposito's attempt to develop a reworking of biopolitics from within inevitably encounters certain limits and raises further questions—particularly for those interested in the question of borders.

Esposito and the Limits of Affirmative Biopolitics

The upshot of Esposito's attempt to think biopolitics affirmatively means, as Campbell (2008, xl) puts it, recognizing that 'harming one part of life or one life harms all lives'. This vitalist embrace and affirmation of life, as we have already seen, is characteristic not only of Esposito's thought, but also that of Negri and Deleuze (and Guattari). While one possible line of critique might be that Esposito simply ends up reiterating a position that he has sought to differentiate himself from, this argument would be to overlook the method by which he arrives at that end point. Unlike other vitalist thinkers, particularly Negri, Esposito goes to great lengths in order to work through rather than sidestep the violent potentialities of thanatopolitical and zoopolitical drift. Yet, unlike Agamben, Esposito's commitment to the affirmative arguably offers a clearer articulation of the possibility for conceptualizing another history and politics: 'what is missing', Esposito writes of the negative thanatopolitical disposition, 'is a living relationship with our common origin, in its dual aspects of donation and risk, exposure and alteration' (Esposito 2012b, 269). Via the paradigm of immunity, Esposito is able to conjoin the thanatopolitical and affirmative potentiality of biopolitics in a way that, at least in the reading offered here, is both novel and compelling: 'From this point of view', he continues, 'we can even accept that the "material" of all politics has always been biopolitics – but with the addendum that its qualitative intensification, and also its thanatopolitical drift, only began with the immunitary "turn"' (Esposito 2012b, 269).

An arguably more significant potential line of critique of Esposito's affirmative biopolitics, however, is one that pushes the question of what kind of politics (and ethics) his position ultimately entails and performs. In this regard, Cary Wolfe (2012) identifies what he considers to be two blind spots in Esposito's embrace of a vitalist approach to 'life'. The first concerns the flat ontology that such a position would appear to assume and advocate: 'The only alternative that Esposito seems to be able to imagine . . . is a sort of neovitalism that ends up radically dedifferentiating the field of "the living" into a molecular wash of singularities that all equally manifest "life"' (Wolfe 2012, 59). Wolfe is wary that a bland commitment to 'life' effectively flattens all living beings and insinuates a political and ethical equivalence between them: if all forms of life are equal, he asks, then should anthrax microbes not be killed if they threaten children? This leads into Wolfe's second line of critique, which questions the ethical-political dimensions of Esposito's seemingly depoliticizing approach to ethics: 'The problem with the recourse to "life" as the ethical *sine qua non* is that it bespeaks the desire for a nonperspectival ethics, ethics imagined fundamentally as a noncontingent view from nowhere, a view which—for that very reason—can declare all forms of life of equal value' (Wolfe 2012, 85).

Wolfe's critiques gesture towards a third area of possible concern, which is pertinent to the overarching concerns of this book: Esposito's somewhat ambiguous—even contradictory—stance towards the question of the border and the work that divisions, distinctions, and line-drawing practices perform in his political philosophy. It is clear that Esposito's thought identifies the thanatopolitical potentiality of biopolitics based on immunitary excess as being characterized first and foremost by the violent closure of borders: 'Border closings that do not tolerate anything from the outside, that exclude the very idea of an outside, that do not admit any foreignness that might threaten the logic of the One-and-everything' (Esposito 2008, 63). In this context, as we have seen, the borders to which Esposito's thought refers are multiple and apply variously to the immunitary closures of the self to the other, the subject to *communitas*, and political community to a more expansive understanding of the 'world' as a 'massive living body' (Esposito 2012b, 262). However, while the connection between border closures and thanatopolitical and zoopolitical drift is made plain, a lack of clarity nevertheless creeps into Esposito's approach regarding how this impetus should be responded to in ethical-political terms and the very role of borders and border logics as a basis for that response.

On the one hand, Esposito's vitalist approach to 'life' would seem, as per Wolfe's reading above, to imply the radical abandonment or refusal of borders between all forms of life as a deliberate strategy for deactivating the thanatopolitical *dispositif*. Allied to this position, it would also appear to follow from Esposito's arguments—about the subversive potentiality of *communitas*, the need to embrace an openness to what is held in common with others, and the focus on what is impersonal to all living singularities—that running throughout his oeuvre is an injunction to reject border logics and practices more generally, as discussed above in relation to the arrival of 'irregular' migrants on the shores of EU Member States. However, any position that acknowledges the work that borders do in the thanatopolitical and zoopolitical potentiality of biopolitics *without projecting that work into a response* is politically unsatisfying for the reasons implied by Wolfe: such a stance would evacuate from rather than (re)occupy the ground on which that violent potentiality was possible. In such a position, Esposito's careful diagnostic work in *Bíos, Communitas, and Immunitas*—among other texts—would appear to be somewhat in vain: this would be unnecessary under-labouring for yet another empty 'open borders' rhetoric.

On the other hand, there are moments within Esposito's work, as we have also already seen, which retain a carefully specified commitment to (a particular understanding of) borders. This is particularly notable in respect of his treatment of the immune system, which Esposito presents as a fundamentally Janus-faced border figure: too much protection and an autoimmune crisis may ensue; too little protection and the organism or community will also die. The latter point is crucial because despite Esposito's commitment to an opening up to the common at no point throughout his texts does he advocate the abandonment of the immune system *in toto*. On the contrary, Esposito under-scores that there is always a need for such systems: 'certainly, we need immune systems. No individual or social body could do without them, but when they grow out of proportion they end up forcing the entire social organism to explode or implode' (Esposito 2013, 62). In this direction, then, Esposito defends the immune system as a biopolitical border, but one that nevertheless allows *for* the rediscovery of and negotiation with what lies beyond the limits of ourselves and of our communities. Perhaps surprisingly Esposito's is in the final analysis an argument for borders precisely to maintain the possibility of an encounter with the 'outside': without some notion of the border that very encounter would be unthinkable.

If these twinned poles within Esposito's thought are taken together as double contradictory imperatives then the upshot is potentially significant for new directions in critical border and migration studies. On this reading, a more affirmative biopolitical approach to borders would be one that recon-ceptualizes the border as a porous figure, which maintains an inside/outside distinction while allowing for the 'inside' to open up to the 'outside'. We see the outlines of such a position when Esposito writes: 'The world . . . should not only be thought but "practiced" as an ensemble of differences, or a system of distinctions, in which distinction and difference are not points of resistance to or residues of the processes of globalization but their very form' (Esposito 2013, 65). Here, borders are *not* collapsed into a 'molecular wash' as per Wolfe's reading, but retained and reworked in a more affirmative direction. To reimagine biopolitical borders affirmatively, therefore, would be not to abandon protection of the self, but to protect against too much protection; not to dismantle the border as a biopolitical immune system, but to immunize against the threat of excessive immunization; not to open all borders, but to demilitarize contemporary border security so that that instead of violent forms of self-defence borders are transformed into a conduit for negotiating the exposure to *communitas* on a global scale.

Although it is certainly possible to discern the outlines of such a position within Esposito's thought, I want to suggest that additional work is neverthe-less necessary in order to further develop the grammatical shifts required for an affirmative border imaginary. This is primarily because Esposito's work currently lacks the grammars required to think in more concrete terms about how an affirmative border politics would work with rather than negate bor-ders. With this in mind the following section argues that compatible resources for rethinking borders affirmatively can be found in Derrida's work, particu-larly via his treatment of the figures of 'autoimmunity' and 'hostipitality'. Moreover, I will build towards the suggestion that these conceptual resources provide the basis for alternative headings in the context of possible responses to EUrope's border crisis.

Towards an Affirmative Biopolitical Border Imaginary

Esposito is not alone in drawing upon the paradigm of immunity in order to reconceptualize contemporary politics and the possibility for more affirmative modes of political thought and action.[8] Among other thinkers to engage with this paradigm is perhaps most notably Derrida (2002, 2003, 2005) for whom the concept of autoimmunity became central, particularly in his critical engagements with the question of sovereignty and US Foreign Policy in the post-9/11 context. However, despite this point of contact, the relationship between Esposito and Derrida on the theme of (auto)immunity has not hitherto attracted the attention that it deserves. In many respects this is surprising because with this theme it is possible to place biopolitics and deconstruction—two strands of contemporary European thought that have developed independently—in closer conversation with each other.

The small number of interdisciplinary commentators who have already gestured in this direction are somewhat divided on the issue of where this conversation might lead. On Campbell's (2008) reading, the two thinkers diverge fundamentally because Derrida collapses immunity and autoimmunity, whereas Esposito seeks to maintain a separation between the two frames. Campbell (2008, xix) argues that this means Derrida is destined to see autoimmunity as an essentially 'destructive' force, whereas for Esposito a more affirmative reading of immunity—one that is distinct from an autoimmune crisis—is possible, as previously discussed. Esposito (2008, 6) endorses Campbell's view when he comments in an interview with Campbell that Derrida's characterization of autoimmunity is ultimately 'tragic'. By contrast, Michael B. Naas' (2008, 28) reading of the figure of autoimmunity in Derrida's work views it as entirely commensurate with an understanding of deconstruction as a 'philosophy of affirmation'.[9] Similarly, Lemm (2013, 6) and Revel (2014, 112) see the possibility for a more complementary engagement between Esposito's thought and Derridean deconstruction precisely around the question of what a more affirmative approach to biopolitics might involve. For Revel (2014, 112), a deconstructive engagement with biopolitics is one that is simultaneously 'critical and affirmative'. Moreover, she sees in deconstruction not an approach to the common that seeks to erase difference and borders, but an onto-political mode of thought that is sensitive to context: 'An affirmative and positive thinking of biopolitics would thus be a thinking of the yet-to-come forms of the becoming differential of singularities, that is, the slow invention of a new common as the incessantly (re)worked-out space of subjectivization and of resistant ways of life' (Revel 2014, 124).

With Lemm (2013) and Revel (2014), the following discussion suggests that the differences between Esposito and Derrida should not be overstated and that the latter can assist the former in the task of developing a more affirmative border imaginary within the horizon of biopolitics. Deconstruction, with its attentiveness to the aporetic nature of autoimmunity and what Derrida refers to as 'hostipitality', halts any sense of the politics of escape associated with the bland vitalism about which Wolfe warns, but has not been connected with the biopolitical paradigm more generally. By bringing Esposito's search for an affirmative biopolitics into conversation with Derrida's deconstructive approach, the wager here is that this intersection offers a productive site for imagining a more affirmative border politics that does not eschew the thanatopolitical and zoopolitical potentiality of biopolitics, but works with it.

The Productive Dimension of Autoimmunity

As discussed in Chapter 5, autoimmunity for Esposito is cast primarily as a negative phenomenon: the apogee of the thanatopolitical potentiality immanent within biopolitics. By contrast, for Derrida, as we shall see, autoimmunity is presented as a condition that is potentially productive, but he does not connect it to biopolitics. Whereas the former thinker advocates a vitalist move towards an immanent embrace of life and a philosophy of the impersonal in response to autoimmunity, the latter reappropriates that condition and explores its affirmative potentiality. What is common to both thinkers is that autoimmunity is fundamentally a border concept: a threshold figure that helps us to reconceptualize borders and the work that they do. The argument I seek to make is that thinking biopolitical borders via the lens of autoimmunity—as understood by Derrida—enables a deconstruction of and movement beyond discourses that either simply seek to close off borders in a securitizing move or alternatively open them up in an equally hyperbolic way. The lesson that I see in Derrida's treatment of autoimmunity is that both discourses ultimately entail a problematic politics of escape, which has potentially important repercussions for critical border and migration scholars.

According to Naas (2008, 124), Derrida first used the term autoimmunity explicitly in his essay 'Faith and Knowledge' reprinted in *Acts of Religion* (2002). Later, this concept became a central motif in his writings post-9/11, especially in *Rogues* (2005) and throughout various interviews (Naas 2008, 124). In the latter context, Derrida, like Esposito, understands the term in relation to biomedical knowledge: 'that strange behavior where a living being, in a quasi-*suicidal* fashion, "itself" works to destroy its own protection, to immunize itself against its "own" immunity' (Derrida 2003, 94). However, autoimmunity is a term that connects with Derrida's earlier work on supplementarity and deconstruction more generally if understood as a critique of the performative fiction 'of the self-same of any same': in other words the notion of bordered self-identity as if it were pure in its presence and sovereign in its unconditionality (Naas 2008, 37).[10] Derrida's deconstructive approach argues that the relationship between identity, self, and other is always already fundamentally open to the future, the event, and therefore to the unknown.[11] Indeed, as Pheng Cheah (2009, 77) puts it, the central message of deconstruction is that there is no simple present: a straightforward idea, but with manifold implications.

From a deconstructive perspective the sovereign identity or 'ipseity'[12] of a finite being is inescapably exposed and risks being undone and undermined because of the fact that it alone cannot give itself time: 'it is always self-divided in the very constitution of its self through the iterability that allows it to relate to the same as itself' (Cheah 2009, 77). On this basis, Derrida (2005) has developed a theory of sovereignty as the attempt to immunize against the other by shielding—or bordering—itself from the law, language, time, and space: in other words, anything that would challenge its claim to self-presence (Naas 2008, 127). The work of deconstruction is to both illuminate the fact that sovereign self-identity is a performative fiction and acknowledge the indebtedness of the self to the other: 'our being is ... ontologically, hauntologically, autoimmune. The life cannot do without the spectre; life cannot do without nonlife; identity without difference ...' (Naas 2008, 129–30).

At base, Derrida uses the term 'autoimmunity' to refer to the way in which the self is not and never can be pure, but is always already contaminated by the other; not sovereign and bordered, but inescapably open and compromised; not independent from, but dependent upon—indeed inseparable from—the other. As Naas (2008, 125) explains, autoimmunity is understood by Derrida to be a condition that is at work in *all* discourses of sovereign identity: 'a force that turns on and disables force or power, autoimmunity at once destroys or compromises the integrity and identity of sovereign forms and opens them up to their future—that is, to the unconditionality of the event' (Naas 2008, 125). For this reason, as Bora Isyar argues, 'autoimmunity is at work everywhere ... destroying the integrity and self-identity of all forms' (2014, 55). It is a condition that 'reveals the powerlessness and instability of all self-identification and exposes the fact that all living organisms are in desperate need of the "other"' (Isyar 2014, 55).

Particularly in his later works, Derrida appears to concur with the 'negative' or thanatopolitical reading of autoimmunity adopted by Esposito that sees the condition as a threat to the immune system and the identity of the bordered self. For example, in the context of the aftermath of 9/11, as we saw above, Derrida (2003, 94) famously argued that the counter-terrorism discourses and practices of the West risk acquiring the very anti-democratic and terroristic characteristics that they purport to be fighting against in a 'quasi-*suicidal* fashion'. With this emphasis it is perhaps possible to read a tragic element into Derrida's argument, but such a reading is only partial and fails to grasp the complex nuance of that position.

Unlike Esposito, it is clear that Derrida also sees in autoimmunity a possibility or chance for a post-immunitary politics that turns around an alternative identity/difference problematic. Thus, in *Rogues*, Derrida (2005, 152) argues:

> Autoimmunity is not an absolute ill or evil. It enables an exposure to the other, to *what* and to *who* comes—which means that it must remain incalculable. Without autoimmunity, with absolute immunity, nothing would ever happen or arrive; we would no longer wait, await, or expect, no longer expect one another, or expect any event.

In other words, as the work of Naas (2008, 131) has sought to emphasize, the crisis of autoimmunity is not only a threat—as Esposito would have it—but also an opportunity: 'a threat insofar as it compromises the immune system that protects the organism from external aggression, but...a chance for an organism to open itself up to and accept something that is not properly its own...in a word, the other, which is but the cutting edge, the living edge, of the self' (Naas 2008, 131). This reading of the Derridean approach is supported by Cheah (2009, 79) for whom autoimmunity refers to the inescapable constitutive exposure of the self to the other as a weak affirmative force: 'the structural relation to alterity that renews temporality and enables a life to live on'.

In 'Faith and Knowledge', Derrida offers a fuller account of the affirmative ethical-political implications of autoimmunity for an understanding of political community, as follows:

> Nothing in *common*, nothing immune, safe and sound...without a risk of autoimmunity...This death-drive is silently at work in every community, every auto-co-immunity...Community as common auto-immunity: no community <is possible> that would not cultivate its own auto-immunity, a principle of self-destruction ruining the principle of self-protection (that of maintaining its self-integrity intact), and this is in view of some sort of invisible and spectral survival. This self-contesting attestation keeps the auto-immune community alive, which is to say, open to something other and more than itself: the other, the future, death, freedom, the coming or the love of the other, the space and time of a spectralizing messianicity beyond all messianism. (Derrida 2002, 87)

On this basis, in an argument that predates Esposito's similar position in *Communitas* and elsewhere, Derrida argues that the (non)essence of community is that it is always already open to more than itself and that it is precisely this openness—not the immunitary move to close borders—that enables communities to survive. Another way of making this point is to acknowledge, as a number of writers inspired by Derrida have done, that no community or culture ever has a pure identity, but is shaped by and is itself imbued with a range of differences or constitutive outsides (Isyar 2014, 49). As Engin Isin remarks, the hallmark of the Derridean approach to community as 'common auto-immunity' above is that it is a 'thesis of impurity . . . the assertion of the impossibility of any social group . . . being able to identify itself with itself without any relation or reference to the other' (Isin 2014, 110).

The upshot of thinking political community in terms of autoimmunity from the affirmative Derridean position is that we are presented with the same border paradox arrived at by Esposito's treatment of *communitas*: the idea that 'there can be no community without autoimmunity, no protection of the safe and sound without a perilous opening of borders' (Naas 2008, 131). Despite their differences, both Esposito and Derrida end up arguing that too much border security and that which is attempting to secure itself will come to jeopardize and pose a threat to itself; too little border security and equally the self will be undermined and rendered insecure in a quasi-suicidal move. However, I would suggest that Derrida's thought arguably goes further than Esposito's by offering additional critical resources for illustrating and understanding this constitutive double bind in his treatment of hospitality—or rather 'hostipitality' as he prefers to call it. Furthermore, it is in the autoimmune figure of hostipitality that I argue Derrida's thought perhaps offers the most instructive opening for an alternative biopolitical border imaginary that is affirmative while recognizing the potential for thanatopolitical and zoopolitical drift of the kind diagnosed by Esposito. Ultimately, this figure also offers the basis for a critical response to EUrope's border crisis as I have sought to diagnose it.

Hostipitality

The Derridean approach to hospitality and its ethical-political implications has already attracted a range of engagements (see, for example, Baker 2013; Brown 2010; Bulley 2009; Vaughan-Williams 2007). However, in a slightly different albeit complimentary direction to these debates, the argument advanced here is that the Derridean figure of 'hostipitality' reveals what is at stake ethically and politically by the condition of autoimmunity, how this is fundamentally a question of the border and a technology of power, and why scholars of critical border and migration studies, in particular, may benefit from the paradigm of thought it entails and performs. Moreover, given the rise of humanitarianism as a discourse that increasingly structures the field of EUropean border security and migration management policy and practice, I also want to suggest that the theme of hospitality/hostipitality is especially apposite in this specific empirical context.

As is well known, Derrida's (2000, 2002, 2003) engagement with the concept of hospitality is via a deconstructive reading of Kant's paradigmatic figure of the foreigner, who, according to the cosmopolitan ideal, has the right to an albeit limited form of hospitality (Vaughan-Williams 2007). Without entering into the detail of extant debates about the nature and 'accuracy' of Derrida's reading of Kant, what interests me here is the way in which the basic logic of hospitality is precisely that of autoimmunity: this connection holds the key to understanding how the latter holds affirmative potentiality. Hospitality, according to Derrida, is structured according to two contradictory imperatives, which reflect conditional and unconditional poles.

On the one hand, there is a conditional or possible dimension to hospitality: 'hospitality must wait, extend itself toward the other, extend to other the gifts, the site, the shelter and the cover; it must be ready to welcome . . . to host and shelter, to give shelter and cover . . . and institute . . . a welcoming apparatus' (Derrida 2002, 361). Elsewhere, Derrida (2003, 128) describes this as a form of tolerance: 'a conditional hospitality, the one that is most commonly practiced by individuals, families, cities, or states. We offer hospitality only on the condition that the other follow our rules, our way of life, even our language, our culture, our political system, and so on.' This conditional hospitality—'hospitality under surveillance' (Derrida 2003, 128)—is one that Derrida associates with the Kantian cosmopolitan ideal: one that can be regulated, formalized, and written into law.

On the other hand, however, Derrida (2002, 361) also identifies an unconditional or impossible aspect to the experience of hospitality: 'to be hospitable is to let oneself be overtaken . . . to be ready not to be ready, if such is possible, to let oneself be overtaken, to not even let oneself be overtaken, to be surprised in a fashion almost violence'. Without this element of surprise or lack of preparedness, Derrida argues that there would be no such thing as hospitality as such, only a technologized welcoming: 'hospitality consists in welcoming the other that does not warn me of his coming' (Derrida 2002, 381). Indeed, the unconditional or impossible element is absolutely central on Derrida's view because hospitality worthy of the name cannot be merely an exchange or act of reciprocity, only an experience whereby *in extremis* the host may run the risk of being threatened or entirely taken over by the guest:

> pure hospitality opens or is in advance open to someone who is neither expected nor invited, to whomever arrives as an absolutely foreign *visitor*, as a new *arrival*, non-identifiable and unforeseeable, in short, wholly other. I would call this a hospitality of *visitation* rather than *invitation*. The visit might actually be very dangerous, and we must not ignore this fact, but would a hospitality without risk, a hospitality backed by certain assurances, a hospitality protected by an immune system against the wholly other, be true hospitality? Though it's ultimately true that suspending or

suppressing the immunity that protects me from the other might be nothing short of life-threatening. (Derrida 2003, 129)

It is because an experience of unconditional hospitality entails the thanato-political possibility of hostility and violence—'the visit might actually be very dangerous'—that Derrida recasts hospitality as 'hostipitality'. Derrida (2003, 129) is all too well aware that unconditional or pure hospitality cannot be organized, legislated for, or acquire an institutional status politically: 'no one can write it into its laws'. Yet, he argues that without the unconditional or impossible notion of hospitality there could be no such thing as a conditional or possible experience of it: 'we would have no concept of hospitality in general and would not even be able to determine any rules for conditional hospitality' (Derrida 2003, 129). As Madeleine Fagan (2013) has sought to emphasize, Derrida argues that the realm of the ethical-political is located precisely in the transaction between the conditional and the unconditional:

> I cannot expose myself to the coming of the other and offer him or her anything whatsoever without making this hospitality effective, without, in some concrete way, giving *something determinate*. This determination will thus have to re-inscribe the unconditional into certain conditions. Otherwise, it gives nothing. What remains unconditional or absolute . . . risks being nothing at all if conditions . . . do not make of it some thing. *Political, juridical, and ethical responsibilities have their place, if they take place, only in this transaction . . . between these two hospitalities, the unconditional and the conditional.* (Derrida 2003, 130, emphasis added)

Herein lies the brilliance of Derrida's diagnosis of the way in which conditions of autoimmunity allow for both an affirmative and a thanatopolitical poten-tiality: it is a risk for the self to be entirely open to the other and yet also a risk for the self to be entirely closed to the other; both borderlessness and closed borders result in an autoimmune crisis. What the Derridean position advo-cates in ethical-political terms, as indicated in the lengthy quotation above, is a negotiation of the conditional and unconditional poles of hostipitality: a double register of ethical-political thought and action is required. With the autoimmune figure of hostipitality, Derrida grasps the paradoxical logic of the border—also at play in Esposito's thought—whereby in order to be open, hospitable, and welcoming to the other it is also necessary for there to be a border between self and other and the possibility for that relationship to be marked by violence. To repeat, an affirmative border imaginary that takes seriously the potentiality for thanatopolitical and zoopolitical drift is not one that abandons the border between self and other. If this were to happen then hospitality would no longer be possible because there has to be a differ-ence in the identities of host and guest. At the same time, unconditional hospitality undermines this very distinction and this is why it can only ever be experienced via its conditional manifestation.

What we are left with is an argument about the need to acknowledge and live with the uncomfortable fact that ourselves, our communities, our cultures are always already open and dependent on the other and that we are indebted to the other for our identity and sense of self, and owe hospitality to the other as a result; but that at the same time we must negotiate the equally difficult fact that in order to be hospitable to the other we need borders that mark out our identity as different from the other and that in the attempt to be hospitable the other may threaten us up to the very point of our ability to receive and host the other. In this way, the autoimmune logic of hostipitality I believe offers critical border and migration scholars an alternative and affirmative paradigm of the border, which deconstructs extant dichotomies between borders/migration, control/escape, closure/openness, violence/agency, and death/life while remaining cognizant of the thanatopolitical and zoopolitical potentialities as diagnosed by Esposito. Moreover, taken seriously, it is not a normative or utopic argument about what *should* or *ought* to happen: if, as Derrida argues, deconstruction is the case then we see the condition of auto-immunity all around us in both its affirmative as well as its thanatopolitical and zoopolitical guises. Thus, as Naas puts it, despite the impossibility of unconditional hospitality and the violent riskiness that it necessarily involves, we nevertheless witness and ourselves experience hospitality 'through the most everyday and unremarkable gestures' (Naas 2008, 22). Perhaps an affirmative imaginary of the border is an ethical-political disposition that better nurtures those gestures while at the same time one that also recognizes the inevitable violence that they are based on and further give rise to. Further still, maybe there are times such as ours that demand interventions designed to recalibrate the relationship between thanatopolitical and affirmative potentialities.

Affirmative Headings for EUropean Border Security and Migration Management

Derrida's own work has addressed the condition of autoimmunity, specifically as it relates to the historical and geocultural context of EUrope. In *The Other Heading* (1992), he explores the autoimmune structures that have conditioned the possibility for and continue to haunt expressions of EUropean identity.

Writing more than twenty years ago, Derrida (1992) acknowledged and anticipated the various ways in which alterity is increasingly perceived as threatening EUrope: as witnessed in the strength of certain nationalist discourses fuelled by a politics of fear, the recurring activities of the far right and manifestations of racism and xenophobia, the rise of extremist immigration and asylum policies, tougher border security measures, and countless other attempts at social immunization. As Isyar (2014) has put it, these policies and practices are all diagnosed by Derrida precisely as being symptomatic of a lack of openness to the (non-EUropean) other both inside and outside the geographical limits of what is conventionally seen as EUrope. Derrida's response to these conditions, which, as we have seen in previous chapters, have intensified and diversified more recently, was to reiterate that as with all political communities EUrope is not ipseic or sustainable as a sovereign entity, but is given rise to as a result of multiple competing identities both extrinsic and intrinsic to itself: 'What is proper to a culture is never to be identical to itself. Not to not have any identity, but to be able to identify itself, to say "me" or "we" only in the non-identity to itself, or, if you prefer, only in the difference with itself . . . What differs and diverges from itself would also be a difference from and with itself, a difference both internal and irreducible to being at home' (Derrida 1992, 9–10). Thus, Derrida draws attention to the way in which what is presented as a threat to EUropean identity is in fact not distinct from and thereby external to, but fundamentally a part of that identity: EUrope is constituted by and therefore intrinsically indebted to alterity. Moreover, as Stuart McLean (2014, 66) shows, Derrida is not merely arguing that EUrope is dependent on the other located outside or beyond itself, but that EUrope's own culture, identity, and sense of self is imbued with difference to itself given by a multitude of Graeco-Latin, Arab, Jewish, and Turkish influences, to name only a few prominent examples.

What Derrida posits then as 'another heading' for EUrope is one that takes inspiration from this alternative rendering of alterity: not as a threat coming from the outside, but one that already sees the self as 'contaminated', albeit in a positive way.[13] Such affirmative contamination allows for a different course to be charted from within the context of already existing horizons rather than from some other imagined starting point: 'It is necessary to make ourselves the guardians of an idea of Europe, of a difference of Europe, *but* of a Europe that consists precisely in not closing itself off in its identity and in advancing itself in an exemplary way to what it is not, toward the other heading or the heading of the other' (Derrida 1992, 29). Again, we see in this passage autoimmunity working positively in Derrida's thought: as an affirmative technology of power, which gives 'hope for a different Europe whose identity is constituted by being always already different from and non-identical to itself, a Europe-to-come' (Isyar 2014, 50). Autoimmunity operates as a technology of power in this context precisely because it works to challenge, mitigate, and erode 'the forces of identity that sustain self-sameness': in other words, 'autoimmunity opens us to the other; it opens Europe to non-Europe' (Isyar 2014, 55). Furthermore, autoimmunity has a spatial as well as a temporal characteristic in Derrida's argument not only because it challenges the inside/outside distinction that makes possible the argument that alterity is a threat against which EUrope needs to immunize itself against, but also because it provokes further reflection on the role of territorial limits and their negotiation. In this vein, Sam Weber (2014) reflects on the significance of the term 'heading' or 'cap' in the original French title of Derrida's essay, which he suggests connotes EUrope's distinctive tendencies to desire and have the capacity to go beyond itself: 'It is a continent always on the verge of becoming incontinent: of exceeding its limits, whether through colonial expeditions, interventions, annexations, external or internal wars, or through political, social and cultural changes that would leave it unrecognisable' (Weber 2014, 17). On this basis, the possibility of 'another heading' for EUrope, as imagined by Derrida, would be one marked by a non-EUrocentrism: a disposition that worked affirmatively with autoimmune conditions (Naas 2008, 84).

A more affirmative heading for EUropean border security and migration management is perhaps difficult to imagine in the context of contemporary thanatopolitical and zoopolitical drift, as traced in Chapters 3 and 4. Indeed, it might be argued that for all the philosophical gymnastics performed by the likes of Esposito and Derrida what remains most important is concrete political action that puts a halt to the violent methods by which 'irregular' migrants are (re)produced both as security threats and as lives to be saved for the purposes of humanitarian governance. However, one of the motivations of this study has been to explore different ways of thinking about these issues and the intractable problems underpinning them: to offer alternative diagnoses in the hope that this might lead to new and potentially more affirmative lines of enquiry for political judgement and action. While the translation of figures such as the commons, impersonal politics, and autoimmune hostipitality into concrete praxis may appear somewhat anodyne in the final analysis, I nevertheless consider the attempt to sketch out their implications to be an important aspect of this programme of work. In this regard, the Derridean theme of the double register of conditionality and unconditionality is potentially helpful and its application to the issues discussed in earlier chapters may raise the following critical points.

An affirmative approach to EUrope's border crisis within the conditional register would be one associated with many of the policy suggestions already put forward by NGOs, migrant activist networks, and critical academic and non-academic commentators. This line of response is one that operates primarily within the existing juridical-political order and, as such, runs a risk of perpetuating underlying dynamics instead of overcoming them, but a deconstructive position is ultimately not one that rejects the notion that there is a place for this kind of strategy. In this context, there is no shortage of practical suggestions for how instances of border violence and injustice against 'irregular' migrants might be addressed. These suggestions might be said to include, *inter alia*, the reversal of the trend of the externalization and outsourcing of

EUropean border security and its renationalization; the demilitarization of EUropean border security and the disaggregation of militarized and humanitarian logics of governmentality; the exposure of the policies, activities, and management of Frontex to greater debate in the EU Parliament and public scrutiny; the cessation of illegal push-back operations and the establishment of safe corridors notably across the Mediterranean and Aegean seas; the return and opening up of legal channels for migrants seeking work in EUrope; the improvement of material conditions of detention and renationalization of migrant processing centres; the provision of long-term health-care programmes for 'irregular' migrants in detention; the granting of permission for lawyers, academics, politicians, journalists, and other concerned members of the public to access detention centres for the purpose of monitoring material conditions; public campaigns to highlight the violence and injustices endured by migrants in the name of 'EUropean' citizenship and security; the desecuritization and repoliticization of migration as an issue in contemporary political life; the recognition of the complicity of EUropean colonialism—past and present—in the creation of conditions that stimulate migratory dynamics to EUrope; efforts to tackle structural inequalities globally that also shape those dynamics; and the enactment of democratic limits on some of the most excessive practices of border surveillance and security.

Alongside these conditional measures, however, a deconstructive approach would also seek to emphasize the importance of a negotiation with the unconditional: not as a programme or blueprint, but as a work of thought that strategically seeks to recover the ground of the ethical-political. In this regard, the Derridean notion of pure hospitality offers a marked contrast to the cynical immunitary appropriation of (a perverse form of) hospitality associated with humanitarian border security and the 'migrant-centredness' of the EU Commission's GAMM. While an experience of unconditional hospitality can never be provided for in policy, legislation, or practice, it nevertheless acts as a critical and affirmative check on the worst excesses of contemporary border violence carried out in the name of hospitality. Indeed, it might be argued that in today's EUrope—perhaps even more so than when Derrida was writing several decades ago—the right to invitation (never mind the right to visitation) has itself been violently curtailed: a recovery of that right in the name of the unconditional might at least be a start. In a similar vein, while it would be foolish to abandon a conditional commitment to human rights, both Derrida and Esposito urge us to be wary of their appropriation in the service of immunitary policies and practices. Both thinkers call for radical, experimental approaches beyond the horizon of human rights and the exclusionary *dispositif* of the person underpinning it. Again, the unconditional position is and must remain a vanishing horizon, but Esposito's impersonal politics resonates with what Derrida sees as an already existing point of contact between singularities (rather than sovereign subjects), which offers an alternative affirmative ethical-political register:

> If I feel in solidarity with this particular Algerian who is caught between the F.I.S [*Front Islamique du Salut*] and the Algerian state, or this particular Croat, Serb, or Bosnian, or this particular South African, this particular Russian or Ukrainian, or whoever—it's not a feeling of one citizen towards another, it's not a feeling peculiar to a citizen of the world...No...what binds me to them—and this is the point; there is a bond, but this bond cannot be contained within traditional concepts of community, obligation or responsibility—is a protest against citizenship, a protest against membership of a political configuration as such. (Derrida 1994, 47–8)

While the general implications of this ethos have been discussed elsewhere (Campbell 2003; Vaughan-Williams 2007), the turn to singularity and the impersonal calls for a response to violence and injustice against 'irregular' migrants not on the basis of their nationality, motivation for seeking entry to the EU, or indeed any other identity-based criteria for that matter (including that of being 'human'), but precisely *as* singularities with whom we feel a bond. In such a feeling there is perhaps a deconstruction of the opposition between the 'EU citizen' on the one hand and the 'irregular' migrant on the other, and an opening of both out and onto the common: another trace of the unconditional.

In conclusion, although the radical openness to the other implied by both Derrida and Esposito is orientated towards yet another impossible pole, it is possible to imagine how a movement in that more affirmative direction would be to in a certain sense recover the borders of EUrope. By this I do not mean to insinuate a nostalgia for some idealized image of the geopolitical borders of EUrope in the past—far from it. However, because EUropean border security and migration management practices have undergone a series of spatial-temporal displacements, the encounter between 'EUrope'—citizens and politicians as well as border security authorities—and 'irregular' migrants has also become ever more diffused and spectral. Perhaps an affirmative approach to border security and migration management on the terrain of biopolitics might seek to recover that encounter in all its manifold complexities so that it can be identified, interrogated, and used as a productive site for reminding EUrope of its constitutive difference and indebtedness to those it otherwise attempts to immunize itself against. Inevitably, this involves a huge risk and vulnerability, but the thought of Esposito and Derrida suggests that so does excessive immunization. Perhaps EUrope's border crisis—epitomized by the 2013 Lampedusa incident—should be seen, to paraphrase Esposito, as an opportunity to shatter the mirror in which EUrope is reflected without seeing anything but itself.

Notes

1. Papadopoulos et al. (2008, 203) trace their emphasis on the need to 'escape from zones of misery' and to work with the 'excess of experience' to Negri's history of capitalism from the perspective of workers' mobility.
2. Indeed, this move may ultimately be ever more worrisome politically because the notion that 'irregular' migrants have 'agency' is one that authorities complicit in some of the most egregious border violence are already well aware of: this is what they are attempting to control. Hence, any theoretical perspective that seeks to develop a critique of such violence on the basis of the assumed 'autonomy of migration' is politically impotent (see Chapter 3).
3. Such a position marks out the argument presented here from that of Mezzadra and Neilson (2013, 291) for whom the border is essentially destructive of the common.
4. McNevin (2013) argues that both Agamben (1998) and Agambenian-inspired literature on the one hand and the 'autonomy of migration' approach associated with Papadopoulos et al. (2008) and Hardt and Negri (2001, 2004) on the other hand take the biopolitics of sovereign power as a given. Instead, she urges a sociological turn to a more 'grounded approach' that focuses on the ambivalence of 'irregular' migrants' experiences and claims. Whereas McNevin urges an empirical turn in this regard, I take a step back and try to offer a complementary conceptual diagnosis of what is at stake in the ambivalence to which she refers by drawing on Esposito's deconstruction of the 'thanatopolitical' versus 'vitalist' strands of (post)biopolitical thought.
5. Such a deconstructive approach to borders is in my view subtly albeit vitally distinctive because it seeks to avoid the 'politics of escape' that R. B. J. Walker (2010) has warned of.
6. This is of particular concern for the purposes of the present chapter precisely because Negri's materialist rendering of biopolitics has shaped extant attempts to conceptualize alternative imaginaries to that of the control-biased thanatopolitical paradigm in critical border and migration studies.
7. Muhle's (2014) critique also applies to the move by the AoM approach to posit migrants as 'autonomous' subjects that are somehow above and beyond Foucaultian power relations. For example, this is evident when Papadopoulos et al. (2008, 43) assert: 'We cannot understand social change and people's agency is we always see them as *already* entangled in and regulated by control.'
8. In his 'Translator's Introduction' to *Bíos*, Campbell (2008) lists other contemporary thinkers engaging with the immunitary paradigm—albeit to varying degrees—as including Luhmann, Haraway, Baudrillard, and Derrida.
9. In his last interview, Derrida said: 'Deconstruction is always on the side of the *yes*, the affirmation of life' (quoted in Cheah 2009, 79).
10. Naas (2008, 141) argues that the logic of autoimmunity is detectable already in Derrida's discussion of the logic of the supplement in 'Structure, Sign, and Play in the Discourse of the Human Sciences' [1966].
11. A fuller exegesis of Derridean deconstruction is beyond the more modest scope of the present discussion, which focuses more specifically on the concept of

autoimmunity. I have presented my own reading of deconstruction elsewhere Vaughan-Williams 2005, 2007, 2009: Lundborg and Vaughan-Williams 2015.

12. Cheah and Guerlac (2009, 16) refer to ipseity as the 'power of a self to constitute itself by gathering itself unto itself and mastering itself'; similarly, Naas (2008, 126) argues 'sovereignty, power, autonomy, automobility, autotely: these words form the matrix that Derrida names *ipseity*'.

13. This notion of positive contamination is reminiscent of Esposito's example of the mother's affirmative hosting of the foetus. With this example we also see that hospitality, though implicit, is also central to Esposito's attempt to articulate a more affirmative biopolitical thought.

References

Adorno, Francesco Paolo. 2014. 'Power Over Life, Politics of Death: Forms of Resistance to Biopower in Foucault'. In *The Government of Life: Foucault, Biopolitics, and Neoliberalism*, edited by Vanessa Lemm and Miguel Vatter, pp. 98–111. New York, NY: Fordham University Press.

Agamben, Giorgio. 1994. 'We Refugees'. *Symposium* 49: pp. 114–19.

Agamben, Giorgio. 1998. *Homo Sacer: Sovereign Power and Bare Life*. Stanford, CA: Stanford University Press.

Agamben, Giorgio. 1999. *Remnants of Auschwitz: The Witness and the Archive*. New York, NY: Zone Books.

Agamben, Giorgio. 2000. *Means Without End: Notes on Politics*. Minneapolis, MN: University of Minnesota Press.

Agamben, Giorgio. 2004a. *The Open: Man and Animal*. Stanford, CA: Stanford University Press.

Agamben, Giorgio. 2004b. 'Interview With Giorgio Agamben—Life, A Work of Art Without an Author: The State of Exception, the Administration of Disorder and Private Life'. *German Law Journal* 5 (5): pp. 609–14.

Agamben, Giorgio. 2009. *The Signature of All Things: On Method*. New York, NY: Zone Books.

Agamben, Giorgio. 2013. 'What Is a Destituent Power?'. *Environment and Planning D: Society and Space* 32: pp. 65–74.

Agnew, John. 1994. 'The Territorial Trap: The Geographical Assumptions of International Relations Theory'. *Review of International Political Economy* 1: pp. 53–80.

Agnew, John. 2003. *Geopolitics: Revisioning World Politics*. London and New York, NY: Routledge.

AGSI. 2013. 'Italy: Statement Over Lampedusa Video Highlights'. Available online at: <http://www.statewatch.org/news/2013/dec/asgi-lampedusa.pdf> (accessed 26 May 2014).

Albert, Mathias, David Jacobson, and Yosef Lapid. 2001. Eds. *Identities, Borders, Orders: Re-Thinking International Relations Theory*. Minneapolis, MN: University of Minnesota Press.

Amnesty International. 2013. 'Scapegoats of Fear: Rights of Refugees, Asylum-Seekers and Migrants Abused in Libya'. Available online at: <http://www.amnesty.org/en/library/info/MDE19/007/2013/en> (accessed 7 April 2014).

Amoore, Louise. 2006. 'Biometric Borders: Governing Mobilities in the War on Terror'. *Political Geography* 25: pp. 336–51.

References

Amoore, Louise. 2007. 'Vigilant Visualities: The Watchful Politics of the War on Terror'. *Security Dialogue* 38: pp. 215–32.

Andersson, Ruben. 2014. 'Hunter and Prey: Patrolling Clandestine Migration in the Euro-African Borderlands'. *Anthropological Quarterly* 87: pp. 119–49.

Arendt, Hannah. 1951. *The Origins of Totalitarianism*. New York, NY: Schocken Books.

Baker, Gideon. 2013. *Hospitality and World Politics*. Basingstoke and New York, NY: Palgrave Macmillan.

Balibar, Étienne. 1998. 'The Borders of Europe'. In *Cosmopolitics: Thinking and Feeling Beyond the Nation*, edited by Pheng Cheah and Bruce Robbins, pp. 216–33. Minneapolis, MN: University of Minnesota Press.

Balibar, Étienne. 2009. 'Europe as Borderland'. *Environment and Planning D: Society and Space* 27 (2): pp. 190–215.

Basham, Victoria and Nick Vaughan-Williams. 2013. 'Gender, Race, and Border Security Practices: A Profane Reading of "Muscular Liberalism"'. *British Journal of Politics and International Relations* 15 (4): pp. 509–27.

BBC News. 2013a. 'Italy Boat Sinking: Hundreds Feared Dead off Lampedusa'. Available online at: <http://www.bbc.co.uk/news/world-europe-24380247> (accessed 1 January 2015).

BBC News. 2013b. 'Lampedusa Wreck: EU seeks Mediterranean Migrant Sea Patrols'. Available online at: <http://www.bbc.co.uk/news/world-europe-24440908> (accessed 1 January 2015).

BBC News. 2015. 'Abandoned Migrant Ship Ezadeen Reaches Italy'. Available online at: <http://www.bbc.co.uk/news/world-europe-30653742> (accessed 25 January 2015).

Bialasiewicz, Luiza. 2011. Ed. *Europe and the World: EU Geopolitics and the Transformation of European Space*. Hampshire and Berlington, VT: Ashgate.

Bialasiewicz, Luiza. 2012. 'Off-Shoring and Out-Sourcing the Borders of Europe: Libya and EU Border-Work in the Mediterranean'. *Geopolitics* 17: pp. 843–66.

Bigo, Didier. 2001. 'The Möbius Ribbon of Internal and External Security(ies)'. In *Identities, Borders, Orders: Re-Thinking International Relations Theory*, edited by Mathias Albert, David Jacobson, and Yosef Lapid, pp. 91–116. Minneapolis, MN: University of Minnesota Press.

Bigo, Didier. 2007. 'Detention of Foreigners, States of Exception, and the Social Practices of Control of the Banopticon'. In *Borderscapes: Hidden Geographies and Politics at Territory's Edge*, edited by Prem Kumar Rajaram and Carl Grundy-Warr, pp. 57–101. Minneapolis, MN: University of Minnesota Press.

Bigo, Didier and Elspeth Guild. 2005. Eds. *Controlling Frontiers: Free Movement Into and Within Europe*. Hampshire and Burlington, VT: Ashgate.

Bigo, Didier, Sergio Carrera, Elspeth Guild, and R. B. J. Walker. 2007. 'The Changing Landscape of European Liberty and Security: Mid-Term Report on the Results of the CHALLENGE Project', Research Paper No. 4. Available online at: <http://www.libertysecurity.org/article1357.html> (accessed 10 April 2009).

Borderline Europe. 2013. 'At the Limen: The Implementation of the Return Directive in Italy, Cyprus and Spain'. Available online at: <http://www.borderline-europe.de/sites/default/files/features/2014_Final_brochure_at-the-limen.pdf> (accessed 7 April 2014).

Bröckling, Ulrich, Susanne Krassman, and Thomas Lemke. 2010. Eds. *Governmentality: Current Issues and Future Challenges*. London and New York, NY: Routledge.

Brown, Garrett Wallace. 2010. 'The Laws of Hospitality, Asylum Seekers and Cosmopolitan Right: A Kantian Response to Jacques Derrida'. *European Journal of Political Theory* 9 (3): pp. 308–27.

Brown, Michael and Claire Rasmussen. 2010. 'Bestiality and the Queering of the Human Animal'. *Environment and Planning D: Society and Space* 28: pp. 158–77.

Bulley, Dan. 2009. *Ethics as Foreign Policy: Britain, the EU, and the Other*. London and New York, NY: Routledge.

Butler, Judith. 2004. *Precarious Life: The Powers of Mourning and Violence*. London and New York, NY: Verso.

Calarco, Matthew. 2008. *Zoographies: The Question of the Animal From Heidegger to Derrida*. New York, NY: Columbia University Press.

Campbell, David. 2003. 'Deterritorialized Loyalty: Multiculturalism and Bosnia'. In *Political Loyalty and the Nation-State*, edited by Michael Waller and Andrew Linklater, pp. 43–58. London and New York, NY: Routledge.

Campbell, Timothy. 2008. 'Translator's Introduction: Bios, Immunity, Life: The Thought of Roberto Esposito'. In Roberto Esposito *Bíos: Biopolitics and Philosophy*. Minneapolis, MN: University of Minnesota Press.

Campbell, Timothy. 2011. *Improper Life: Technology and Biopolitics From Heidegger to Agamben*. Minneapolis, MN: University of Minnesota Press.

Carrera, Sergio. 2007. *The EU Border Management Strategy: FRONTEX and the Challenges of Irregular Immigration in the Canary Islands*. Brussels: Centre for European Studies.

Cheah, Pheng. 2009. 'The Untimely Secret of Democracy'. In *Derrida and the Time of the Political*, edited by Pheng Cheah and Suzanne Guerlac, pp. 74–96. Durham, NC and London: Duke University Press.

Cheah, Pheng and Suzanne Guerlac. 2009. *Derrida and the Time of the Political*. Durham, NC and London: Duke University Press.

Clough, Patricia and Craig Willse. 2011. Eds. *Beyond Biopolitics: Essays on the Governance of Life and Death*. Durham, NC and London: Duke University Press.

Coleman, Mathew and Kevin Grove. 2009. 'Biopolitics, Biopower, and the Return of Sovereignty'. *Environment and Planning D: Society and Space* 27 (3): pp. 489–507.

Collard, Rosemary. 2012. 'Cougar–Human Entanglements and the Biopolitical Un/Making of Safe Space'. *Environment and Planning D: Society and Space* 30: pp. 23–42.

Connolly, William. 2004. 'The Complexity of Sovereignty'. In *Sovereign Lives: Power in World Politics*, edited by Jenny Edkins, Véronique Pin-Fat, and Michael J. Shapiro, pp. 23–41. London and New York, NY: Routledge.

Coole, Diana. 2013. 'Agentic Capacities and Capacious Historical Materialism: Thinking with New Materialisms in the Political Sciences'. *Millennium: Journal of International Studies* 41 (3): pp. 451–69.

Côté-Boucher, Karine, Federica Infantino, and Mark B. Salter. 2014. 'Border Security as Practice: An Agenda for Research'. *Security Dialogue* 45: pp. 196–208.

Council of Europe. 2014. 'Report to the Greek Government on the Visit to Greece Carried out by the European Committee for the Prevention of Torture and Inhuman or Degrading Treatment or Punishment (CPT), from 4 to 16 April, 2013'. Available

References

online at: <http://www.refworld.org/docid/543f7ba54.html> (accessed 27 December 2014).

Coutin, Susan. 2005. 'Being En Route'. *American Anthropologist* 107: pp. 195–206.

Culler, Jonathan. 1982. *On Deconstruction: Theory and Criticism After Structuralism.* Ithaca, NY: Cornell University Press.

De Genova, Nicolas and Nathalie Peutz. 2010. Eds. *The Deportation Regime: Sovereignty, Space, and the Freedom of Movement.* Durham, NC and London: Duke University Press.

De La Durantaye, Leland. 2012. 'The Paradigm of Colonialism'. In *Agamben and Colonialism*, edited by Marcelo Svirsky and Simone Bignall, pp. 229–38. Edinburgh: Edinburgh University Press.

Debrix, François. 2013. 'Topologies of Vulnerability and the Proliferation of Camp Life'. Unpublished paper presented at the Association of American Geographers Annual Meeting, Los Angeles, CA.

Debrix, François and Alexander Barder. 2012. *Beyond Biopolitics: Theory, Violence, and Horror in World Politics.* London and New York, NY: Routledge.

Deleuze, Gilles and Félix Guattari. 2004. *A Thousand Plateaus: Capitalism and Schizophrenia.* London and New York, NY: Continuum.

Derrida, Jacques. 1981. 'Plato's Pharmacy'. In *Dissemination*, pp. 61–72. London: The Athlone Press.

Derrida, Jacques. 1982. *Positions.* Chicago, IL: University of Chicago Press.

Derrida, Jacques. 1992. *The Other Heading: Reflections on Today's Europe.* Bloomington, IN: Indiana University Press.

Derrida, Jacques. 1994. 'Nietzsche and the Machine: Interview With Jacques Derrida by Richard Beardsworth'. *Journal of Nietzsche Studies* 7: pp. 7–66.

Derrida, Jacques. 2000. *Of Hospitality.* Stanford, CA: Stanford University Press.

Derrida, Jacques. 2002. *Acts of Religion.* London and New York, NY: Routledge.

Derrida, Jacques. 2003. 'Autoimmunity: Real and Symbolic Suicides: An Interview With Jacques Derrida'. In *Philosophy in a Time of Terror: Dialogues With Jürgen Habermas and Jacques Derrida*, edited by Giovanni Borradori, pp. 85–136. Chicago, IL and London: University of Chicago Press.

Derrida, Jacques. 2005. *Rogues: Two Essays on Reason.* Stanford, CA: Stanford University Press.

Derrida, Jacques. 2008. *The Animal That Therefore I Am.* New York, NY: Fordham University Press.

Derrida, Jacques. 2009. *The Beast and the Sovereign: Volume 1.* Chicago, IL: Chicago University Press.

Dijstelbloem, Huub and Albert Meijer. 2011. Eds. *Migration and the New Technological Borders of Europe.* Basingstoke and New York, NY: Palgrave Macmillan.

Diken, Bülent. 2004. 'From Refugee Camps to Gated Communities: Biopolitics and the End of the City'. *Citizenship Studies* 8: pp. 83–106.

Dillon, Michael. 2003. 'Virtual Security: A Life Science of (Dis)Order'. *Millennium: Journal of International Studies* 32: pp. 531–58.

Dodds, Klaus. 2013. '"I'm Still Not Crossing That": Borders, Dispossession and Sovereignty in Frozen River (2008)'. *Geopolitics* 18 (3): pp. 560–83.

Doty, Roxanne. 2009. *The Law Into Their Own Hands: Immigration and the Politics of Exceptionalism*. Tucson, AZ: University of Arizona Press.

Edkins, Jenny and Véronique Pin-Fat. 2005. 'Through the Wire: Relations of Power and Relations of Violence'. *Millennium: Journal of International Studies* 34 (1): pp. 1–25.

Edkins, Jenny and R. B. J. Walker. 2000. Eds. 'Zones of Indistinction: Territories, Bodies, Politics', Special Issue of *Alternatives: Global, Local, Political* 25 (1).

Elbe, Stephan. 2010. *Security and Global Health: Toward the Medicalization of Insecurity*. Cambridge: Polity Press.

Elden, Stuart. 2006. 'Contingent Sovereignty, Territorial Integrity and the Sanctity of Borders', *The SAIS Review of International Affairs* 26 (1): pp. 11–24.

Esposito, Roberto. 2008. *Bíos: Biopolitics and Philosophy*. Minneapolis, MN: University of Minnesota Press.

Esposito, Roberto. 2010. *Communitas: The Origin and Destiny of Community*. Stanford, CA: Stanford University Press.

Esposito, Roberto. 2011. *Immunitas: The Protection and Negation of Life*. Cambridge: Polity Press.

Esposito, Roberto. 2012a. *Third Person: Politics of Life and Philosophy of the Impersonal*. Cambridge: Polity Press.

Esposito, Roberto. 2012b. *Living Thought: The Origins and Actuality of Italian Philosophy*. Stanford, CA: Stanford University Press.

Esposito, Roberto. 2013. *Terms of the Political: Community, Immunity, Biopolitics*. New York, NY: Fordham University Press.

Esposito, Roberto and Timothy Campbell. 2008. 'Rene—An Interview With Roberto Esposito'. *Diacritics* 36 (2): pp. 49–56.

EU Commission. 2010a. 'Delivering an Area of Freedom, Security and Justice for Europe's Citizens: Action Plan Implementing the Stockholm Programme'. Available online at: <http://eur-lex.europa.eu/LexUriServ/LexUriServ.do?uri=COM:2010:0171:FIN:en:PDF> (accessed 5 October 2014).

EU Commission. 2010b. 'The EU Internal Security Strategy in Action: Five Steps Towards a More Secure Europe'. Available online at: <http://eur-lex.europa.eu/LexUriServ/LexUriServ.do?uri=COM:2010:0673:FIN:EN:PDF#page=2> (accessed 5 October 2014).

EU Commission. 2011a. 'The Global Approach to Migration and Mobility'. Communication From the Commission to the European Parliament, the Council, the European Economic and Social Committee and the Committee of the Regions, 18/11/11 COM (2011) 743 Final. Available online at: <http://ec.europa.eu/home-affairs/news/intro/docs/1_EN_ACT_part1_v9.pdf> (accessed 20 November 2011).

EU Commission. 2011b. 'Communication on Migration'. Available online at: <http://ec.europa.eu/home-affairs/news/intro/docs/1_EN_ACT_part1_v11.pdf> (accessed 3 January 2012).

EU Commission. 2011c. 'Establishing the European Border Surveillance System (EUROSUR)'. Available online at: <http://ec.europa.eu/home-affairs/policies/borders/docs/20110128EUROSURCSWPSEC2011145%20final.pdf> (accessed 3 January 2012).

EU Commission. 2011d. 'Smart Borders: Options and the Way Ahead'. Available online at: <http://www.ipex.eu/IPEXL-WEB/dossier/dossier.do?code=COM&year=2011& number=0680> (accessed 26 May 2014).

EU Commission. 2011e. 'Commission Staff Working Document on the Third Annual Report on Immigration and Asylum'. Available online at: <http://ec.europa.eu/ dgs/home-affairs/e-library/documents/policies/immigration/pdf/general/com_2012_ 250_final_1_en_act_part1_v5.pdf#zoom=100> (accessed 26 May 2014).

EU Commission. 2013a. 'Commission Report Calls for Forward-Looking Policies on Migration'. Available online at: <http://europa.eu/rapid/press-release_IP-13-552_en. htm> (accessed 7 October 2014).

EU Commission. 2013b. 'Communication From the Commission to the European Parliament and the Council on the Work of the Task Force Mediterranean'. Available online at: <http://ec.europa.eu/dgs/home-affairs/what-is-new/news/news/docs/ 20131204_communication_on_the_work_of_the_task_force_mediterranean_en.pdf> (accessed 7 April 2014).

EU Commission. 2014a. 'Report From the Commission to the European Parliament, the Council, the European Economic and Social Committee, and the Committee of the Regions: Report on the Implementation of the Global Approach to Migration and Mobility 2012–13'. Available online at: <http://europeanmemoranda.cabinetoffice. gov.uk/memorandum/report-from-the-commission-to-the-european-parliament- the-council-the-european-economic-social-committee-1395699448> (accessed 7 October 2014).

EU Commission. 2014b. 'Communication From the Commission to the European Parliament and the Council: The Final Implementation Report of the EU Internal Security Strategy 2010–2014'. Available online at: <http://ec.europa.eu/dgs/home- affairs/e-library/documents/basic-documents/docs/final_implementation_report_of_ the_eu_internal_security_strategy_2010_2014_en.pdf> (accessed 7 October 2014).

EU Council. 2008. 'European Pact on Immigration and Asylum'. Available online at: <http://register.consilium.europa.eu/doc/srv?l=EN&f=ST%2013440%202008% 20INIT> (accessed 5 October 2014).

EU Council. 2010. 'The Stockholm Programme: An Open and Secure Europe Serving and Protecting Citizens'. Available online at: <http://eur-lex.europa.eu/legal- content/EN/TXT/PDF/?uri=CELEX:52010XG0504(01)&from=EN> (accessed 5 October 2014).

European Surveillance. 2011. 'Assessment of Public Health Issues of Migrants at the Greek–Turkish Border'. Available online at: <http://www.eurosurveillance.org> (accessed 7 April 2014).

Fagan, Madeleine. 2013. *Ethics and Politics After Poststructuralism: Levinas, Derrida, and Nancy*. Edinburgh: Edinburgh University Press.

Fanon, Franz. 2001. *The Wretched of the Earth*. London: Penguin.

Fassin, Didier. 2009. 'Another Politics of Life Is Possible'. *Theory, Culture, and Society* 26 (5): pp. 44–60.

Fassin, Didier. 2012. *Humanitarian Reason: A Moral History of the Present*. Berkeley, CA: California University Press.

Fassin, Didier and Mariella Pandolfi. 2013. *Contemporary States of Emergency: The Politics of Military and Humanitarian Interventions*. New York, NY: Zone Books.

Feldman, Allen. 2010. 'Inhumanitas: Political Speciation, Animality, Natality, Defacement'. In *In the Name of Humanity: The Government of Threat and Care*, edited by Ilana Feldman and Miriam Ticktin, pp. 115–50. Durham, NC and London: Duke University Press.

Feldman, Ilana and Miriam Ticktin. 2010. Eds. *In the Name of Humanity: The Government of Threat and Care*. Durham, NC and London: Duke University Press.

Foucault, Michel. 1998. *The Will To Knowledge: The History of Sexuality: Volume 1*. London: Penguin.

Foucault, Michel. 2000. 'Confronting Governments: Human Rights'. In *Essential Works of Michel Foucault Volume 3: Power*, edited by James Faubion, pp. 474–5. New York, NY: The New Press.

Foucault, Michel. 2003. *Society Must Be Defended: Lectures at the Collège de France 1975–6*. London: Penguin.

Foucault, Michel. 2007. *Security, Territory, Population: Lectures at the Collège de France 1977–1978*. Basingstoke and New York, NY: Palgrave Macmillan.

Foucault, Michel. 2008. *The Birth of Biopolitics: Lectures at the Collège de France 1978–9*. Basingstoke and New York, NY: Palgrave Macmillan.

Frontex. 2013. 'Africa–Frontex Intelligence Community Joint Report'. Available online at: <http://www.statewatch.org/news/2014/oct/eu-frontex-africa-intell-2013.pdf> (accessed 24 January 2015).

Fundamental Rights Agency. 2013. *Fundamental Rights at Europe's Southern Sea Borders*. Available online at: <http://fra.europa.eu/en/publication/2013/fundamental-rights-europes-southern-sea-borders> (accessed 26 May 2014).

Gammeltoft-Hansen, Thomas. 2011. 'Outsourcing Asylum: The Advent of Protection Lite'. In *Europe and the World: EU Geopolitics and the Transformation of European Space*, edited by Luiza Bialasiewicz, pp. 129–52. Hampshire and Berlington, VT: Ashgate.

Garelli, Glenda and Martina Tazzioli. 2013. 'Arab Springs Making Space: Territoriality and Moral Geographies for Asylum Seekers in Italy'. *Environment and Planning D: Society and Space* 31: pp. 1004–21.

Gregory, Derek. 2006. 'The Black Flag: Guantánamo Bay and the Space of Exception'. *Geografiska Annaler* 88B: pp. 405–27.

Gros, Frederic. 2014. 'The Fourth Age of Security'. In *The Government of Life: Foucault, Biopolitics, and Neoliberalism*, edited by Vanessa Lemm and Miguel Vatter, pp. 17–28. New York, NY: Fordham University Press.

The Guardian. 2013. 'Libya Turns Zoo Into Migrant Processing Centre as More Head for EU', 13 October 2013. Available online at: <http://www.theguardian.com/world/2013/oct/13/libya-zoo-migrant-centre-eu-refugee> (accessed 7 April 2014).

Guild, Elspeth. 2009. *Security and Migration in the 21st Century*. Cambridge: Polity.

Guild, Elspeth and Sergio Carrera. 2013. 'EU Borders and Their Controls: Preventing Unwanted Movement of People in Europe?' CEPS Essay 6 (14). Available online at: <http://www.ceps.eu/ceps/dld/8597/pdf> (accessed 7 April 2014).

Hardt, Michael and Antonio Negri. 2001. *Empire*. Cambridge, MA and London: Harvard University Press.

References

Hardt, Michael and Antonio Negri. 2004. *Multitude: War and Democracy in the Age of Empire*. London: Penguin.

Hayes, Ben. 2009. 'Neoconopticon: The EU Security-Industrial Complex', Statewatch. Available online at: <http://www.statewatch.org/analyses/neoconopticon-report.pdf> (accessed 7 April 2014).

Hayes, Ben and Mathias Vermeulen. 2012. 'Borderline: The EU's New Border Surveillance Initiatives'. Available online at: <http://www.statewatch.org/news/2012/jun/borderline.pdf> (accessed 23 March 2013).

Heller, Charles and Chris Jones. 2014. 'Borders, Deaths, and Resistance'. *Statewatch Journal* 23 (3/4). Available online at: <http://www.statewatch.org/subscriber/protected/statewatch-journal-vol23n34.pdf> (accessed 7 October 2014).

Howell, Allison. 2011. *Madness in International Relations: Psychology, Security, and the Global Governance of Mental Health*. London and New York, NY: Routledge.

Human Rights Watch. 2009. 'Pushed Back, Pushed Around: Italy's Forced Return of Boat Migrants and Asylum Seekers, Libya's Mistreatment of Migrants and Asylum Seekers'. Available online at: <http://www.hrw.org/sites/default/files/reports/italy0909web_0.pdf> (accessed 28 March 2015).

Human Rights Watch. 2011a. 'EU—Put Rights at Heart of Migration Policy', 20 June 2011. Available online at: <http://www.hrw.org/news/2011/06/20/eu-put-rights-heart-migration-policy> (accessed 3 January 2012).

Human Rights Watch. 2011b. 'The EU's Dirty Hands: Frontex Involvement in Ill-Treatment of Migrant Detainees in Greece'. Available online at: <http://www.hrw.org/reports/2011/09/21/eu-s-dirty-hands-0> (accessed 26 April 2014).

Human Rights Watch. 2012. 'Joint Letter to UN Special Rapporteur on Health: Human Rights of Immigrants and Sex Workers in Greece'. Available online at: <http://www.hrw.org/news/2012/05/09/joint-letter-un-special-rapporteur-health> (accessed 28 March 2015).

Huysmans, Jef. 2000. 'The European Union and the Securitization of Migration'. *Journal of Common Market Studies* 38 (5): pp. 751–77.

Huysmans, Jef. 2006. *The Politics of Insecurity: Fear, Migration and Asylum in the EU*. London and New York, NY: Routledge.

IOM. 2014. *Fatal Journeys: Tracking Lives Lost During Migration*, edited by Tara Brian and Frank Laczko, Geneva: International Organization for Migration. Available online at: <http://publications.iom.int/bookstore/free/FatalJourneys_CountingtheUncounted.pdf> (accessed 25 January 2015).

Isin, Engin. 2014. 'We, the Non-Europeans: Derrida With Said'. In *Europe After Derrida: Crisis and Potentiality*, edited by Agnes Czajka and Bora Isyar, pp. 108–19. Edinburgh: Edinburgh University Press.

Isyar, Bora. 2014. 'A Roman Europe of Hope: Reading Derrida With Brague'. In *Europe After Derrida: Crisis and Potentiality*, edited by Agnes Czajka and Bora Isyar, pp. 49–60. Edinburgh: Edinburgh University Press.

Johnson, Corey, Reece Jones, Anssi Paasi, Louise Amoore, Alison Mountz, Mark B. Salter, and Chris Rumford. 2011. 'Intervention: Rethinking the Border in Border Studies'. *Political Geography* 30: pp. 61–9.

Johnson, Heather. 2013. 'The Other Side of the Fence: Reconceptualizing the "Camp" and Migration Zones at the Borders of Spain'. *International Political Sociology* 7: pp. 75–91.

Jones, Chris. 2014a. 'Border Guards, Planes, "Thermal Vision Vans", and Heartbeat Detectors—Who is Equipping Frontex?', Statewatch. Available online at: <http://www.statewatch.org/analyses/no-245-frontex-tech.pdf> (accessed 7 October 2014).

Jones, Chris. 2014b. 'Smart Borders: *Fait Accompli*?', Statewatch. Available online at: <http://www.statewatch.org/analyses/no-253-smart-borders.pdf> (accessed 7 October 2014).

Jones, Chris. 2014c. '11 Years of EURODAC', Statewatch. Available online at: <http://www.statewatch.org/analyses/no-235-eurodac.pdf> (accessed 7 October 2014).

Keller, Ska. 2014. 'New Rules on Frontex Operations at Sea'. Available online at: <http://www.statewatch.org/news/2014/apr/ep-green-keler-mep-frontex-operations-at-sea.pdf> (accessed 26 May 2014).

Khosravi, Shahram. 2007. 'The "Illegal" Traveller: An Auto-Ethnography of Borders'. *Social Anthropology* 15 (3): pp. 321–34.

Khosravi, Shahram. 2010. *Illegal Traveller: An Auto-Ethnography of Borders*. Basingstoke and New York, NY: Palgrave Macmillan.

Kinnvall, Catarina and Paul Nesbitt-Larking. 2013. 'Securitising Citizenship: (B)ordering Practices and Strategies of Resistance'. *Global Society* 27 (3): pp. 337–59.

Kitagawa, Shinya. 2011. 'Geographies of Migration Across and Beyond Europe: The Camp and the Road of Movements'. In *Europe and the World: EU Geopolitics and the Transformation of European Space*, edited by Luiza Bialasiewicz, pp. 201–22. Hampshire and Berlington, VT: Ashgate.

Kumar Rajaram, Prem and Carl Grundy-Warr. 2007. Eds. *Borderscapes: Hidden Geographies and Politics at Territory's Edge*. Minneapolis, MN: University of Minnesota Press.

Lakoff, Andrew and Stephen Collier. 2010. 'Infrastructure and Event: The Political Technology of Preparedness'. In *Political Matter: Technoscience, Democracy and Public Life*, edited by Bruce Braun and Sarah Whatmore, pp. 243–66. Minneapolis, MN: University of Minnesota Press.

Lemke, Thomas. 2011. *Biopolitics: An Advanced Introduction*. New York, NY: New York University Press.

Lemke, Thomas. 2014. 'The Risks of Security: Liberalism, Biopolitics, Fear'. In *The Government of Life: Foucault, Biopolitics, and Neoliberalism*, edited by Vanessa Lemm and Miguel Vatter, pp. 59–74. New York, NY: Fordham University Press.

Lemm, Vanessa. 2013. 'Introduction: Biopolitics and Community in Roberto Esposito'. In Roberto Esposito, *Terms of the Political: Community, Immunity, Biopolitics*. New York, NY: Fordham University Press.

Lemm, Vanessa and Miguel Vatter. 2014. *The Government of Life: Foucault, Biopolitics, and Neoliberalism*. New York, NY: Fordham University Press.

Libya Herald. 2013. 'Inside Tripoli Zoo's Prison for Illegal Immigrants'. 26 August 2013. Available online at: <http://www.libyaherald.com/2013/08/26/inside-tripoli-zoos-prison-for-illegal-immigrants/> (accessed 7 April 2014).

Lundborg, Tom and Nick Vaughan-Williams. 2015. 'New Materialisms, Discourse Analysis, and International Relations: A Radical Intertextual Approach'. *Review of International Studies* 41 (1): pp. 3–25.

Mainwaring, Cetta. 2012. 'Centring on the Margins: Migration Control in Malta, Cyprus, and the European Union'. Unpublished DPhil thesis completed at the University of Oxford.

Maquet, Paloma and Julian Zartea. 2013. 'Sanctions for Stowaways: How Merchant Shipping Joined the Border Police'. *Statewatch Journal* 23 (2): pp. 38–42.

Martin, Marie. 2014. 'Extension of Mobility Partnerships With Euro-Mediterranean Partners', Statewatch. Available online at: <http://www.statewatch.org/news/2013/jan/mp-article.pdf> (accessed 7 October 2014).

Masters, Cristina. 2009. 'Femina Sacra: The "War on/of Terror", Women and the Feminine'. *Security Dialogue* 40 (1): pp. 29–49.

McLean, Stuart. 2014. 'Other Shores: Insularity, Materiality and the Making (and Unmaking) of "Europe"'. In *Europe After Derrida: Crisis and Potentiality*, edited by Agnes Czajka and Bora Isyar, pp. 61–79. Edinburgh: Edinburgh University Press.

McNevin, Anne. 2013. 'Ambivalence and Citizenship: Theorising the Political Claims of Irregular Migrants'. *Millennium: Journal of International Studies* 41: pp. 182–200.

Médicin Sans Frontières. 2013. 'Violence, Vulnerability and Migration: Trapped at the Gates of Europe'. Available online at: <http://www.msf.ie/document/violence-vulnerability-and-migration-trapped-gates-europe> (accessed 7 April 2014).

Mezzadra, Sandro and Brett Neilson. 2013. *Border as Method, or, the Multiplication of Labor*. Durham, NC and London: Duke University Press.

Migrants at Sea. 2014. 'Interview With Frontex Director Laitinen'. Available online at: <http://migrantsatsea.org/2014/03/24/interview-with-frontex-director-laitinen/> (accessed 26 May 2014).

Migreurop. 2012. 'At the Margins of Europe: The Externalization of Migration Controls', *Annual Report 2010–11*. Available online at: <http://www.migreurop.org/article2069.html?lang=fr> (accessed 2 June 2012).

Migreurop. 2014. 'Frontex Between Greece and Turkey: At the Border of Denial'. Available online at: <http://www.migreurop.org/article2533.html?lang=fr> (accessed 22 January 2015).

Minca, Claudio. 2005. 'The Return of the Camp'. *Progress in Human Geography* 29: pp. 405–12.

Minca, Claudio. 2006. 'Giorgio Agamben and the New Biopolitical *Nomos*'. *Geografiska Annaler* 88B: pp. 387–403.

Minca, Claudio. 2007. 'Agamben's Geographies of Modernity'. *Political Geography* 26: pp. 78–97.

Minca, Claudio and Nick Vaughan-Williams. 2012. 'Carl Schmitt and the Concept of the Border'. *Geopolitics* 17 (4): pp. 756–72.

Morgenthau, Hans. 1948. *Politics Among Nations: The Struggle for Power and Peace*. New York, NY: A. A. Knopf.

Muhle, Maria. 2014. 'A Genealogy of Biopolitics: The Notion of Life in Canguilhem and Foucault'. In *The Government of Life: Foucault, Biopolitics, and Neoliberalism*, edited by Vanessa Lemm and Miguel Vatter, pp. 77–97. New York, NY: Fordham University Press.

Murray, Alex. 2010. *Giorgio Agamben*. London and New York: Routledge.

Naas, Michael. 2008. *Derrida From Now On*. New York, NY: Fordham University Press.

Nancy, Jean-Luc. 1993. 'Abandoned Being'. In *The Birth to Presence*, pp. 36–47. Stanford, CA: Stanford University Press.

Negri, Antonio. 1993. *Insurgencies: Constituent Power and the Modern State*. Minneapolis, MN: University of Minnesota Press.

Negri, Antonio. 2004. *Negri on Negri: Antonio Negri in Conversation With A. Dufourmantelle*. London and New York, NY: Routledge.

Negri, Antonio. 2008. *Reflections on Empire*. Cambridge and Malden, MA: Polity Press.

NPR. 2013. 'Tripoli Zoo Sees Different Kind of Cage—One With Migrants'. Available online at: <http://www.npr.org/blogs/parallels/2013/11/12/244550320/tripoli-zoo-sees-different-kind-of-cage-one-with-migrants> (accessed 7 April 2014).

Nunes, João. 2013. *Security, Emancipation and the Politics of Health: A New Theoretical Perspective*. London and New York, NY: Routledge.

Nyers, Peter. 2013. 'Liberating Irregularity: No Borders, Temporality, Citizenship'. In *Citizenship and Security: The Constitution of Political Being*, edited by Xavier Guillaume and Jef Huysmans, pp. 18–34. London and New York, NY: Routledge.

Open Access Now! 2013. 'Migrant Detention Centres in Europe: Open the Doors! We Have the Right to Know! Campaign of Parliamentary Visits 2013'. Available online at: <http://www.migreurop.org/IMG/pdf/open_access_-_country_reports_-_08102013_-_en-2.pdf> (accessed 26 May 2014).

Open Society. 2011. 'Case Watch: A Victory for Refugee Protection in Europe'. Available online at: <http://www.soros.org/voices/case-watch-victory-refugee-protection-europe> (accessed 5 January 2012).

PACE. 2012. 'Lives Lost in the Mediterranean Sea: Who Is Responsible?' Available online at: <http://assembly.coe.int/committeedocs/2012/20120329_mig_rpt.en.pdf> (accessed 26 May 2014).

PACE. 2013. 'Frontex: Human Rights and Responsibilities'. Available online at: <http://assembly.coe.int/ASP/Doc/XrefViewPDF.asp?FileID=19719&Language=EN> (accessed 26 May 2014).

Papadopoulos, Dimitris, Niamh Stephenson, and Vassilis Tsianos. 2008. *Escape Routes: Control and Subversion in the 21st Century*. London: Pluto Press.

Parker, Noel and Nick Vaughan-Williams et al. 2009. 'Lines in the Sand? An Agenda for Critical Border Studies'. *Geopolitics* 14 (3): pp. 582–7.

Parker, Noel and Nick Vaughan-Williams. 2012. 'Critical Border Studies: Broadening and Deepening the "Lines in the Sand" Agenda'. *Geopolitics* 17 (4): pp. 727–33.

Peers, Steve. 2014. 'New EU Rules on Maritime Surveillance: Will They Stop the Deaths and Push-Backs in the Mediterranean?' Available online at: <http://www.statewatch.org/analyses/no-237-maritime-surveillance.pdf> (accessed 26 May 2014).

Peoples, Columba and Nick Vaughan-Williams. 2015. *Critical Security Studies: An Introduction*, Second Edition. London and New York, NY: Routledge.

Philo, Chris and Chris Wilbert. 2000. 'Animal Spaces, Beastly Places: An Introduction'. In *Animal Spaces, Beastly Places: New Geographies of Human–Animal Relations*, edited by Chris Philo and Chris Wilbert, pp. 1–34. London and New York, NY: Routledge.

PICUM. 2010. 'Main Concerns About the Fundamental Rights of Undocumented Migrants in Europe'. Available online at: <http://picum.org/picum.org/uploads/pub lication/Annual%20Concerns%202010%20EN.pdf> (accessed 5 January 2012).

PICUM. 2012. 'Migrants' Uprising at Detention Centre of Komotini'. Available online at: <http://picum.org/en/news/bulletins/38190/> (accessed 27 December 2014).

PICUM. 2014. 'Deportation Causes Protest Among Passengers on Plane'. Available online at: <http://picum.org/en/news/bulletins/43511/#cat_25597> (accessed 31 December 2014).

Pro Asyl. 2012a. '"I Came Here for Peace": The Systematic Ill-Treatment of Migrants and Refugees by State Agents in Patras'. Available online at: <http://www.proasyl.de/ fileadmin/fm-dam/p_KAMPAGNEN/Flucht-ist-kein-Verbrechen/Patras-Webversion04 D-DS-k_03.pdf> (accessed 7 April 2014).

Pro Asyl. 2012b. 'Walls of Shame: Accounts From the Inside: The Detention Centers of Evros'. Available online at: <http://www.proasyl.de/fileadmin/fm-dam/q_ PUBLIKATIONEN/2012/Evros-Bericht_12_04_10_BHP.pdf> (accessed 7 April 2014).

Pro Asyl. 2013. 'Pushed Back: Systematic Human Rights Violations Against Refugees in the Aegean Sea and at the Greek–Turkish Land Border'. Available online at: <http:// www.proasyl.de/fileadmin/fm-dam/l_EU_Fluechtlingspolitik/proasyl_pushed_back_ 24.01.14_a4.pdf> (accessed 7 April 2014).

Prokkola, Eeva-Kaisa. 2013. 'Technologies of Border Management: Performances and Calculations of Finnish/Schengen Border Security'. *Geopolitics* 18: pp. 77–94.

Prozorov, Sergei. 2005. 'X/Xs: Towards a General Theory of the Exception'. *Alternatives: Global, Local, Political* 30 (1): pp. 81–112.

Prozorov, Sergei. 2013. 'Powers of Life and Death: Biopolitics Beyond Foucault'. *Alternatives: Global, Local, Political* 38 (3): pp. 191–3.

Prozorov, Sergei. 2014. *Agamben and Politics: A Critical Introduction*. Edinburgh: Edinburgh University Press.

Puggioni, Raffaela. 2014. 'Against Camps' Violence: Some Voices on Italian Holding Centres'. *Political Studies* 62 (4): pp. 945–60.

Rajaram, Prem Kumar and Carl Grundy-Warr. 2004. 'The Irregular Migrant as *Homo Sacer*: Migration and Detention in Australia, Malaysia, and Thailand'. *International Migration* 42: pp. 33–64.

Rasmussen, Claire. 2013. 'Review Essay: *The Beast and the Sovereign*, Biopolitics and Derrida's Menagerie'. *Environment and Planning D: Society and Space* 31: pp. 1125–33.

Razack, Sherene. 2008. *Casting Out: The Eviction of Muslims From Western Law and Politics*. Toronto: University of Toronto Press.

Revel, Judith. 2014. 'Identity, Nature, Life: Three Biopolitical Deconstructions'. In *The Government of Life: Foucault, Biopolitics, and Neoliberalism*, edited by Vanessa Lemm and Miguel Vatter, pp. 112–24. New York, NY: Fordham University Press.

Rose, Nikolas. 2007. *The Politics of Life Itself: Biomedicine, Power, and Subjectivity in the Twenty-First Century*. Princeton, NJ and Oxford: Princeton University Press.

Rumford, Chris. 2006. 'Introduction: Theorising Borders'. *European Journal of Social Theory* 9 (2): pp. 155–69.

Rumford, Chris. 2009. Ed. *Citizens and Borderwork in Contemporary Europe*. London and New York, NY: Routledge.

Sakai, Naoki and Jon Solomon. 2006. Eds. *Translation, Biopolitics, Colonial Difference*. Hong Kong: Hong Kong University Press.

Salter, Mark. 2012. 'Theory of the /: The Suture and Critical Border Studies'. *Geopolitics* 17 (4): pp. 734–55.

Scheel, Stephan. 2014. 'Rethinking the Autonomy of Migration: On the Appropriation of Mobility Within Biometric Border Regimes'. Unpublished PhD thesis completed at the Open University.

Schmitt, Carl. 2005. [1922] *Political Theology: Four Chapters on the Concept of Sovereignty*. Chicago, IL and London: University of Chicago Press.

Shapiro, Michael. 2012. *Studies in Trans-Disciplinary Method: After the Aesthetic Turn*. London and New York, NY: Routledge.

Shewly, Hosna. 2013. 'Abandoned Spaces and Bare Life in the Enclaves of the India–Bangladesh Border'. *Political Geography* 32: pp. 23–31.

Shukin, Nicole. 2009. *Animal Capital: Rendering Life in Biopolitical Times*. Minneapolis, MN: University of Minnesota Press.

Sidaway, James. 2006. 'On the Nature of the Beast: Re-Charting Political Geographies of the European Union'. *Geografiska Annaler* 88B: pp. 1–14.

Squire, Vicki. 2011. 'The Contested Politics of Mobility: Politicizing Mobility, Mobilizing Politics'. In *The Contested Politics of Mobility: Borderzones and Irregularity*, edited by Vicki Squire, pp. 1–26. Basingstoke and New York, NY: Palgrave Macmillan.

Squire, Vicki. 2014. 'Desert "Trash": Posthumanism, Border Struggles, and Humanitarian Politics'. *Political Geography* 38: pp. 11–21.

Squire, Vicki. 2015. 'Reshaping Critical Geopolitics? The Materialist Challenge'. *Review of International Studies* 41 (1): pp. 139–59.

Statewatch. 2012. 'Summary of the Special Report of the European Ombudsman in Own-Initiative Inquiry OI/5/2012/BEH-MHZ Concerning Frontex'. Available online at: <http://www.statewatch.org/news/2014/feb/eu-omb-frontex-report.pdf> (accessed 26 May 2014).

Statewatch. 2014. 'Refugee protests in Europe: fighting for the right to stay'. Available online at: <http://database.statewatch.org/article.asp?aid=33230> (accessed 31 December 2014).

Stierl, Maurice. 2014. 'Migration Resistance as Border Politics: Counter-Imaginaries of EUrope'. Unpublished PhD thesis completed at the University of Warwick.

Sundberg, Juanita. 2011. 'Diabolic *Caminos* in the Desert and Cat Fights on the Río: A Posthumanist Political Ecology of Boundary Enforcement in the United States–Mexico Borderlands'. *Annals of the Association of American Geographers* 101: pp. 318–36.

Ticktin, Miriam. 2011. *Casualties of Care: Immigration and the Politics of Humanitarianism in France*. Berkeley, CA and London: University of California Press.

Times of Malta. 2014. 'Mare Nostrum mission has to end'. Available online at: <http://www.timesofmalta.com/articles/view/20140815/world/mare-nostrum-mission-has-to-end-and-eu-must-take-over-italy-says.531961> (accessed 20 August 2014).

Tondini, Matteo. 2010. 'Transcript of Interview with Mr Ilkka Laitinen, Frontex Executive Director'. Available online at: <http://migrantsatsea.files.wordpress.com/2010/11/inex-laitinen-interview-12may20101.pdf> (accessed 26 May 2014).

References

UNHCR. 1951. *The 1951 Refugee Convention*. Available online at: <http://www.unhcr. org/pages/49da0e466.html> (accessed 28 March 2015).

United Against Racism. 2014. 'List of 18,759 documented refugee deaths through "Fortress Europe"'. Available online at: <http://www.unitedagainstracism.org/ campaigns/refugee-campaign/fortress-europe/> (accessed 1 January 2015).

United Nations. 2013a. 'Report of the Special Rapporteur on the Human Rights of Migrants'. Available online at: <http://www.ohchr.org/en/Issues/Migration/ SRMigrants/Pages/AnnualReports.aspx> (accessed 7 April 2014).

United Nations. 2013b. *Trends in International Migration: The 2013 Revision*. New York, NY: UN Publications.

Van Houtum, Henk. 2010. 'Human Blacklisting: The Global Apartheid of the EU's External Border Regime'. *Environment and Planning D: Society and Space* 28: pp. 957–76.

Van Munster, Rens. 2009. *Securitizing Immigration: The Politics of Risk in the EU*. Basingstoke and New York, NY: Palgrave Macmillan.

Vaughan-Williams, Nick. 2005. 'International Relations and the "Problem of History"'. *Millennium: Journal of International Studies* 34(1): pp. 115–36.

Vaughan-Williams, Nick. 2007. 'Beyond a Cosmopolitan Ideal: The Politics of Singularity'. *International Politics* 44 (1): pp. 107–24.

Vaughan-Williams, Nick. 2009. *Border Politics: The Limits of Sovereign Power*. Edinburgh: Edinburgh University Press.

Vaughan-Williams, Nick. 2010. 'The UK Border Security Continuum: Virtual Biopolitics and the Simulation of the Sovereign Ban'. *Environment and Planning D: Society and Space* 28: pp. 1071–83.

Vaughan-Williams, Nick. 2011a. 'Off-Shore Biopolitical Border Security: The EU's Global Response to Migration, Piracy, and "Risky" Subjects'. In *Europe and the World: EU Geopolitics and the Transformation of European Space*, edited by Luiza Bialasiewicz, pp. 185–200. Hampshire and Berlington, VT: Ashgate.

Vaughan-Williams, Nick. 2011b. 'European Border Security After the Arab Spring'. *EU–GRASP Working Paper 24*. Available online at: <http://www.eugrasp.eu/> (accessed 25 May 2013).

Walker, R. B. J. 1993. *Inside/Outside: International Relations as Political Theory*. Cambridge: Cambridge University Press.

Walker, R. B. J. 2000. 'Europe Is Not Where it Is Supposed to Be'. In *International Relations Theory and the Politics of European Integration*, edited by Morten Kelstrup and Michael C. Williams, pp. 14–32. London and New York, NY: Routledge.

Walker, R. B. J. 2010. *After the Globe, Before the World*. London and New York, NY: Routledge.

Walters, William. 2002. 'Mapping Schengenland: Denaturalising the Border'. *Environment and Planning D: Society and Space* 20: pp. 564–80.

Walters, William. 2011. 'Foucault and Frontiers: Notes on the Birth of the Humanitarian Border'. In *Governmentality: Current Issues and Future Challenges*, edited by Ulrich Bröckling, Susanne Krassman, and Thomas Lemke, pp. 138–64. London and New York, NY: Routledge.

Watch The Med. 2014. '"They Want to See Us Drown"—Survivors of a Push-back Operation in the Aegean Sea Report to the Watch The Med Alarm Phone'. Available online at: <http://watchthemed.net/reports/view/84> (accessed 22 January 2015).

Weber, Samuel. 2014. 'Mind the "Cap"'. In *Europe After Derrida: Crisis and Potentiality*, edited by Agnes Czajka and Bora Isyar, pp. 9–29. Edinburgh: Edinburgh University Press.

Wolfe, Cary. 2012. *Before the Law: Humans and Other Animals in a Biopolitical Frame*. Chicago, IL: University of Chicago Press.

Index of Names

Index of Names

General Index